Stephen King's
Modern Macabre

Stephen King's Modern Macabre

Essays on the Later Works

Edited by PATRICK MCALEER
and MICHAEL A. PERRY

McFarland & Company, Inc., Publishers
Jefferson, North Carolina

LIBRARY OF CONGRESS CATALOGUING-IN-PUBLICATION DATA

Stephen King's modern macabre : essays on the later works / edited by Patrick McAleer and Michael A. Perry.
    p.   cm.
Includes bibliographical references and index.

ISBN 978-0-7864-9400-2 (softcover : acid free paper) ∞
ISBN 978-1-4766-1745-9 (ebook)

1. King, Stephen, 1947– —Criticism and interpretation.
I. McAleer, Patrick, 1980– editor.   II. Perry, Michael A., 1973–

PS3561.I483Z884 2014
813'.54—dc23   2014023733

BRITISH LIBRARY CATALOGUING DATA ARE AVAILABLE

On the cover: *The White Commands You,* an interior illustration for *The Dark Tower* © Michael Whelan

Printed in the United States of America

McFarland & Company, Inc., Publishers
  Box 611, Jefferson, North Carolina 28640
    www.mcfarlandpub.com

To Julie, Brenda, and Ann
and
to Karen, Caleb, and Julian

Table of Contents

Table of Contents

Acknowledgments

First and foremost, the editors owe a debt of gratitude to Mary Findley—she is the original driving force behind this volume, and we are thankful that we were afforded the opportunity to complete the task set forth. Additionally, we would like to thank each and every contributor for this volume—you all have been a pleasure to work with.

Michael A. Perry would like to acknowledge his wife and forever partner, Karen—your unconditional support in all things is a blessing and a gift that I do not take lightly. I can't wait to see what we do next. My boys, Caleb and Julian, for being Boys with a capital B. I would also like to thank my parents. My mom for reading to me nearly every night as a child. My dad for modeling what it means to be a lifelong reader and for placing a huge book called *The Stand* in my lap so many years ago. Who would have thought I could have turned that into a career?

Patrick McAleer would like to acknowledge his friend, love, and partner Kim Socha—you are always supportive of everything that I do, and I thank you for bearing with me as I took time away from our wonderful days and evenings to work on this volume, and I am especially thankful to you for bearing with me and my shifting attitudes while editing and writing. You are a treasure, and I hope to repay your kindness and understanding each and every day. I would, of course, also like to thank my parents, Lee and Denise, who have, simply put, been wonderful folks and friends.

Introduction

A More Subtle Macabre

MICHAEL A. PERRY *and* PATRICK MCALEER

"After having a two-hundred pound babysitter fart on your face and yell Pow! The Village Voice holds few terrors."[1]

We open with a passage from Stephen King's memoir, *On Writing: A Memoir of the Craft.* Interrupted, as it was, by a drunk man operating a minivan along the quiet Maine road where King liked to walk, his memoir offers this collection a marker of sorts between his early and later work. The other marker, less dramatic but more practical, comes with his change of publishers in 1996, from Viking to Scribner (with *Bag of Bones* [September 1998] as the first installment with Scribner). Both roughly mark a transition period for scholarship on King, as extensive criticism and analyses of King's "recent" works (some of which are almost twenty years old) have only been collected sporadically over the last twenty years or so. However, King continues to write, and scholars continue to blur the line between literary and popular distinctions insofar as critical analysis of his work is concerned. Indeed, the volume you have in your hands marks what will undoubtedly be one of many subsequent collections that begin to assess King's later work as he continues to navigate American culture and, increasingly, enable scholars to redefine, reclassify, and reconsider the ever-evolving horrorscape presented in his growing body of work—a collection of recent texts that, while certainly including elements of horror, or the horrific, may rest more along the lines of American Gothic and supernatural/speculative fiction.

In 2003, the literary establishment began the process of "reconsidering" King as he was awarded the National Book Foundation's Medal for Distinguished Contribution to American Letters. In his acceptance speech, much of which centered on his wife, Tabitha, he stated: "For far too long the so-called popular writers of this country and the so-called literary writers have stared at each other with animosity and willful lack of understanding."[2] Thus addressing the elephant in the room head on, and possibly remembering the weight of the "two-hundred pound babysitter," King went on to further contextualize the relevance of challenging established modes of criticism and the evaluative properties assigned to various types of literature. As King scoffed at the notion that writing fiction is akin to "mental masturbation," he goes on to say that his primary goal with writing was to be "an honest writer."[3] And if we are to be honest about King's fiction, we would all do well to consider that *just* horror, either as a literary label or an adjective for day-to-day life, is not always a truthful, or honest, classification.

The essays located herein contain a similar sentiment as they seek to further critical discussion on King's work and often challenge preconceived notions of just who and what King represents. Indeed, it is hard to not begin from a defensive standpoint when engaged in a sustained critical piece of scholarship that addresses King, as evinced in many of the essays you will be reading. However, we assume the audience for this particular text does not need convincing that this is a legitimate exercise. Moreover, critical endeavors stemming from King's work are nothing new. A number of early popular culture scholars such as Gary Hoppenstand, Ray Browne, and Tony Magistrale have successfully argued for the importance of King's work and began forging a path of scholarly discourse that continues to this day. And, as King's work increasingly pushes at the borders of horror into the gothic and supernatural/speculative genres, King's popularity continues to grow, both with the general public and with scholars. Courses dedicated to critical analyses of his works, including one taught by one co-editor of this book and referenced in the second essay of this collection, are becoming more common in colleges and universities around the world, much to our delight.

Understandably, critical analyses of Stephen King's fiction, from an academic and general readership standpoint, primarily concerns King's first fifteen years of publication (1974–1989). Possibly, scholars have simply had more time in which to reflect upon his early works. Another reason: King's early canon can be more easily categorized into the genre of horror. In fact, Tony Magistrale argues that the '90s mark a bit of a content transition for King as "the books of the 1990s [by King] are not similar in subject matter to the narratives that originally established King's reputation in the 1970s and 1980s."[4] Notably, around the time King begins to explore and push the boundaries of the horror genre, while maintaining in nearly all his work a sense of the horrific, published scholarly attention diminishes. Coincidentally, this coincides with the number of King's "constant readers" continuing to grow. But due to the sheer volume of his work, even self-proclaimed King scholars, many who have contributed to this volume, cannot claim to have read *all* of his work (although one of the editors has certainly tried, even spending $50 here and there on eBay for rare copies of King's "lost" works like "Weeds," "Man with a Belly," and "The Blue Air Compressor," to name a few). Many readers know King for his early horror works and tend to remain unaware of his more recent work, just as many readers no doubt are familiar with more contemporary works, such as *Duma Key* (2008) and *11/22/63* (2011), and have not yet read back far enough into his canon. While anecdotally this may hold up, King scholarship does appear to stick to his earlier works. As mentioned, part of the explanation may simply be that his recent work is, well, recent, and the Academy simply requires time to consider work that is no longer clearly identifiable via genre (especially an expected one). In other words, critical analyses of his horror writing offers King scholarship a safe place, but to analyze him as a contributor to American letters alongside other winners of the same award presents a greater challenge to established modes of critical hierarchies.

Evidently, there are no current scholarly books that examine the full spectrum of King's work, including both his novels and films—he has simply produced too much and, presently, is not slowing down. However, as Magistrale rightly contends, the study of King is immensely useful, especially from a cultural standpoint: "in the past forty years, Stephen King has supplied America with a national portrait. [But] It is not always a flattering one [...] as it reveals our historical and cultural foibles and scars."[5] The "usefulness" of King study, combined with the daunting task of deciding what to consider, so far have resulted in King scholarship to fall into one of three major categories: somewhat broad/generalized reviews of King's fiction, superb scholarship on King's fiction from the early selections of King's canon, or strong criticism of both King's early and more recent fiction but with the balance of the

3

scales tipped towards King's older compositions. When books are published, they often (and rightly) seek thematic groupings that allow for an in-depth look at a portion of King's work: recently published books, such as Magistrale's *Hollywood's Stephen King* (2003) and *The Films of Stephen King: From* Carrie *to* Secret Window (2008), for example, focus solely on films adapted from King's novels or short stories. Other works include *Stephen King: A Literary Companion* by Rocky Wood (2011), *Respecting* The Stand: *A Critical Analysis of Stephen King's Apocalpytic Novel,* by Jenifer Paquette (2012), and two titles from one of the editors of this book, Patrick McAleer (*Inside the Dark Tower Series* [2009] and *The Writing Family of Stephen King* [2011]).[6] This particular collection, however, seeks to begin the process of (re)creating a fourth major category of King Scholarship.

In Part I, "King in the World Around Us," each contributing author places King's work within a larger cultural context by examining the question of genre, the inclusion of King in the literature classroom, his column in *Entertainment Weekly,* and the role of fear in American culture. Jennifer Jenkins begins, in "Fantasy in Fiction: The Double-Edged Sword," by exploring the effects of *story* as a tool that King utilizes to create a fundamental and intimate connection between him and his reader to infuse his texts with life and to avoid inert productions. Her essay considers the embedded intertextuality between *IT* and *11/22/63* as but one of many metaphors and reflections of faith, imagination, and (readerly) activity that result from reading King's fiction. Michael A. Perry, in "King Me: Inviting New Perceptions and Purposes of the Popular and Horrific into the College Classroom," then examines his experiences teaching the fiction of Stephen King in a college classroom, and how his placement alongside particular texts (namely the more "literary" writings of Toni Morrison) allow for a deeper understanding of and appreciation for King's honest and "real" writing as well as add new critical insight into the more conventional literary texts that accompany the pairing. Next, Scott Ash, in "A Taste for the Public: Uncle Stevie's Work for *Entertainment Weekly,*" studies, and scrutinizes, King's columns; the chapter discusses how King adeptly utilizes his position as a literary and cultural critic while simultaneously abusing such power often in an attempt to remain seen as "just one of the guys," or good ol' "Uncle Stevie." Mary Findley, in "The World at Large, America in Particular: Cultural Fears and Societal Mayhem in King's Fiction Since

1995," considers the vast reach of King's canon and theorizes a perceived gap between King's early works and his contemporary writings, arguing that King has not necessarily changed as a writer despite his movement away from his traditional/typical horror story.

Part II, "Spotlight on *The Dark Tower*," pursues multiple avenues of inquiry in regards to King's *Dark Tower Series*, over half of which was published during the latter half of his career. Michele Braun, in "Roland the Gunslinger's Generic Transformation," traces three predecessors to Roland Deschain, beginning with Charlemagne's knight in the eleventh century, to Orlando in the sixteenth century text *Orlando Furioso* by Ludovico Ariosto, to Childe Roland of Robert Browning's poem "Childe Roland to the Dark Tower Came." Throughout, Braun traces how changing genres and heroic conventions shape the narratives. T. Gilchrist White, in "'Childe Roland to the Dark Tower Came': The Heroic Aspects of the Gunslinger," offers additional insights into this character of Roland and considers how *The Dark Tower* series positions Roland into the role of a hero despite some of his less-than-heroic deeds. Jennifer D. Loman, in "Riddles Wrapped in Mystery Inside Enigmas: Anglo-Saxon Literature as the Key to Unlocking the Series' End," looks to the Anglo Saxons and their fascination with, and use of, riddles as a means of understanding the numerous puzzles King's Constant Reader faces throughout the Roland's quest. Georgianna O. Miller, in "A Rose, a Stone, an Unfound Door: Metaphor and Intertextuality in *The Dark Tower* Series," offers an intertextual discussion of King's work alongside Dante and T.S. Eliot. In particular, Eliot's "The Waste Land" and each text's use of the tarot deck figure heavily into her analyses.

In Part III, "Writing into the Millennium," we begin the long and difficult task of examining, in a variety of ways, the recent work of Stephen King. From baseball to television, from the American vernacular to adaptations, essays in this part begin what is bound to be a long and fruitful discussion. Abigail L. Bowers and Lowell Mick White, in "Survival of the Sweetest: Little Miss Bosox and the Saving Grace of Baseball in *The Girl Who Loved Tom Gordon*," explore the novel's central framing device of chapters as innings, and examine King's text alongside other works that offer baseball as more than just a subject, but infuse the spirit of the game into the very narrative. Alexandra Reuber, in "More Than Just Ghost Lore in a Bad Place: Mikael Håftröm's Cinematographic Translation of *1408*," navigates one of the more recent cinematic adaptations of King's work—*1408*—and primarily discusses how the film provides an in-depth analysis of a father, Mike Enslin, mourning the loss of his child (where King's original text arguably fails), in addition to examining the manifestations of his pain and guilt that populate and transform the titular room 1408. Philip L. Simpson, in "'Born in Sin': Millennial Anxiety in *Storm of the Century*," examines King's teleplay and argues that the choice the town faces in the narrative places a mirror upon millennial anxieties of a post–9/11 society and the lengths communities will go to preserve a sense of "safety." Patrick McAleer, in "The Fallen King(dom): Surviving Ruin and Decay from *The Stand* to *Cell*," bridges the gap between early and later King through an examination of the multi-genre depictions of the apocalyptic throughout King's oeuvre. He argues that rather than focus on the devastation present in so many of the narratives, the focus ought to be on how the characters put into this situation endure and survive. Jennifer Alberico provides the final words of this collection in "'The Word Pool, Where We All Go Down to Drink': The Irresistible Pull of Language in *Lisey's Story*," and she offers a close consideration of language in King's text, particularly the potential for the invented vocabulary of his characters to transcend the world of the book and enter into the real world of his Constant Reader.

The scope of this collection is wide, but the potentiality of scholarship on King's recent work abounds. Indeed, as scholars continue to approach King's oeuvre from the last twenty years, consider the immense size of King's publications between 1994 and 2013: Among these titles, a curious party would undoubtedly be able to find essays on, say, *The Green Mile* (1996); however, finding scholarly analysis on the novels *Insomnia* (1994), *Rose Madder* (1995), *Desperation* (1996), *Bag of Bones* (1998), *Hearts in Atlantis* (1999), *Dreamcatcher* (2001), *Black House* (with Peter Straub; 2002), and *From a Buick 8* (2002) would yield but a handful of articles. As such, King scholars are left with numerous gaps to navigate, including King's venture into the realm of the graphic novel, particularly his work *The Dark Tower* (2007–2013), *The Stand* (2008–2012), *The Talisman* (2009–2010), *American Vampire* (2010), *N.* (2010), and *Road Rage* (2012, a collaboration with his son Joe Hill). There are also numerous electronic texts that are quite often left alone, including *Riding the Bullet* (2000), *Ur* (2009), *Mile 81* (2011), *A Face in the Crowd* (2012, with Stewart O'Nan), and *Discordia* (*The Dark Tower*; online video game;

2010). In addition, readers and scholars seem to be also at a loss with respect to academic treatments of King's musical *Ghost Brothers of Darkland County* (2012, in collaboration with John Mellencamp), King's "lost" and unfinished serial story *The Plant* (2000), and his recent rediscovery of his poetic voice via the selections "Mostly Old Men" (2009), "The Bone Church" (2009), "Tommy" (2010), and *The Dark Man* (2013), which was originally written in 1969 but has been reintroduced to King's Constant Reader as an illustrated text. There are also the visual adaptations to contend with, including *The Dead Zone* television series (2002–2007), *Kingdom Hospital* (2004), *Desperation* (2006), *Nightmares and Dreamscapes* (2006), *Dolan's Cadillac* (2009), *Haven* (based on *The Colorado Kid*, 2010), *Bag of Bones* (2011), *Carrie* (2013), and *Under the Dome* (2013), not to mention the short stories collected in *Just After Sunset* (2008) in addition to the uncollected tales "Premium Harmony" (2009), "Under the Weather" (2010), "Herman Wouk Is Still Alive" (2011), "The Little Green God of Agony" (2011, which was also adapted into an online graphic novel format in 2012), "The Dune" (2011), "In the Tall Grass" (2012, another collaboration with his son Joe Hill), "Batman and Robin Have an Altercation" (2012), "Afterlife" (2013), and "Summer Thunder" (2013).

Pausing for a moment in the wake of such a list, it is no wonder that the potentiality for King study abounds. And the list is not yet complete. Indeed, one must also consider that a bulk of King's magnum opus, *The Dark Tower*, was written well after King had established his immense popularity among his audience. To be sure, the first three books of this series—*The Gunslinger* (1982), *The Drawing of the Three* (1987), and *The Waste Lands* (1991)—were published alongside some of King's more appealing, or popular, works, namely *Pet Sematary* (1983), *Misery* (1987), and *Needful Things* (1991), perhaps aiding with an initial interest in the works, especially among scholars (notably James Egan, author of several articles on *The Dark Tower* appearing in journals and edited collections published in the late 1980s and early 1990s). However, the later texts—*Wizard and Glass* (1997), *Wolves of the Calla* (2003), *Song of Susannah* (2004), *The Dark Tower* (2004), and *The Wind Through the Keyhole* (2012)—have certainly earned attention from King's readers, akin to those who waited eagerly for J.K. Rowling to complete her seven-book *Harry Potter* series in 2007, but even Bev Vincent's *The Dark Tower Companion* (2013; a revised version of his 2004 *The Road to the Dark Tower*), as well as the aforementioned *Inside the Dark Tower Series* have their limits (as encapsulating and analyzing a 4,000-page series cannot be done fully with just two books).

Still, while there are, thankfully, some conversations starting regarding *The Dark Tower*, the rest of King's current canon remains largely outside of the academic spotlight. These texts include *The Colorado Kid* (2005), *Cell* (2006), *Lisey's Story* (2006), *Blaze* (2007, published under the pseudonym Richard Bachman), *Duma Key* (2008), *Under the Dome* (2009), *Blockade Billy* (2010), *Full Dark, No Stars* (2010), *11/22/63* (2011), *The Joyland* (2013), *Dr. Sleep* (2013), *Mr. Mercedes* (2014), and *Revival* (2014). Although *The Colorado Kid* spawned the television show *Haven* and *Under the Dome* has also been adapted to television (albeit not necessarily more accurately than *Haven* which is just loosely based upon *The Colorado Kid*), the message remains: a great deal of work remains to be done. The babysitter is no longer part of the story—*The Village Voice* is silent—so now is the time for the Constant Readers to make their voices heard. Pow!

Notes

1. Stephen King, *On Writing* (New York: Pocket Books, 2000), 7.
2. Stephen King, "Acceptance Speech," *National Book Award Acceptance Speech*, 2003, http://www. nationalbook. org/nbaacceptspeech_sking.html.
3. Ibid.
4. Tony Magistrale, *Stephen King: America's Storyteller* (Santa Barbara: Praeger, 2010), 17.
5. Tony Magistrale, preface to *Stephen King: America's Storyteller*, ix.
6. Hardly an exhaustive list. Please see bibliography at end of this book.

PART I

King in the World
Around Us

Fantasy in Fiction
The Double-Edged Sword

JENNIFER JENKINS

> *"Sometimes a story is just a story."*
> —Jake Epping, *11/22/63*

In my first year as a graduate student, the question of the greatest import seemed to be "Why study literature?" Why indeed. Not so very long ago, I was involved in a conversation with someone who first asked, "What is your major?" and who then, when I told him it was English, replied, "Well, it's only slightly less useless than philosophy." Further conversation provided some minimal insight. One, this person was of the opinion that, beyond the very basics of reading and writing, further study in English was really quite useless. A story, he argued, will never change the world the way the internet, and computers, or medical science would. A story, after all, is just a story. An entire gamut of retorts sprung to mind, and I was seconds away from delivering an hour-long treatise on the importance of building critical thinking skills, learning the tools and devices of rhetoric and even the power of a properly placed comma. Instead, what came out was this: "You've never read Stephen King, have you?"

The rest of the conversation was fairly unremarkable. No lives were changed, no blood was shed, and ultimately, no consensus as to the importance of literature was reached. The important bit, and the reason it serves as an opening here, is that out of a vast and wide ranging canon—out of texts that have fundamentally changed the way we as a society view the world—when asked to articulate why stories are important, I thought not of the Bible, or of Talmud, which would have been quick and defensible selections. Despite years of training and study in the field of English, it was not Shakespeare, nor Milton, nor even Morrison who carried the weight of defending the importance and impact of story. Instead, for a brief moment, I was eight years old and hiding under my blankets with a flashlight in the dead of night as the story of The Loser's Club and their nemesis, Pennywise, unfolded in the dark and cavernous tunnels beneath Derry. It was there I for the first time glimpsed at something I would later discover embedded into all of King's works: a question and a consequence. The question: what does it mean to see not just the concrete, but the indefinable? To spot the hazy lines of the world which exists under, over, and around the reality we perceive from moment to moment? Further, once that sub-world has been spotted, and the pattern captured, to what extent do the consequences prove transformative? In the context of these questions, fantasy (and horror) becomes not just some made up thing, but a bridge that potentially connects reality (the experience) with history (the narrative).

What we see influences what we experience, and what we experience will, in turn, transport and transform us if we choose to follow the trail laid out before us and adeptly use the tools given to us along the way. As each of us sees and experiences things differently, the trail is often different for all, but the vehicle—the story, if you will—is a pretty standard thing in that it has existed for as long as we have and has evolved along with us. Love or hate the works or the man, the self-proclaimed "literary equivalent of a Big Mac and fries" often shows a keen awareness of this creative force we call story. Indeed, the question of creation, of myth, of *story*, is something returned to time and time again. Paintings open portals to other worlds (*Rose Madder, Duma Key*), novels act as mediums for ghosts (*Bag of Bones*), and typewriters have the potential to eat their users' families ("The Word Processor of the Gods"). In almost all instances, fantasy acts not necessarily as narrative, but the gateway to it, and to further understanding. Of his earlier works, one of the most striking examples of this theme is seen in *IT*, and when King revisits the idea of story and creation in *11/22/63*, the story inevitably lands in Derry, and invites us to consider not just the struggles of an English teacher suddenly gifted with an opportunity to change our country's story (for what is history if not the story of how we came to be where we are?), but also takes us back and asks us to consider this earlier work as well. But first, we're introduced to Jake Epping, the protagonist of *11/22/63*.

Jake is a 35-year-old English teacher who spends the better part of his days trying to get his students to read and grading an endless cycle of moderately interesting essays while trying not to dwell too much on how tired and routine it all is. When we first meet him, he's a guy clearly intent on going through the motions, doggedly dragging his fabled red pen from one paper to the next, until one day he reads an essay by a developmentally disabled GED student named Harry Dunning. Here we're given our first glimpse into art gone stunningly, and startlingly, right. While Harry is neither the most grammatically gifted writer, nor the best speller, the story he weaves is powerful enough to stop Epping cold and hold him from the opening lines: "*It wasnt a day but a night. The night that change my life was the night my father murdirt my mother and two brothers and hurt me bad.*"[1] The night that changed Harry's life will also turn out to be the night that changes Jake Epping's life. The story brings Epping to tears, and he admits "Everything that followed—every terrible thing—flowed from those tears."[2]

The essay leads Harry to earning his first ever A+ "Because it was good, and because his pain had evoked an emotional reaction in me [Jake], his reader. And isn't that what A+ writing is supposed to do? Evoke a response?"[3] It is ultimately this response that serves as a catalyst for what follows in King's story when Jake discovers that there's a doorway into the past (the late 1950s) in his favorite local diner. The owner of the diner, Al Templeton, has been trying to use this doorway to save John Kennedy from being assassinated, but before he can pull it off, he is diagnosed with cancer. Because he knows he won't be able to stop Kennedy from dying in his condition, he recruits Jake and does his best to convince him to finish the job and save the world from the radical reconfiguration caused by a single man with a gun. This puts Jake in an interesting position. Rather than being the unwitting buyer of a painting or owner of a people eating word processor, he actually has some idea of what he is getting himself into. He knows he's got a chance to change the story, and not just the big story, but the little one as well. "'Go on,' Templeton tells him, 'I need you to do this.'"[4] And of course, Epping does go on and goes forth, even if he at first only has a hazy idea of what he might be getting into. Like a reader caught in the grip of the opening lines of a novel, Epping sets aside his daily life as a high school English teacher and steps into a world where he can spend years exploring a place and time, and potentially return to the "real" world where only two minutes have passed, yet Epping returns older and changed from the experience, with his world still largely intact and relatively unchanged. The experience of the reader has suddenly been made manifest. Is it any wonder that, despite his reservations, he chooses to go forward with things, if only to see what it might be like to *really* tumble down the rabbit hole, step the magic wardrobe, or drive a Ford Sunliner down a highway in the latter-end of the fabled '50s? It's an impulse that isn't all that different than the impulse that brings many to books, and the effects, while not quite the same, are similar enough run parallel.

Much has been made of the psychological effects of both reading and writing. In *Experiencing Narrative Worlds*, Richard Gerrig explores both the "effects authors can achieve and the mechanisms by which they achieve them"[5] as a means of capturing the experience of the audience. He suggests that not only can the reader be affected by the experience of reading a text, but that the reader is also, in some ways, transported by it. As Gerrig puts it, "One of the hoariest bits of advice with respect to travel is 'When in Rome, do as the Romans do.' In essence, we are admonished to refit ourselves for local customs. Certainly if we plan to travel in good faith, we must be sure we are willing to behave as Romans do for the duration of the trip,[6] which is a notion Jake Epping wholly endorses on his second foray into the world of the past,[7] and indirectly induces us to follow. So then, if we're willing and faithful travelers where Stephen King is concerned, we inevitably come up against the double-edged blade of our own stories and are asked to take a long and hard look at both the creative and destructive powers of our stories, and the effect they have on us. Like Epping, we suit up for the longer journey, getting settled in as he buys his second root beer, gets a proper haircut, and heads for Derry. It is time to change the world, and for Epping, all bets are off, because he's stepped into a story where he can actually do it.

Under ordinary circumstances, "we are strictly prohibited from affecting the course of action in narrative worlds."[8] While we may argue about how the world may be changed in a circumstance where Kennedy is not assassinated, no one reading *11/22/63* has an expectation that it will actually change the course of history. But, for a brief time, we are nevertheless pulled through a portal in time to a particular day in 1958, where the world was younger, sweeter, and full of more promise than anyone at the time could have realized. In 1958, John Kennedy and Martin Luther King are still alive, gas is pennies to the gallon, and our fast paced world of internet/Kardashians/cell phones isn't even a remote possibility. Most importantly of all, Harry Dunning hasn't yet seen his life explode into a bloody and shattered mess. And Jake Epping, English teacher and now time-traveler, is the guy who can make sure that he never does. Assuming King has done his job, we want to make sure of it, too. There is an investment on behalf of the reader, who has strapped in and, much like Jake when he steps into his first shop in 1958, we are prepared to not only "do as the Romans do," in a passive sense, but we're also physically engaged. Anne Paul, in her *New York Times* article titled "Your Brain on Fiction," offers an interesting perspective on the phenomenon of reader interaction with narrative:

> The brain, it seems, does not make much of a distinction between reading about an experience and encountering it in real life; in each case, the same neurological regions are stimulated. Keith Oatley, an emeritus professor of cognitive psychology at the University of Toronto (and a published novelist), has proposed that reading produces a vivid simulation of reality, one that "runs on minds of readers just as computer simulations run on computers." [...] The novel, of course, is an unequaled medium for the exploration of human social and emotional life. And there is evidence that just as the brain responds to depictions of smells and textures and movements as if they were the real thing, so it treats the interactions among fictional characters as something like real-life social encounters.[9]

The encounters of Jake's early travels are a bit reversed from this: rather than the scripted page feeling real, reality feels like a scripted page as "characters" go "off-script" in response to changes in his responses or their surroundings. In other words, Jake Epping is not simply time travelling; he has been transported into the story and made an agent of change. And it's no coincidence that on his quest to forever alter the destiny of the world that Epping first has to travel to Derry, because "in Derry, reality is a thin skim of ice over a deep lake of dark water."[10] In a world already rife with contradiction, layers of nostalgic levels of prosperity cover a simmering mess of class warfare, racism, and poverty; Derry is a microcosm of the United States in the '50's, and it's picturesque streets a cover for miles of dark sewers that run underneath the concrete. Jake Epping says, "There was something wrong with that town, and I think I knew it from the first,"[11] and indeed, if ever there were a place that embodies the blurred line between what we experience in real life versus what we experience in our heads, Derry is it. And It, of course, is Derry. Though Jake never encounters the thing that sleeps and feeds in Derry, he can feel it as few of the people who live there can. This is interesting for a couple of reasons. First, because anyone familiar with Derry knows that the children of the town are the ones who are most clearly aware and vulnerable to It; second, because It can be seen an extended metaphor in and of itself about the inherent dark powers of myth and story. It is a thing born of the darkness beyond the ends of the universe, but for the children of Derry, It is a fairytale monster straight out of Grimm's with no last-minute saves, no friendly woodsmen, and no happily ever after. Jake, as a traveler outside his own narrative, has no way of knowing any of this, but he intuits it long before he speaks to anyone in Derry, and well before he runs into two players in a script from another story. And while he can sense the edges of that story, he never quite grasps it. Instead, it was "as if I had gripped the rim of some vast understanding. Or peered (through a glass darkly, you understand) into the actual clockwork of the universe."[12]

If Jake had gotten the full story, he may well have been better prepared for the consequences of changing that fabled day in Dallas, 1963. In front of him are children who have peered into a world in which reality and fantasy collide, the lines blurring until both can be glimpsed. And like Jake Epping, Bev Marsh and Richie Tozier have traveled down the fabled rabbit hole, and will do so again at a later date, and though their story is separate from the larger narrative that takes place in *11/22/63*, they were driven by the same sorts of impulses that he is: to save something, to stop the course of Derry's narrative, and shift it into a better direction. And, for a little while at least, they did. The atmosphere in 1958 Derry is almost, but not quite, a town under siege. Through only the broad strokes, Jake does pick up a few things about the previous year, a time when the town had been held in a grip of terror, which "began, so far as I know or can tell, with a boat made from a sheet of newspaper floating down a gutter swollen with rain."[13]

The paper boat, made by a six-year-old boy named George with his big brother, Bill, serves both as the opening for *IT* and a symbol of a child's innocent desire to imagine and create—racing down the rain filled gutters in an effort to fly and escape the mundane, propelled as much by the imagination of boy who runs behind it as it is by the natural force of the wind, the water current, and the rain. Like any child who wanders into the forest during a fairytale, George has no real sense of danger, and much like Jake Epping, he has only a hazy idea of the forces that surround him. In Derry, there is a creature that feeds, not on actual flesh, but on emotion and fantasy, particularly negative emotions and fantasies. In a less literal sense, this creature serves as a negative embodiment of creative work: it's sole purpose is to consume the elements around it and be filled by that which is consumed. For longer than Derry existed, this force had made a home there: "It had spent Its long, long existence inflicting pain, feeding on it," [14] but never Itself having experienced either pain or fear.

Here, King approaches the effects of story and myth from multiple angles at once. Yes, they inform our ideologies, help us to communicate, and yes, quite often they entertain us. But they can also be dark and scary, and leave us a little afraid. Not only that, but as many a theorist has suggested, we all encounter and experience stories in different ways, and so with It, King gives us a shape shifting creature that can become literally anything and be experienced in multiple ways nearly simultaneously. Countless other possible metaphors aside, with this creature and the surrounding narrative, we're treated to a serious and occasionally thoughtful examination of the inherent power of myth as seen and experienced through the eyes of children, possibly the most avid consumers of our darkest and most twisted fairytales. Indeed, children's fears tend toward basic, concrete, and even physical manifestations; to wit, fear of darkness and monsters are an intrinsic part of growing up. Within *IT*, It feeds, not specifically on the children themselves, but on their fears and desires, using myths and stories to control, cull, and then ultimately feed off of the children It hunts. It changes Its shape in accordance with what most frightens its target, becoming a werewolf, or an initially sweet but slightly creepy (and homicidal) old lady, a vampire, a mummy, or a psychotic killer clown, and so on. The cycle doesn't stop there, however. The passage of childhood forces a break from those older, simpler myths and new, less definable fears gained in their stead. This means that for adults, the influences of It are more subtle, more complex fears that cannot be symbolized as easily—racism, poverty, failure, and so on are used to manipulate and mold the adults into tools that can be used for the hunt. It is not so much that adults lose the creative and imaginative forces that define childhood, but rather that the creative impulse evolves into something new and often less *singularly* powerful. Either way, both young and old are caught in an endless cycle that, when examined at a distance yields a pattern that can be traced like a script that runs, not on a single climax, but on a series of them, each occurring once every 28 years or so, catalyzed by a creature that has no single face.

Ultimately, It is a conglomeration of the entire town's darkest fears and desires, all of which are recognized on some level but ignored in the day to day lives of the adults who live there. They have forced themselves to not see It because for all the terror it brings, the presence of It also brings them a sense of security. As long as they keep within the guidelines set to them and don't try to upset the order It imposes, the town prospers. Only the children are fully aware that there is something more sinister going on than a migrant serial killer, and they exist almost completely below the sightline of the adults. This partial visibility works in It's favor, and the simpler, more concrete fears of children are easier to draw from, allowing It to feed off their fear and destroy them. And for this reason, It prefers to hunt children rather than focusing on the adults of the town. But if It can be used as a metaphor for the dark and destructive aspects of myth and fantasy, then the children of Derry, particularly the members of The Loser's Club, are a reminder of the healing, cathartic properties of myth. For these children, it can be argued that the trauma they suffer is what ultimately helps them to sharpen the tools they will eventually use to hurt and later defeat It. In "Nightmares of Childhood: The Child and the Monster in Four Novels by Stephen King," Sara Alegre writes extensively about the trauma each child in this circle of friends (and enemies) suffers and how it relates to their experiences with It:

> Ben, Mike, Stan, [Bill], Eddie, Richie and Beverly are drawn together because they have seen "It," each in a form particularly suited to family circumstances, early childhood traumas or the imaginary horrors enjoyed in fiction. Four of these children are already enduring the attacks of another kind of monster: Ben, Eddie and Mike are being mercilessly persecuted by the school bully, Henry, himself a badly abused child; Eddie is also the victim of an overprotective mother and Beverly of her father's sexual abuse.[15]

Faced with a world already dark and lonely without the added complications, they are uniquely suited toward not only being pulled into by a fantasy, but also they're all extremely adept at creating their own worlds and rules as a means of escapism. The members of The Loser's Club spend their summer days hidden away in The Barrens, an undeveloped area that largely serves as a drainage mechanism for the town's sink and bath water. Described as a scar-like mark in the otherwise developed town of Derry, The Barrens is a wild, and sometimes even dangerous place that they nevertheless make their own. The world they create for themselves in the Barrens allows them to temporarily leave behind their victimhood, and serves as the other (happier, lighter, cathartic) side of the creative force where they lose themselves in playing games, in building dams and underground clubhouses, and constructing boundaries within which they are safely the heroes of their own stories. And the leader of them all, the hero that ties the others together, is none other than Bill Denbrough, brother of George, who made the boat that sent the younger boy to his death, and who one day grows up to become a bestselling novelist by using the horrors he and his friends survived in their childhoods as a catalyst to enchant readers into similar experiences. As King says about the younger Denbrough before his death, "Bill was good at reading and writing, but even at *his* age George was wise enough to know that wasn't the only reason why Bill got all A's on his report cards, or why his teachers liked his compositions so well. *Telling* was only part of it. Bill was good at seeing."[16] Seeing, as we have already set forth, is an integral part of engaging the senses when both writing and reading fiction, and each of the children in their club is adept to a degree, but Bill, the child who will one day be a novelist, is the one who sees the clearest. It is not just a thing that feeds on children; It has become a naturalized part of Derry's (hi)story, a parasite that has drained all that is good from childhood stories and left only the nightmares behind. To defeat It, they must not only overcome their own fears, they have to overcome the inertia of Derry as well.

It is Bill who convinces his friends that they must be the ones who change the story of Derry after the horrific death of his brother, and it's through Bill that the voice of the Turtle speaks most clearly. Rules are set out, fantasy pitted against fantasy, and the confrontation started. Once the children understand that their greatest weapon is their belief in their myths, they use that knowledge to their advantage learning to, as the Turtle later tells Bill to "believe in all the things you have believed in, believe that if you tell the policeman you're lost he'll see that you get home safely, that there is a Tooth Fairy who lives in a huge enamel castle, and Santa Claus below the North Pole, making toys with his trove of elves, believe that your mother and father will love you again, that courage is possible."[17] The battle was temporarily won by the children learning to use their fears to trap It in a shape, and then fight It using the weakness of the shape assumed—ie. silver ball bearings to defeat the werewolf, "battery acid" to defeat the giant, menacing eyeball, and so on.

It is perhaps only fitting then, that two of the children who harnessed their own creative power to defeat (if not destroy) It sense a similar ability to "see" in Jake Epping. He is not one of them, and he does not hear the voice of their Turtle, but he, like them is trying to set things right. And so, while it is Harry Dunning's essay that serves as a catalyst and motivates Jake to push forward with his new and strange adventure when he first encounters the portal in Al Templeton's diner, it is Richie and Bev who steer Epping in the right direction on his test case (attempting to change Harry Dunning's past and seeing if this results in change in the "real world"), and it is Bev who asks him if he knows the Turtle. A figure that weaves its way through most of King's work, the Turtle is, on one level, the creator of the universe, and on another, the ultimate muse through which all creative and imaginative thoughts flow, connecting the children to one another despite the counterforces at work in Derry. All of this—the Turtle, It, Derry and its various citizens—can serve an extended metaphor for the way myths and histories are seen, as well as the effect of such myths on the people who believe them. When the people of Derry are part of Its structure and stuck inside what Mike Hanlon calls "the feeding pen," then the values of that system hold sway over all of them and a culture of insular fear and suspicion rules. Only by examining these values and the system itself are the children able to determine its rules and use those rules as a way to bring down the system in hopes of instituting a new one in Derry. It, the mindless consumer that gobbles up small children and paralyzes adults with fear, is the status quo of the town, an ignorable level of discomfort that occurs every once and awhile but is left to stand because people believe everything is otherwise more or less okay, even though the outside reality suggests that a 27-year cycle of fear and violence is anything but normal.

The Turtle, the indifferent creator of the universe, encourages the challenge of the status quo, but cannot (or will not) do the challenging. However, Bill and his friends have learned the power of creating myths and use that power to disrupt the standing history in favor of some new order. Yet this ability comes with a price: having seen what lives under

Derry, they are forever unable to unsee it. Though they forget the specifics eventually, their dreams—the ultimate conveyor of myth—always remind them, even if they forget once they're awake. To cap it off, even though they have the ability to create (or re-create) myth, that ability does not necessarily suggest that change is ever permanently for the better. Instead, we are told it is "Best to *believe* there will be happily ever afters all the way around—and so there may be; who is to say there will not be such endings? Not all boats which sail away into darkness never find the sun again, or the hand of another child,"[18] and invited to create our own myth, suggesting that we all have our status quos that put us to sleep and allow us to sleep walk through the world, the writers, the artists, and the world changers. Pennywise lives, even for those who would reveal the truth within the lie ... and remove the haze of myth from their reality.

While most of Derry's story is left implied or unstated, most of the resistance that Epping encounters stems back to it. All but blind to the troublesome and occasionally terrifying psychotic turns that take place in the city limits, the people of Derry are far more hostile to potential outsider influence than they are to the heavy drinking (sledge)hammer wielding fathers who occasionally murder their children, for it is the outsider who sees what they themselves no longer can. There are dark forces working in their midst that have been there so long they are not only a part of the narrative of Derry, but, rather, they *are* Derry. For these forces to be defeated, they have to first be acknowledged and then the surrounding society has to change in response. In the end, though, destroying It is a good thing in much the same the way that Kennedy not being assassinated is a good thing; destroying It also means the destruction of Derry. In a larger context, this same pattern can be seen in the broader world of the United States in the 1950s. From the outside, it looks idyllic. Prices are down, personal safety and security are up, and the food tastes better. On the other hand, racial equality is laughable in many sectors, gender equality fares only a little better, and underneath the feel good sense of security lies a disquieting sense of wrongness not unlike the muck that flows through the sewers of Derry. To change this risks destroying the society it stems from, and every good thing that came out of it afterward. For all that we can see about what is good and what is bad, how prepared are we as readers to grapple with the consequences that stem from making even minor changes?

Of course, this treatment of text as a real thing happening as we read it is a fairly limited thing. For while we may flinch internally at the whistle of an impending hammer blow, we are in no danger of getting injured. We are expected to fully embrace Jake Epping's thoughts and feelings, or agree with his course of action regarding both Harry Dunning and Kennedy, but we are most certainly maneuvered into taking active roles as we at least *consider* those thoughts, feelings, and actions. In the course of that consideration, are we not then also compelled to examine ourselves in relation to that the narrative? Probably, yes. Chances are good that if our brain is as actively engaged as current research suggests it is while we're reading, we're considering *something*. I hesitate to suggest that King wants us to ponder any one specific thing as we follow Jake's story, but it is certainly a cautionary tale. Remember, we are first situated with Jake as a reader who reacts to a story, and is then given the improbable chance to change that story, which he does. This small success then leads him down a path where everything that followed, "every terrible thing—flowed from those tears."[19] In other words, to go back to where we started this discussion, particularly through King's recent tale *11/22/63*, stories have power. Authors can use it, whether knowingly or not, to have myriad effects on their readers. Often times, this effect is a good thing—research abounds for the ways in which reading affects us cognitively, emotionally, spiritually, and politically. It can also, as Jake finds out, be a not so good thing. While Jake does save Harry Dunning and his family from Harry's murderous father, Harry is ultimately killed in Vietnam and never has the chance to actually meet Jake in the future and take GED courses. And while Jake also does manage to save Kennedy, and briefly savor his success, his return to the "real" world nets him a failed Civil Rights movement and resultant chaos that leads to the destruction of the United States as we know it, much as the destruction of It causes Derry to disintegrate. Both are well intentioned acts, and while they operate at different levels (Derry at least, might someday recover) that they share a similar outcome suggests that whatever else we may be, we are never fully in control of that which we create, for good or bad.

As I mentioned, often for King, the creative process and the things that come out of it are dual- natured. We can craft a story with the best of intentions, and we can also read other stories and be genuinely affected by them in ways that we may not have expected. Generally speaking, King's ultimate response to this relationship between art, the artist, and the audience is to show both sides of the proverbial coin, let us plunge forward into the situation, and then ultimately carry us through to the other side, a little older, possibly a little wiser, and more often than not a little worse for wear. Though King freely admits he has strong opinions about some of the other themes that run through the novel (political extremism is a big one), I don't think those opinions should lead us to dismiss or otherwise trivialize the idea of narrative power and how a person (whether reader or author) deals with it. Indeed, any given story may not change the world. It will not perfect the democratic process, revolutionize the way we shop, or cure cancer. A story won't even let us time travel (though if science is right, maybe it brings us closer to that than we think). What it will do, and what Stephen King is especially good at, is offer us insight into ourselves. The way we think, the way we create, and the whys of how we do both. Rhetoric and narratives are tools that allow us to explore these insights, and thereby in and of themselves, they are neither necessarily good nor bad. Are they useful? Certainly. Do those insights then change us? Most definitely. Given that, and that the product of these tools is of a dual-nature for all parties involved, then in all probability no story is ever *just* a story. But be careful with it; it cuts both ways.

Notes

1. Stephen King, *11/22/63* (New York: Scribner, 2011), 6. And note that all errors within this quotation reflect the awkward writing of Henry Dunning and are not typographical mistakes.

2. Ibid., 7.

3. Ibid., 6.

4. Ibid., 28.

5. Richard Gerrig, *Experiencing Native Worlds: On the Psychological Activities of Reading* (New Haven, CT: Yale University Press, 1993), 2.

6. Ibid., 11.

7. King, *11/22/63*, 250.

8. Gerrig, *Experiencing Native Worlds*, 24.

9. Anne Paul, "Your Brain on Fiction," *The New York Times*, March 17, 2012, http://www.nytimes.com/2012/03/18/opinion/sunday/the-neuroscience-of-your-brain-onfiction.html?pagewanted=all&_r=0.

10. King, *11/22/63*, 150.

11. Ibid., 121.

12. Ibid., 137.

13. Stephen King, *IT* (New York: Signet, 1987), 3.

14. Ibid., 1094.

15. Sara Martín Alegre, "Nightmares of Childhood: The Child and the Monster in Four Novels by Stephen King," *Atlantis*, 23, no. 1 (2001): 110.

16. King, *IT*, 13.

17. Ibid., 1047.

18. Ibid., 1100.

19. King, *11/22/63*, 27.

King Me

Inviting New Perceptions and Purposes of the Popular and Horrific into the College Classroom

Michael A. Perry

Stephen King is taught throughout academia in both English and film departments, often in classes that focus on the genre of horror—a label that King himself simultaneously embraces and frustrates with increasing vigor.[1] Likewise, the approach offered herein seeks to complicate perceptions of King by pairing him with a few of his more "literary" contemporaries and predecessors. This project, which stems from issues born of my decision to pair Toni Morrison and King in a special topics seminar, addresses ways to include King into literary curricula without devolving into a debate over canonization. Upon examining how King and Morrison value an intimate connection to their readership while frustrating literary and popular classifications, attention turns to Mark Twain and Ambrose Bierce, which leads to a focus on broader thematic elements—honesty, truth, probability and reality—culminating in an examination of King's *The Colorado Kid*. Ultimately, this essay constitutes a meditation on the possibilities of what can be achieved if we question the origins of our preconceptions and find the courage to invite one of our most prolific and increasingly diverse authors into literary studies discourse.

When Carrie Met Sula

Encouraged by the possibility of applying rigorous critical analysis to popular texts, yet troubled not only by the implications of removing popular texts from their original context but also by the false binary between popular and literary that such a division signifies, I sought to examine the effects of relocating popular texts into the classroom and blur the boundaries between literary and popular fiction. As such, I designed a special topics course, titled "When *Carrie* Met *Sula*: Blurring the Line Between 'Literary' and 'Popular' Works with Toni Morrison and Stephen King." Many students (and I would venture to guess faculty) navigate the imaginary border between the "popular" and the "literary" on a daily basis and are perfectly suited to pursue this dynamic. As such, the combination of Morrison and King opens a dialogue that challenges our perceptions of the supposed solid distinctions between the two. Ultimately, and importantly, when considered side-by-side, striking similarities arise which provide a greater understanding of what it means to be an American writer.

When Carrie met Sula in my classroom, students displayed both excitement and trepidation at the pairing. Many assumed we would proceed by using each author to solidify and define, rather than blur and complicate, the boundary between literary and popular texts. Instead, I began by asking students to view two of contemporary America's most influential writers in a new context. The first step was to consider the popular aspects of Morrison and the literary aspects of King. This, however, simply flipped rather than blurred the line. Therefore, the second and most crucial step was to focus the act of interpretation, of analysis, on the reading experience alongside that of text itself. Such redirection began a semester-long exploration (one that, for me, continues) of not only Morrison and King, but also the larger questions of how we approach texts designated as literary or popular and how such designation informs the reading experience.

Presently, both Morrison and King enjoy large, devoted audiences for their work. Both authors stand out as quintessentially American. Yet, to speak of them in the same sentence inevitably invites resistance. More so than differences in race or gender, the classifications of their respective oeuvres chiefly account for this reality. To counter this resistance, I have students read both authors' acceptance speeches for the National Book Foundation award—an identical honor that they received only seven years apart. Fascinatingly, the similarities do not end there. Despite obvious contrasts in style, both writers challenge the literary establishment, engage in storytelling, muse upon the role writing plays in their lives, and reflect upon the importance of honesty in fiction. Both King and Morrison challenge established traditions embodied in what King calls the "Old Boy network" and what Morrison calls the "Ivory Tower." King directly challenges the divide between the literary and the popular in his acceptance speech: "For far too long the so-called popular writers of this country and the so-called literary writers have stared at each other with animosity and willful lack of understanding."[2] Despite King's dissatisfaction with the arbitrary distinction, he does not argue that there is no difference between the two. Rather, he takes issue with the way we go about evaluating each genre and locates blame within the writers themselves. Morrison further challenges the divide, although more subtly, as she argues that "when the voice [of the narrative] is not the separate, isolated ivory tower voice of a very different kind of person but an implied 'we' in narration," one's perceptions of the "artist as supreme individual" can be disrupted.[3] This disruption allows the reader, according to Morrison, to engage the author on equal footing and enjoy a more intimate connection with the text.

While encouraging readers to approach both authors on equal ground, it is important to provide the disclaimer that such an exercise is meant to neither reify distinctions between literary and popular fiction nor render them useless. Instead, I contend that achieving the freedom to feel as though we have the right to approach any given text from a popular or literary standpoint, despite its classification, expands our "horizon of expectations" for both author and text.[4] By initially focusing discussion upon how we read, what we read, and why we read (essentially applying tenets of reader response and reception theories), resultant class discussions articulate the implications of the preconceptions we bring to a text. Indeed, observations students bring to the class ("Doesn't King just write horror novels about psycho prom queens and rabid dogs?" "I heard Morrison is really hard to 'get.'") illuminate more about the reader than they do either author or text.

By directing her readers to an implied "we," Morrison displays the importance she places upon her readership. She appreciates the relevancy of individual responses, especially responses that stem from consideration of one's reading experience. Elizabeth Long, in her study of book clubs, addresses the fear that members of King's "Old Boy network" and Morrison's "Ivory Tower" have of embracing individual reader response as she notes how "the open-ended multiplicity of actual reader's readings is especially alarming to scholars invested in a tradition of great books, because it threatens to destabilize the very textual building blocks of their authority."[5] In this sense, pairing King with Morrison, while certainly not meant to dismantle the tradition of great books, certainly threatens the too often comfortable "Othering" imposed upon King by academia.

To put it succinctly, we can read King with the same rigorous critical view scholars apply to literary texts, and we can read Morrison with the same sense of "reading for escape," for "fun," that often marks King's readership. Simply telling students how to approach texts, however, is not enough. That is why throughout the course of the semester I have students read two novels side-by-side, thus letting the texts and the reading experience of each text implicitly engage in a dialogue within each individual reading experience. While reading *Carrie* alongside *The Bluest Eye*, readers not only picked up upon thematic concerns such as standards of beauty, gender inequality, and the perversion of religion, but they also pointed out how King's first novel (much like Morrison's) is actually quite experimental in its use of multiple points of view, which include excerpts from fake "real" books and moments of non-linear reflection.

The striking amount of similarities translates to each author's frustration at the limitations of critics. Morrison, as she talks about translating blues rhythms and themes into her fiction, muses "I wish there were ways in which such things could be talked about in criticism."[6] King, admittedly using more crass language, recalls his first bout with a critic: "After having a two-hundred pound babysitter fart on your face and yell *Pow! The Village Voice* holds few terrors."[7] Essentially putting into perspective his first critical beating, he employs humor. But underneath the humor is an edge that comes out more blatantly in his acceptance speech. Upon deriding judges of the National Book Foundation for taking pride in not reading popular authors, he deadpans: "What do you think? You get social or academic brownie points for deliberately staying out of touch with your own culture?"[8] Importantly, King once again avoids entering into a canon debate. Instead, he derides critics for shirking in their duty to know the culture they critique and challenges them to reassess "how" they evaluate only after they have engaged the texts they dismiss. Like Morrison, King simply wants critics to approach his work from the perspective of what he is trying to accomplish.

Frustration at being misread by critics is certainly not unique to King and Morrison; however, their decision to highlight the concerns of their readers displays a kinship that not only respects but also honors their readership. Without their readers, both authors imply that their work would be meaningless. Morrison goes as far to state "If anything I do, in the way of writing [...] isn't about the village or the community or about you, then it is not about anything."[9] As such, Morrison directly ties the value of her text to the response of her readers. King, in his memoir, offers a similar sentiment as he addresses a poem authored by his wife, Tabitha King: "Her poem made me feel that good writing can be simultaneously intoxicating and idea-driven."[10] What both authors share is a belief that writing ought to connect with a life lived—it ought to speak to a community of readers. King continues: "There was also a work ethic in the poem [...] that suggested writing poems had as much in common with sweeping the floor as with mythy moments of revelation."[11] The combination of creative impulse and practical concerns, which speaks to both the spontaneity of creation and the calculated translation of that spontaneity onto the page, is similarly reflected in Morrison as she reminds us that fiction, while "it may be more interesting," is "not random."[12]

Probably the most striking resemblance between King and Morrison resides in their philosophy of what it means to be a writer. King offers that writing is "telepathy of course," which he goes on to describe as a meeting of the minds between the reader and the author.[13] To illustrate, he offers a descriptive paragraph in which sits a rabbit in a cage on a table with the number eight marked on its back. He offers many details but the one that stands out above the rest: "It's an eight. This is what we're looking for, and we all see it. I didn't tell you. You didn't ask me. I never opened my mouth and you never opened yours."[14] The wordless communication King alludes to transcends both time and space: "We're not even in the same *year* together, let alone the same room ... except we *are* together. We're close. We're having a meeting of the minds."[15] The fascinating aspect of King's narrative is how seemingly obvious his point is (a good writer doesn't need to tell his reader what to see, what to think) while, at the same time, how profound (consider two minds in different times, different places, interacting in the same moment). Morrison, in a similar reference to telepathic connection, refers to "the dance of an open mind when it engages another equally open one."[16] Together, we have a meeting of the minds, across time and space, enabled by the interaction of author, reader, and text. Approaching the reading experience as a form of telepathy, a metaphorical dance, allows students to further assess their positions relative to each author.

To be clear, I make no assertion that King and Morrison are alike, that they write in the same manner, or that they have the same agendas; rather, I contend that our classification of each author necessarily infects (yes, I say infect, not affects) our reading. When Bourdieu writes that "taste classifies and it classifies the classifier," to use terminology appropriate to King, we should all be afraid, very afraid, as such a dichotomy instills far too much power in the institutions that put forth criteria for such classifications in the first place.[17] This pairing complicates normative modes of classification and challenges Bourdieu's observation that taste is singular rather than pluralistic, and often, contradictory. Regardless of how we perceive their respective classifications, further analysis of King's and Morrison's decision to focus on reader response over critical response informs their respective reflections upon the nature of literary realism as it pertains to honesty and truth in fiction that makes use of the supernatural.

In Fear of Mark Twain

Ever since my experience teaching "When Carrie Met Sula," the site for the original pairing of King and Morrison, I have found ways to further blur the boundary between popular and literary fictions. As such, King surfaced twice during the course of an American literature survey I offered a year later: first during a reading of Mark Twain wherein Twain attacks the work of James Fenimore Cooper's *Deerslayer* and later alongside the Gothic renderings of Ambrose Bierce and his peculiar views upon probability and reality. King's resurfacing redirected my attention to an unresolved thematic connection between King and Morrison: their perceived role of honesty and truth in fiction.

I titled this section "In Fear of Mark Twain" because it is my contention that since Twain, American writers have, in part, lived in fear of his missive against poor James Fenimore Cooper—a spirited attack on *Deerslayer*, where he implicitly defines realism by explaining what it is not (even though he never explicitly uses the term). Of the eighteen rules Twain says Cooper violates, I have included four: first, "a tale shall accomplish something and arrive somewhere"[18]; second, "personages in a tale ... shall exhibit a sufficient excuse for being there"[19]; third, "when the author describes the character of a personage in his tale, the conduct and conversation of that personage shall justify said description"[20]; and fourth, "the author shall make the reader feel a deep interest in the personages of his tale and in their fate."[21] What Twain argues against is a lack of control on the author's part. Cooper's failure, according to Twain, is a failure to yield to the law of physics and verisimilitude (in dialogue and setting) and to rely solely on coincidence while seemingly believing that such things appear natural. Combined, Twain's rules appear to look for honesty and truth in narrative by asserting that a tale that meanders with random characters who act in "unnatural" ways is not only dishonest but also precludes the reader from feeling a "deep interest" in the narrative. What angers Twain so much about Cooper is the implication that Cooper claims to be offering a realistic portrayal of life and is unaware of just how ridiculous and uncontrolled his narration can appear.

The parallels between Twain's missive and King's reflections upon what makes "good" writing in his memoir abound and are what initially led me to this pairing. The more I considered the connections, the more I observed that along with Morrison, all three authors share a desire to be "honest" in their writing while still adhering to the tenets of their respective genres. King wants his characters to "do things *their* way."[22] Not his way. King gives life to his characters when he talks of them as living beings. This means he tries, regardless of the reality of the situation (whether telekinesis, rabid dogs, or the death of a spouse) to have characters in his novels react to their respective situations in ways that seem honest: "In the end, the important question has nothing to do with whether the talk in your story is sacred or profane; the only question is how it rings on the page and in the ear."[23] In this way, King places the legitimacy of his writing not upon established critical criteria, but rather on more ephemeral responses from actual readers—a perspective Twain offers as well ("the reader shall feel a deep interest").[24] King goes as far as to say that a writer ought to pay "attention to how the real people around you behave and then [tell] the truth about what you see."[25]

In this way, the quest to offer what they perceive as "honest" narratives (an inability that frustrates Twain in regards to Cooper) ties King and Morrison together in heretofore untold ways. A quick glance at their respective novels shows their tendency to employ supernatural elements into their fictional worlds, although Morrison certainly veers more toward what is popularly called magical realism. Morrison grants that while her work falls "into that realm of fiction called fantastic, or mythic, or magical, or unbelievable," she remains "[un]comfortable with these labels [and considers that her] single gravest responsibility (in spite of that magic) is not to lie."[26] Not lying in art is really about being honest with oneself. And if an author's "truth" is best expressed through the supernatural, through ghosts and monsters, then such narratives can still represent an "honest" narrative even when it diverges from common perceptions of reality. In this sense, lying is contextual, as is dishonesty. That a ghost exists as the embodiment of a dead child is not dishonest, nor can it be simply called magical realism. Maybe emotional realism is a better descriptor. Consider the manifestation of telekinesis in an adolescent female: what is "honest" about King's portrayal is that the resultant narrative derives from his quest to relate the truth of Carrie's situation.

Morrison meditates on the role truth and the fantastic play in her narratives and draws an important line: "[T]he crucial distinction for me is not the difference between fact and fiction, but the distinction between fact and truth."[27] In other words, facts inform but do not necessarily reflect truth—a narrative seeks to communicate the truth behind the fact. Or, narrative is truth, more so than fact, as facts can be manipulated and taken out of context. The story must, in its quest for truth, write itself, and the distinction between what is fact and what is truth ought to remain implicit to the narrative. This ability of the story to write itself is reflected in King's distrust of plot: "first, because our *lives* are largely plotless [...] second, because I believe plotting and the spontaneity of real creation aren't compatible."[28] In other words, according to King, an honest narrative and a plotted narrative are not necessarily compatible in that lives are indeed "plotless." Granted, after a life lived, we may reflect back and discover a "plot" within our lives, but that only comes after the life has been lived. Likewise, we can return to a text that is not plot heavy and still discover a plot, but it is a constructed artifice that necessarily simplifies the narrative.

Rather than plotting, King asserts he listens to his characters and they tell him where the story will go. Similarly, Morrison wants to "make the story appear oral, meandering, effortless, spoken—to have the reader *feel* the narrator without *identifying* that narrator."[29] Morrison's impetus to create the affect of a story told meshes with King's hesitancy toward plot. However, a marked difference lies with each author's use of narrators. King's narrators often clearly represent individual character's points of view, with changes in points of view clearly indicated on the page. Morrison, on the other hand, asserts that she tries to create the "illusion" that it is the characters' point of view when it is not: "it's really the narrator who is there but doesn't make herself known in that role."[30] She continues to remark that she likes "the feeling of a *told* story, where you hear a voice but you can't identify it, and you think it's your own voice."[31] Despite differences in approach, both King and Morrison craft narrators who they deem unfold the narrative in what they see as "truthful" (placing emphasis on the realities of character) rather than "artificial" (placing emphasis on demands of plot) ways.

This preoccupation with communicating "truth" to the reader guides both authors into realms of the fantastic, because within the heightened reality both authors find truth within how characters act rather than the reality of the situation. King, in his speech at the National Book Foundation, offers an example wherein an elevator full of people begins a free-fall worth quoting at length for its candid claims of authenticity: "in my opinion, no one is going to say, 'Goodbye, Neil, I will see you in heaven.' [...] In my book or my short story, they're far more apt to bellow, 'Oh shit' at the top of their lungs."[32] While not necessarily meditating on the creative process, King offers an implicit nod toward literary realism—a tradition that, like Twain, looks with a weary eye upon heightened language. But more than language, King places emphasis on the "honesty" of character action over the authorial impulse to embellish the narrative, whatever circumstances exist. He also displays a keen sense of humor by connecting his narrative to his audience that plays on his mystique as a master of horror and connects him with Twain on another level.[33]

Despite their ability to tell a story and work an audience, neither King nor Twain claim to be able to explain "the how" of their craft. King dryly observes: "Fiction writers, present company included, don't understand very much about what they do—not why it works when it's good, not why it doesn't when it's bad."[34] The irony, of course, is that this pronouncement precedes a 300-page memoir titled, *On Writing*. Twain, in

"The Art of Authorship," offers a similar sentiment: "I am not sure that I have methods in composition. I do suppose I have—I suppose I must have—but they somehow refuse to take shape in my mind."[35] While King and Twain offer conciliatory remarks about the creative process, both are simultaneously outspoken and quite specific about their craft, especially when addressing the act of storytelling. Most striking is King's observation that stories come from "two previously unrelated ideas [that] come together and make something new under the sun. [The writer's] job isn't to find these ideas but to recognize them when they show up."[36] This observation recalls the concept of reading as telepathy and illuminates that the dance is not limited to an interaction between reader and author, but also occurs earlier in the creative process as a dance between author and memory (both personal and public).

Twain, whose ability to tell a story is well known in the annals of American literature, embarks on a similar dance as he employs a mix of self and memory, a mix of fact and truth, wherein even his "factual" name gives way to a construction that represents his "true" identity. This merging of fact and truth, of real life events with creative re-imaginings, is reflected in the two titular characters from the initial pairing of King and Morrison: Carrie and Sula. King details the sad stories of the two women for whom he bases Carrie White's character—the resultant narrative, his first novel *Carrie*, essentially is his translation of the fact of those two girls into the "truth" of Carrie White. Morrison is more evasive as she admits that Sula is inspired by a real person named Hannah Peace, qualifying that the memory of her is that of a four-year-old girl's impressions and images. In spite of this, she proclaims, "I'm not going to ask my mother who she really was [...] That way I can explore two worlds—the actual and the possible."[37] Indeed, it is the merging of the actual and the possible, of memory and imagination, and of fact and fiction, that inform each narrative.

Of course, offering a definition of truth or attempting to understand exactly what truth signifies for each author would be an exercise in futility. As such, allow me to turn to Ambrose Bierce, a contemporary of Twain and author of—in addition to countless tales of the Civil War, the supernatural, and horror—*The Devil's Dictionary*, wherein he offers the following definition of truth: "An ingenious compound of desirability and appearance. Discovery of truth is the sole purpose of philosophy, which [...] has a fair prospect of existing [...] to the end of time."[38]

Despite the obvious sarcasm, Bierce's definition acutely observes the tenuous and subjective nature of truth as well as the human desire to understand it. The role of the writer, as both King and Morrison illustrate, is similar in part to Bierce's philosophers who will still be meditating upon truth when the sun goes dark and the oceans dry up. And the best way to pursue this goal is not to directly talk about it, but, according to King, to communicate it implicitly to the reader "by interpreting 'write what you know' as broadly and inclusively as possible."[39] Writing what one knows, combined with the freedom of merging memory and imagination, leads King to assure his reader that even "plumbers in space is not such a bad set up for a story."[40] It can even be a probable one, if the narrative itself unfolds in an honest way.

Whether or not a narrative includes the fantastic or the supernatural has nothing to do with the probability of the actual narrative. In fact, discerning how to account for probability in narrative fiction can lead a writer to overcompensate, which is exactly what Twain calls out Cooper for doing: he is guilty of attempting to make his story "too" probable to the point that it no longer feels real. Probability is far more nuanced as Bierce observes: "Fiction has nothing to say to probability: the capable writer gives it not a moment's attention, except to make what is related *seem* probable in the reading—*seem* true."[41] Taken this way, fiction is about creating a world that the reader *believes* is real. King, referencing the skepticism an interviewer took with his account of how stories are found, said it did not matter if the interviewer believed it, "as long as he believed that *I* believe it."[42] King's readers do not have to accept telekinesis as a reality in order to consider his novel probable— they need only believe that the characters believe. The same could be said of Pilate's lack of a navel in *Song of Solomon*. In a sense, it all comes back to perception; as Morrison notes, "When I hear someone say, 'Truth is stranger than fiction,' I think that old chestnut is truer than we know, because it doesn't say that truth is truer than fiction; just that it's stranger, meaning that it's odd."[43] Another way of putting it is to say that Morrison, while recognizing the strange and complicated nature of truth, understands that within her fiction she must try to find less "strange" ways to communicate it to her readers. Ironically, this leads her, like King, to employ more fantastical fictional elements rather than remain bound by the generally accepted laws of physics and nature.

Bierce's disdain for fiction bound by such limitations is evident as he takes umbrage with the critics' taste for realism and their disdain for the supernatural, culminating in a fascinating re-contextualization of probability and truth: "Probability? Nothing is so improbable as what is true. It is the unexpected that occurs; but that is not saying enough; it is also the unlikely—one might almost say impossible."[44] Bierce appreciates the absurdity of life and rails against claims of illegitimacy based upon fiction being labeled "improbable" due to its excesses. Morrison articulates a similar sentiment as she notes that truth "may be excessive, it may be more interesting, but the important thing is that it's random— and fiction is not random."[45] In this way, the writer has the advantage of creating a pattern, a sense of organization, that a life-lived does not provide. However, as all four authors (King, Morrison, Twain, and Bierce) imply, to overplan, to overorganize, is to be dishonest. The writer must strike a balance. The multiple pairings I offer here work to expand the bounds of probability and offer ways in which both literary and popular fictions wrestle with the larger concepts of honesty and truth in ways that defy binary categories. The resultant blurring not only opens up King to a wider critical lens but also resituates the proffered literary texts within the blurred site.

The "Real" Colorado Kid

My discussion of honesty, truth, and probability, as well as the very nature of what it means to write from within an American literary system that began, in earnest, with literary realism, ends with King's *The Colorado Kid*. In the text's Afterword, King says "Mystery is my subject here."[46] The fascinating aspect of King's revelation is that he is not offering a mystery, which it appears to be on first glance given it was published in a retro-pulp fiction series as a mystery novel. No doubt using the cultural capital he built up over some fifty plus previous bestsellers, King writes a subversive novel that is actually a meditation on the writing process and the nature of mystery: "consider the fact that we live in a *web* of mystery, and have simply gotten so used to the fact that we have crossed out the word and replaced it with the one we like better, that one being *reality*."[47] One way to read King's assertion here is that a better description of reality would be mystery—that reality is a mystery. If we consider this observation in tandem with literary realism, we can begin to see that King perceives his work, despite its use of the supernatural and the fantastic, as reflecting an honest reality—one that does not shy away from its inherent mysteries.

When I placed *The Colorado Kid* at the end of an American literature survey course, students were enamored by how King's non-definition (like Twain's non-definition earlier) contrasted with the Penguin Dictionary's view of realism, which involves a definition that leaves no room for mystery: "it is a term many now feel we could do without [...] The everyday, the normal, the pragmatic—things as they are [...] no nonsense sleeves rolled up."[48] This definition, while nodding to the inherent challenge of defining such a subjective term, includes the problematic assertion that fiction can communicate "things as they are." Bierce offers a more enigmatic definition of realism: "The art of depicting nature as it is seen by toads. The charm suffusing a landscape painted by a mole, or a story written by a measuring-worm."[49] While certainly tongue in cheek, Bierce's "definition" points to his belief that realism, when stripped of the imagination of the artist and burdened with the need to appear probable, is nothing more than a catalogue of physical objects—a collection of facts without the truth. As such, King's (as well as Morrison's and Bierce's) decision to allow for mystery, for the unexplained and inexplicable, actually constitutes a way of honoring the mysteries of reality. That this observation comes from a tiny paperback that "appears" as almost an afterthought (or sidebar) to his work further demonstrates how dialoguing purportedly popular fiction with the literary not only expands how we read texts but also the larger categories to which the Great Books are assigned.

This dialogue is what makes *The Colorado Kid* such a challenging novel as well as a text that has the potential to capstone an exploration of post–1860 American Literature by calling into question each great literary movement, from realism to modernism to postmodernism. Placed at the end of the semester, King's novel provokes countless questions, beginning with trying to pin down exactly how to classify it. Is it a mystery? A crime novel? A piece of pulp fiction, which the Penguin Dictionary defines as "basically trash, or something very close to it?"[50] In a sense, it is a true piece of horror, far more troubling than monsters and fire-starters, when you consider that a guy left nameless on the beach and in the morgue for so long never gets an end to his story. It speaks to the thousands that go missing everyday without any clues. It speaks to the remaining family, left to wonder forever with only questions and no clear answers. Indeed, the inexplicable nature of his death, the number of "almosts" and so close, the myriad possibilities all of which cancel one-another out, leave the reader frustrated. But the framing of the narrative offers another possibility. It is a story about apprenticeship. About finding oneself. Of course, it is also simply a story about stories ... about story telling.

Moreover, depending on one's perception of the text, King's novel fits into standard definitions of each literary category. It represents American realism as it simply offers a slice of life of two reporters telling an intern a story, one that has no beginning, middle, or end. It also reads as a piece of American modernism, as it certainly breaks the rules of pulp fiction and mystery novels and finds a fresh approach by experimenting in form and style, and also meditates on "language and how to use it and with *writing itself*."[51] Finally, the postmodern implications of what is represented on the cover (the seductive woman and the tag, "Would she learn the dead man' secret?") *mis*represents the narrative between the covers. And, by setting the story within a story years earlier, King is able to comment on the effect technology has not only on detective work (Internet, DNA, databases, even fingerprints) but also on writing itself. Each iteration, each reading of King's text, not only reveals a depth that students are surprised by but also provides vehicles in which to revisit countless questions and concerns that necessarily arise over a survey of nearly a century and a half of American literature.

Let us conclude with a conversation near the end of the novel where the characters talk about the nature of storytelling and that most newspaper features are a lie—that they must be made into a lie to have a beginning, middle, and end. There are only two types of stories, the two old reporters tell their protégée: news stories and feature stories. News stories are "accounts of unfolding events" like slowing "down to look at a wreck on a highway."[52] Features "*are* stories. Everyone one of em has a beginning, a middle, and an end."[53] That makes them happy: "Feature stories are happy stories because they're over. They have *resolution!* They have *closure!*"[54] Here, happiness is not defined by the content of the story, but by the feeling it instills in the reader. One of the old reporters, Vince Teague, goes on: "I never read a feature story that wasn't a lie ... But usually you can make a lie fit on the page."[55] In this sense, the lie to which he speaks represents the very thing both Morrison and King strive to avoid but never actually articulate—that the act of writing fiction, however real, however honest, will always be more structured, more planned (less random) than reality; however, that does not mean that within the narrative there is not some truth—truth that is not outright articulated but exists within the telepathic connection between reader and writer as well as in the mind and memory that dance before (and beneath) the page.

King's rendering of both the mystery and the framed story culminates with the following revelation as to why the reporters kept the mystery to themselves rather than publish it: "[it] would have taken a true unexplained mystery and made it into just another feature story [...] Not by changing any of the facts, but by emphasizing one thing [...] and leavin something else out."[56] King implicitly communicates the power that the writer has when translating observed reality into printed narrative. *The Colorado Kid* marks an evolution in King's oeuvre wherein he increasingly appears to be offering narratives that not only involve writers as characters but also meditate on the process of writing itself. He plays with reader expectation and directly challenges our horizon of expectations—only if we reconsider our initial preconceptions and allow him to enter into the literary curricula. For it requires a class, I assert, to really flesh out all of the possibilities of his little book—not a teacher telling students how to read it, but a meeting of minds, of readers, engaged in a dance. Viewed in concert with Morrison's similar trust in her readers to actively participate with the narrative, Twain's practical concern that writers ought to simply "know" what they write, and Bierce's skepticism toward claiming to offer "real" life on the page, inviting King and his massive oeuvre into the college classroom constitutes an act that could not only blur boundaries between popular and literary fictions but could also have a ripple effect within broader literary studies for years to come.

Notes

1. One only needs to peruse King's literary output over the past decade to see increasing diversity in both subject and style.

2. Stephen King, "Acceptance Speech," *National Book Award Acceptance Speech*, 2003, http://www.nationalbook. org/nbaacceptspeech_sking.html.

3. Toni Morrison, "Rootedness," in *Black Women Writers (1950–1980): A Critical Evaluation*, ed. Mari Evans (Garden City, NY: Anchor/Doubleday, 1984), 343.

4. Here I am broadly referring the work of Hans Robert Jauss in his seminal text

Towards an Aesthetic of Reception. Here, Jauss discusses the "horizon of expectation," or the set of values/expectations a reader brings to a text based upon the reader's pre-conceived notions about certain authors, genres, etc.

5. Elizabeth Long, *Book Clubs, Women and the Uses of Reading in Everyday Life* (Chicago: University of Chicago Press, 2003), 30.

6. Morrison, "Rootedness," 342.

7. King, *On Writing: A Memoir of the Craft* (New York: Pocket, 2000), 7.

8. King, "Acceptance Speech."

9. Morrison, "Rootedness," 344.

10. King, *On Writing*, 55.

11. Ibid.

12. Morrison, "The Site of Memory," in *Inventing the Truth: The Art and Craft of Memoir*, 2d ed., ed. William Zinsser (Boston: Houghton Mifflin, 1985), 113.

13. King, *On Writing*, 95.

14. Ibid., 98

15. Ibid., 98.

16. Morrison, "The Dancing Mind," *National Book Awards Acceptance Speech*, November 6, 1996, http://www. nationalbook.org/nbaacceptspeech_tmorrison.html.

17. Pierre Bourdieu, *Distinction: A Social Critique of the Judgment of Taste*, trans. Richard Nice (Cambridge: Harvard University Press, 1984), 6.

18. Mark Twain, "Fenimore Cooper's Literary Offences" in *The Norton Anthology of American Literature,* 6th ed., Vol. C, ed. Nina Baym (New York: W. W. Norton, 2003), 412.

19. Ibid.

20. Ibid., 413.

21. Ibid.

22. King, *On Writing*, 161.

23. Ibid., 188.

24. Twain, "Fenimore Cooper's Literary Offences," 413.

25. King, *On Writing*, 188.

26. Morrison, "Site of Memory," 113.

27. Ibid.

28. King, *On Writing*, 159.

29. Morrison, "Rootedness," 341.

30. Morrison, "Site of Memory," 121.

31. Ibid.

32. King, "Acceptance Speech."

33. Here I refer to influence of Twain's "How to tell a Story."

34. King, *On Writing*, xvii.

35. Mark Twain, ""The Art of Authorship," in *The Norton Anthology of American Literature*, 6th ed., Vol. C, 407.

36. King, *On Writing*, 25.

37. Morrison, "Site of Memory," 116–7.

38. Ambrose Bierce, *The Devil's Dictionary,* n.d., http://www.thedevilsdictionary. com.

39. King, *On Writing*, 154.

40. Ibid., 159.

41. Ambrose Bierce, "The Principles of Literary Art," in *A Sole Survivor*, eds. S.T. Joshi and David E. Shultz (Knoxville: University of Tennessee Press, 1998), 247.

42. King, *On Writing*, 160.
43. Morrison, "Site of Memory," 113.
44. Ibid., 246.
45. Morrison, "Site of Memory," 113.
46. Stephen King, *The Colorado Kid* (New York: Hard Case Crime, 2005), 182.
47. Ibid., 183.
48. The Penguin Dictionary of Literary Terms and Literary Theory, 4th ed., s.v. "realism."
49. Bierce, The Devil's Dictionary.
50. The Penguin Dictionary of Literary Terms and Literary Theory, 4th ed., s.v. "pulp fiction."
51. Ibid., "modernism."
52. King, *Colorado Kid*, 173.
53. Ibid.
54. Ibid., 174.
55. Ibid.
56. Ibid., 175.

A Taste for the Public

Uncle Stevie's Work for Entertainment Weekly

Scott Ash

In September 2003, critic Harold Bloom and a host of others bemoaned the National Book Foundation's decision to honor Stephen King with its "distinguished contribution" award. In an essay that appeared in *The Boston Globe,* Bloom rehearsed a critique he and others had hurled at King in the past. He declared the Foundation's decision "another low in the shocking process of dumbing down our cultural life."[1] Even Shirley Hazzard, whose novel *The Great Fire* won the National Book Foundation's fiction prize at the same event in 2003, took a swipe. When asked about King's work, she reportedly responded that, given other texts by writers like Shakespeare and Conrad, "I just haven't had time to get around to one".[2] Coincidentally, just a month prior to the award's announcement, King penned his first column on popular culture for *Entertainment Weekly.* Thus, King became at the same time the poster child for all things debased and valueless in American culture and a sanctioned commentator/expert on that culture. This essay examines four years of King's columns in *Entertainment Weekly* to see how he used this forum to address and to evaluate the popular culture that so embraces him but which also appears to despise him. In particular, I argue that he largely resisted the temptation to recreate the high vs. low culture divisions that have been used to diminish his work. By doing so, he followed an alternative and less polemical model of popular culture critique than has often been directed at him, a model that aligns his critical voice with the more moderate tone advocated by W. D. Howells in his famous 1891 piece "Criticism and Fiction."

41

By contrast, Bloom has taken more than a few polemical shots at King's work over the years and his place in the culture. Even in a collection of essays on King that Bloom himself edited, he wrote "Nothing intrinsic in King's work is nearly so important as the overwhelming fact of his popularity. Like television, motion pictures, and computers, King has replaced reading. [...] I see no point in deploring this, and yet we ought not to deceive ourselves: the triumph of the genial King is a large emblem of the failures of American education."[3] Though he attempts not to "deplore," Bloom cannot help himself. Bloom's displays his distaste and distrust of what is popular simply because it is popular. By contrast, for most critics and scholars of popular culture, what is popular is worth studying (as differentiated both from praising or bemoaning) because of its popularity. Novelist Walter Mosley, in his introduction of King at the 2003 award ceremony, represents the other side of the coin, though he esteems the meaning of popularity perhaps too highly. He argues that King's popularity does not reflect a culture having been duped but, instead, reflects a culture declaring what speaks to it, what feeds it: "Universities do not dictate [...] greatness. Day laborers and seamstresses do. Political movements do not define the value of this literature because a well-told tale lives on in spite of the censor and the zealot."[4] Somewhere between Bloom and Mosley is the space Howells charts out in "Criticism and Fiction," the critical path King tries to navigate more often than not.

After the National Book Foundation 2003 award, Bloom condemned King as "an immensely inadequate writer on a sentence-by-sentence, paragraph-by-paragraph, book-by-book basis."[5] Bloom extended his argument to posit that not only is King's work inappropriate for recognition but that it is also bad for readers, bad for the culture. "In a lifetime of teaching," Bloom writes, "I've seen the study of literature debased. There's very little authentic study of the humanities remaining."[6] Thus, it would not be unfair to Bloom to suggest that he also sees those readers, present company included, who have enjoyed or passed on King's work as culturally corrupt themselves or, to use Bloom's words, "immensely inadequate." Given the tone of the comments above, it is clear that Bloom views his authority as a literary/cultural critic as license to educate his audience through a kind of intellectual corporal punishment. More than one hundred years ago, in "Criticism and Fiction," W. D. Howells described such a critical stance: "it is hard to believe that [the critic's] use of the tomahawk and the scalping-knife is a form of conservative surgery. It is still his conception of his office that he should avail with obloquy those who differ with him in matters of taste or opinion; that he must be with those he does not like, and that he ought to do them violence as a proof of his superiority."[7] Howells distrusted the criticism of violence because it offered none of the scientific approach to literature he believed the advent of realism required.

Further, Ray Browne, one of the guiding forces in the emergence of popular culture studies and the Popular Culture Association, describes how essential a scientific methodology has been in overcoming the biases of traditional humanities scholarship. In echo of Howells, and Emerson for that matter, Browne writes that "scientists [build on] the achievements of the past, not looking at the achievements of the past as the desired goal and end-all. Knowledge is to be used and developed, not to be learned, canonized and worshipped as an end in itself."[8] Once taken, a stance that prioritizes the past because it is the past forces the critic to label any attempts to change the roster of those considered authorities as evidence of "the petrifaction of taste."[9] By contrast, Howells's view of the role of the critic in "Criticism and Fiction" is that the critic must help prevent "the pride of caste [from] becoming the pride of taste" and must help identify the literature that "wishes to know and to tell the truth, confident that consolation and delight are there."[10] However, it is not always so easy for the critic to trust the artist and the audience to this degree. The temptation to dictate to the artist and the audience, to serve as a cultural gatekeeper, looms large.

Given the above and the treatment he has received at the hands of Bloom and others, I wondered how King would use his pulpit when he began writing a regular column on popular culture for *Entertainment Weekly* in August 2003. This essay evaluates King's columns from 2003 to 2007, over 60 essays, to examine how he evaluated the popular culture and wore the mantle of critic. More often than not, especially in his early work for *Entertainment Weekly*, King goes for the laugh rather than the cut; he prefers to be inclusive rather than exclusive in his estimations of which popular culture "texts" have value, and which of these texts have something true to say about the way the writer, filmmaker or musician in question "tries to tell just how he has heard men talk and seen them look."[11] However, this is not to say that King has never succumbed to the temptation to look down from on high and pass judgment in a tone and with a style that sounds not unlike Bloom's voice. For example, in an essay on the pleasure to be had from well conceived and executed audio books, King writes "all apologies to Mr. Bloom.... They don't call *it* storytelling for nothing."[12] Here and elsewhere, King shows that he is not above jabbing back by name at those, like Bloom, who have taken a poke at him.

But, by and large, the voice King brings to his *Entertainment Weekly* columns is the one that those in attendance heard during King's acceptance speech to the National Book Foundation in 2003. That is to say, it is a voice that blends the academic and the popular, the serious and the comic, the formal and the conversational. In his acceptance speech, King referred to all writers of fiction as "storytellers," a decidedly pop culture term, but he then defined what "storytellers" do by using some of the terminology of literary Realism. Storytellers "understand that fiction is a lie to begin with. To ignore the truth within the lie is to sin against the craft, in general, and one's own work in particular [...] He or she needs to remember that the truth lends verisimilitude to the lies that surround it."[13] What King says here recalls what Howells says about those he calls "pseudo-realists" who "sin against the living" by ignoring the truth of their moment and by clinging to the romance of an earlier day.[14] Situated in time almost exactly midway between Howells's essay and King's speech, Raymond Chandler applied a similar argument to explain what distinguishes detective fiction that matters and what makes Dashiel Hammett's work, in particular, so strong. Chandler's "The Simple Art of Murder" stresses honesty in art above all: "Hammett gave murder back to the kind of people that commit it for reasons [...] He put these people down on paper as they are, and he made them talk and think in the language they customarily used for these purposes."[15] Thus, Chandler offers a justification for the best detective fiction that does not evade its classification as pulp while still recognizing the honest realism in the work and thus connects the popular and academic cultures.

Similarly, throughout King's acceptance speech, he sprinkled in references to figures and items from both academic and popular culture including Frank Norris, Clive Barker, the New American Library, and Dunkin' Donuts. The point he made in this speech and in the *Entertainment Weekly* articles I will discuss next is that popular culture is not separate from academic culture, nor does it pull high culture down to a baser level. Instead, he argues that they are parts of a larger whole that each resident of the culture must negotiate on his or her own: "giving an award like this to a guy like me suggests that in the future things don't have to be the way they've always been. Bridges can be built between the so-called popular fiction and the so-called literary fiction. The first gainers in such a widening of interest would be the readers, of course, which is us because writers are almost always readers and listeners first."[16] King extends his point and concludes his speech, more than a bit defensively, by chastising the National Book Foundation if it gave him this award in the spirit of tokenism: "What do you think?" King asks. "You get social or academic brownie points for deliberately staying out of touch with your own culture."[17] While Howells would not go as far as King, he does admit that readers, "lettered and unlettered,"[18] have many of the same appetites, and the critic's task is to help all readers sort through those appetites and choose what is most truthful and sustaining and to avoid what is least so. Thus, King does not pay as much attention to the difference between the popular and the literary as between the entertaining and the edifying. Perhaps this is a false dichotomy, but it creates the basis for judging popular and high cultural texts by the same criteria and forms the foundation of much of what King has to say about the popular culture on which he comments.

Perhaps having so often been at the pointed end of the critical stick, King wields it somewhat carefully when given the chance. King demonstrates that concern through the use of a style and a tone that I would characterize as conversational, informal, and intimate (or at least making an attempt at intimacy). In more than ten different essays, roughly twenty percent of the columns I examined, King refers to himself as "Uncle Stevie," as in a column about novelist Meg Gardiner whose work King wanted to promote. He writes that Gardiner's *China Lake* was "the first book I saw by my own U.K. publisher there (yes, Uncle Stevie can brown-nose with the best of them)."[19] By referring to himself as "Uncle Stevie," King appears to want to make himself out to be regular people. In the above example, the tone is somewhat smug and less than convincing. But, in other articles, the effect works more successfully.

"Kick-Back Books," from August 2005, features King using his "Uncle Stevie" alter-ego more effectively to offer book suggestions for the end of the summer. He writes: "Do not fear little Nell (or Nelson); it's your Uncle Stevie to the rescue. Below is my Great Late-Summer Reading List, every book guaranteed to please the mind, eye, and heart."[20] Here, King's tone matches the context of the article. He has a sense for what the end of summer means and feels like for his audience and offers reassurance, in an amiable way, that there is still time to read books that might matter or that will please. Included in his list are *No Country for Old Men* by Cormac McCarthy, *Lost in the Forest* by Sue Miller, and *Killing Floor* by Lee Child, an array spanning academic and popular choices. In a similar vein, King often uses his "Uncle Stevie" persona to remind readers of his elevated status as best-selling author and critic and, at the same time, to undercut that status. When he laments that he cannot get an advance copy of the final Harry Potter installment, he writes "Don't be a sillykins—not even your Uncle Stevie gets that one in advance (although I'm sure you agree that he should, he should)."[21] This passage positions King as a critic whose eagerness for the book mirrors his readers' own excitement. "Uncle Stevie," however, is not reserved only for doling out good news or building connections with his readers. King took issue with *New York Times* book reviewer Michiko Kakutani with the help of "Uncle Stevie." He suggested that Kakutani "has gotten better with age, although she still rates only a low C in your Uncle Stevie's grade book, and most of her counterparts in the Intellectual Smarty Corps would plain-long flunk."[22] Certainly readers can identify with and understand the use of the grading metaphor in King's comment. But, by turning Kakutani into a student to be graded, King demeans her as a professional. In addition, does the use of "Uncle Stevie" make the petulance in this passage with its reference to an "Intellectual Smarty Corps" easier to take? While some readers might enjoy the tone, it seems likely that Kakutani might respond to it in ways not all that dissimilar from how King might have bristled in response to the barbs leveled at him by his critics.

The essay in which the discussion of Kakutani appears focuses on Tom Wolfe's *I Am Charlotte Simmons* and is noteworthy for reasons beyond King's use of his "Uncle Stevie" persona. The essay discusses in an extended way, especially for a popular periodical essay, the nature of popular fiction, its history, and Wolfe's career as well as specific features of *I Am Charlotte Simmons*. In addition, King once again takes the opportunity to build his argument by creating an unusual mixture of ingredients from American culture's cupboard. Beyond Kakutani and Tom Wolfe, King includes references to novelists Scott Smith and Elmore Leonard, "Good Morning America," the periodicals *Literary Review*,

Cosmopolitan, and *Reader's Digest*, and also includes a mention of pop icon Donna Summer.[23] Demonstrations of his omnivorous appetite for cultural texts appear repeatedly throughout his essays, especially in his year-end articles, whether they focus on books, films or music. But beyond that, King's willingness to sample so many cultural offerings regardless of their origins or levels of approval reflects what Howells calls the critic's "true function in the civilized state"[24] which is to serve as a scientific observer of all that he surveys.

After reading these *Entertainment Weekly* essays, I see that King deploys this method around some particular touchstones. He frequently refers to *Huckleberry Finn*, both the novel and the character, as a standard against which to measure other books both positively and negatively. At first, using Twain's work in this way might appear to reflect what Howells calls a "superstitious piety"[25] which the critic uses to elevate the past because it is the past. But, King's metaphoric creation of a cultural bookshelf modifies his references to the past and makes his analysis a question of which texts retain an essence of vitality regardless of their age. In his review of *Harry Potter and the Order of the Phoenix*, an *Entertainment Weekly* article that preceded King's work as a columnist for the magazine, King suggests that "Harry will take his place with Alice, Huck, Frodo, and Dorothy" and that the Potter series will survive its moment of popularity because J. K. Rowling has invented characters who come across as "real children."[26] Further, King invokes comparisons to Lewis Carroll, Mark Twain and J. R. R. Tolkien to say that Rowling, like her predecessors, is no longer writing a series for children and is now "writing them for everyone."[27]

To be sure, King observes, as does Bloom,[28] that Rowling has flaws as a writer and tics as a stylist. But, Bloom states that these shortcomings caused him to suffer "a great deal in the process" of reading *Harry Potter and the Sorcerer's Stone*.[29] By contrast, King argues that Rowling needs to and likely will improve these elements of her work, but he chooses, finally, to focus instead on the force of imagination at the core of her work and his sense that she is a writer enjoying the story she is telling. In that passion resides the vitality that King argues will give the books lasting life and, perhaps, explains why King refers to such books by invoking their main characters' first names alone, i.e. Harry, Alice, Huck, and Frodo. His omission of the titles of the books to which these characters belong echoes the sense of ownership that readers have of the books that have truly mattered to them because they are memorable and vital. It is this vitality, directness, and access to truth that Howells points out as the chief virtue of a text, like General Grant's memoirs, that raises it to the level of texts with more elevated cultural status. Howells writes that Grant's text includes "not a moment wasted in preening and prettifying, after the fashion of literary men; there is no thought of style, and so the style is good as it is in the Book of Chronicles, as it is in the Pilgrim's Progress [sic]."[30] Both Howells and King imagine a bookshelf stocked with items determined by the life they contain and not just by the presence or absence of polish gleaming on their surfaces.

And even when a text does not merit a spot on his imagined bookshelf, King uses *Huckleberry Finn* to create a productive context for his reader to understand the difference between what might be fun and what will matter in the long run. For example, in assessing Ron McLarty's *The Memory of Running* and placing its main character, Smithy, in a literary context, King writes, "Unlike Huck Finn's adventures, Smithy's don't amount to literature, but they are always entertaining and sometimes wildly funny."[31] Here, King acknowledges that sometimes the reader wants to be amused or laugh, and that there is a time for that, so he uses Huck to show that not all texts can hold up to intense scrutiny and that they should not be expected to do so. Howells suggests in a similar vein, somewhat less happily, that though he is "not inclined to despise [literature that amuses alone but offers no truth] in the performance of this office," he knows that people sometimes desire "having their blood curdled for the sake of having it uncurdled again at the end of the book."[32] Finally, *Huckleberry Finn* even proves useful to King across lines dividing media genre. In his December 2004 year-end review of movies, King describes Michael Moore's *Farenheit 9/11* by saying "If *Bowling for Columbine* was Moore's *Tom Sawyer*, *9/11* is his *Huckleberry Finn*—the sort of entertainment where you discover that the clown has lured you into a bramble patch full of tough questions and unpleasant home truths."[33] Mixing media pays dividends for King and his readers. For King, it reinforces his belief in a wide and multi-disciplinary sense of culture; for the reader, King's review might reinforce, challenge, or encourage how a reader views culture. Passages like the ones above show King being inclusive and expansive not at the expense of excellence but in celebration of it wherever it may occur and in whatever form it may appear.

At the same time, the logic King employs to praise elements of popular culture also enables him to differentiate between the popular culture that does and does not matter. In "Do Movies Matter (Part 2)," King uses Francis Ford Coppola's *Dementia 13* and *Godfather III* as illustrations of his point. King describes the first film as having "heart, soul, and the crazy enthusiasm of youth," while the latter is "the work of man who has either used all his talent up or is saving what's left for another day."[34] His larger point is that pop culture texts with lasting value "call out to us in their own voices."[35] King argues that losing the distinction between movies (or any cultural texts) that matter and those that do not would be to lose their connections to the individual. Here, King makes a point Howells would support as well. In "Criticism and Fiction," Howells calls for a literature that must "cease to lie about life" and that does not "put on fine literary airs [...] [that speaks] the dialect, the language, that most Americans know—the language of unaffected people everywhere—and there can be no doubt of an unlimited future, not only of delightfulness but of usefulness, for it."[36] Since the literature/culture that King and Howells praise is "unaffected" and known to "most Americans," they both believe that the critic is less important than the critic might wish to believe.[37] King makes this point in his own particular style by suggesting that the movie-going audience cannot always trust critics to help distinguish between the valuable and the trash because the critics "don't have to pay the babysitter or spring 10 bucks for parking."[38] King's makes a larger point here about how the economic context of culture influences the audience's expectations of, selections of, and responses to culture in whatever form it takes.

King's belief in an active audience/public emerges as a theme in articles beginning with "Don't Go to Sleep" from November 25, 2003. King argues that more and more of America is voluntarily falling into a metaphoric sleep. The essay trolls for reasons why the boomer generation would be looking for the easiest way through the day. And here King is both understanding and critical. He cites economic prosperity, post–9/11 exhaustion, obesity, and fear of a changing and challenging world. In other essays, he points to additional forces that would help the public go to sleep or remain asleep. He includes the censorship of ideas enabled by modern film and other ratings systems and the leadership of Jack Valenti.[39] In a 2005 essay, he argues that the audience and the film studios that believe that celebrity is more important than narrative are audiences and studios experiencing and making hollow cultural products.[40] He reminds his audience that the "brain is the most obedient organ in the body; if you tell it to shut up awready [by settling consistently for less than vital books, films or music] and stop bothering you, it will."[41] To use a different metaphor, he argues we cannot eat only junk food and expect to be fit, though King would certainly not deprive his audience of an occasional bag of pork rinds. Eerily, Howells makes the almost identical point when he writes that what "merely tickle[s] our prejudices and lull[s] our judgement, or that coddle[s] our sensibilities or pamper[s] our gross appetite for the marvelous are not so fatal, but they are innutritious, and clog the soul with unwholesome vapors of all kinds."[42] Indeed, he offers a warning rather than a prohibition.

Despite King's tendency toward more moderate positions, a series of his essays towards the end of 2005 took on a less forgiving tone than they had once employed. The voice of "Uncle Stevie," to which the reader had become accustomed, grew sharper and much less jovial. In "Lights in a Box," King takes aim at television news and its increasingly apparent entertainment agenda. He argues that in pursuit of viewers and ratings, television news, for example, seeks to offend no one so as to attract everyone. Thus, King explains the "news-flation" that generated hosts of undocumented stories about the numbers of dead after Hurricane Katrina and repeated newsflashes about the disappearance and presumed death of Natalee Holloway "while Africa starves and the Mideast burns."[43] But, here, rather than address his audience in a personal way, King takes on the voice of the lecturer. He attempts to use his position as a critic and famous writer to wield authority and inflict some punishment of the kind King, the writer, has received. He writes that "the job of today's newscasters is to be heard in spite of [the culture's] conflicting voices. The danger is that in trying to please everyone, they'll provide no real coverage at all."[44] But the lecturer in King soon gives way to a much angrier speaker.

In "Ready or Not," King fumes about the hypocrisy of reviewers of *United 93* who wondered whether the audience would be ready for its realistic depiction of the violent aftermath of the September 11, 2001, Al Qaeda attacks on America nearly five years after the fact. While King acknowledges that most reviews were very positive, he is much more interested in how the critics could simultaneously wring their hands over *United 93* at the same time as they remained silent about the fact that audiences were making the violent and bloody film *Hostel* a box office success. He characterizes critics' suggestions that the public cannot handle the real violence in its life as attempts to "infantilize the public"[45] and compares the strategy to the Bush administration's attempt to fight a war without having to show the public film or photographs of soldiers returning home wounded or in flag-draped caskets:

> Kimberly Dozier of CBS, injured as part of a news crew that got blown up in Baghdad [...] has been sighted once. In a way that lone sighting sums the whole deal up: It consisted basically of Army personnel, looking like pall-bearers, surrounding what appeared to be nothing but tubes and monitors. [...] Did I want to view her pain, her wounds? God, no. But she deserved more than the bureaucracy gave her (and us).[46]

Earlier in this essay, I examined how Harold Bloom situated his comments on *Harry Potter and the Sorcerer's Stone* in his suffering,[47] and in King's essay cited above, he takes a similar line of approach by placing his critical point of view in the context of "why I was so angry."[48] The kind of scientific distance and perspective that Howells advocated grows thin in both cases.

Perhaps the apex of King's unscientific use of his bully pulpit came in two doses of his *Entertainment Weekly* work, and I do not think it an accident that in both cases his targets are television personalities, the segment of the media community that has become arguably the most powerful seat of cultural criticism in the present moment because of its visibility and pervasiveness. In his first salvo, King condemns Nancy Grace and CNN for producing shows that are "ugly and shameful. As journalism it's immoral, and as entertainment, it's outright pimpery."[49] In particular, he took issue with Grace and CNN's decision to air a taped interview Grace conducted with a mother suspected in the disappearance of her child, an interview during which Grace's questioning was insistent and insensitive. After the interview, but before its airing, that mother killed herself, and King calls the decisions to air the interview, with a news crawl informing the viewers that the woman on their screens had killed herself earlier in the day, "sleaze."[50] He concludes the essay by comparing these currents events to *The Running Man*, a text he authored 35 years earlier, in which "fugitives run until they were executed on national television. I never expected to see anything remotely like it for real, but I never imagined Nancy Grace ... and I've got a pretty nasty imagination."[51] King does not present himself in the best light here in his attack on Nancy Grace as something more monstrous than one of his own creations.

In a similar vein, King intensifies his tone and turns up his volume in an overview of a one-hour stretch of television. By providing snippets of text heard on channel after channel, King creates a reading experience akin to channel surfing. At first, the effect is mostly comic and reminds one of King's "Uncle Stevie" persona as when he refers to then Homeland Security chief Michael Chertoff's "weird cartoon-character voice."[52] But, later in the essay, King shifts the tone of his critique. While it might be funny to some to call Glenn Beck and Bill O'Reilly, respectively, "Satan's mentally challenged" younger and older brothers,[53] I do not hear just the sound of a raspberry but also the crack of a whip. The ad hominem attacks on Grace, Chertoff, Beck, and O'Reilly distance King from the type of critic Howells would want him to be and, therefore, reduce his ability to help his readers see where their access to important insights into and questions about truth might reside.

When he takes on the above posture, King gets in the way of his desire to have his readers see him as "just one more shlub in the popcorn line."[54] He comes much closer to his objective when he speaks from his personal experience to share with his readers something that creates relationship. For example, in "No No No Easy Road," King uses his own substance abuse rehab experience to provide insight into a spate of news stories about celebrities and rehab: "The great thing about [...] [rehab], with its lukewarm showers and nicotine-poisoned air conditioner, was that it took away all the props I had depended on to keep killing myself. It also took away the idea that because I'd been born with a little talent and parlayed it into a fair amount of cash, I was different somehow."[55] Furthermore, over one hundred years ago when Howells wrote "Criticism and Fiction," one of his main concerns was the dangers posed by anonymous criticism.[56] I'm not so sure he would endorse the journalism/criticism of the self that has become the standard today and which King practices so well. But, there are so many echoes of Howells in King's essays that I wonder whether Howells would be forced to admit that King is doing something right.

The final example where an echo of Howells in King's work can be heard came in an October 2007 article written after King returned from a month-long trip to Australia. The focus of the article is King's desire to describe his need for and the benefits of a cultural "purge." Interestingly, given King's honesty about his own history with substance abuse and rehab,[57] King's sojourn in Australia came after a June 2007 article in which he compared his connection to popular culture in terms of addiction.[58] He writes that for him, and by extension for us, getting out of touch is

> a necessary thing for someone who has spent most of his life plugged into the zeitgeist. The silence out there is deafening … and that quiet pause gave me a chance to realize how much of what we watch, read, and listen to is—shall I be honest?—disposable crap. […] And too much entertainment—yes, even the good stuff—makes it easy to forget what entertainment is for in the first place: to delight and amuse.[59]

In a similar vein, Howells wrote that he would not judge the reader for indulging himself in "gratifications […] of the simple sort,"[60] but when these moods "lastingly established themselves in him, I could not help deploring the state of that person."[61] Both men remind their respective audiences that what might serve as an occasional indulgence cannot provide sufficient substance to provide enduring sustenance.

So, if the critic for Howells must be a scientist, then perhaps King's annual "entertainment fast"[62] is analogous to the process by which the scientist recalibrates his instruments. By showing his readers one model of navigating the cultural terrain and maintaining a sharp eye for what will or will not sustain him, King reminds his readers that they must do the same for themselves. Thus, his work for *Entertainment Weekly*, when it was at its best, did not use its platform to dictate to the public what it must do or think. It did not seek to draw an indelible line between high and popular culture. Instead, King invites the public to make its choices for itself in a state of self-awareness.

Notes

1. Harold Bloom, "Dumbing Down American Readers." *The Boston Globe*, September 24, 2003, http://www.boston.com/news/globe/editorial_opinion/oped/articles/2003/09/24/dumbing_down_american_readers/.

2. "Stephen King Honored at Book Awards," CNN.com, November 20, 2003, http://www.cnn.com/ 2003SHOWBIZ/ books/11/20/nationalbookawards.ap/index.html.

3. Harold Bloom, "Introduction," in *Stephen King: Modern Critical Views*, ed. Harold Bloom (Philadelphia: Chelsea House, 1998), 2.

4. Walter Mosley, "Introduction of Stephen King," *The National Book Foundation*, 2003, http://www. nationalbook. org/nbaacceptspeech_sking_intro.html.

5. Bloom, "Dumbing Down."

6. Ibid.

7. W.D. Howells, "Criticism and Fiction," in *Criticism and Fiction and Other Essays by W. D. Howells*, eds. Clara Marburg Kirk and Rudolf Kirk (Westport, CT: Greenwood, 1959), 20.

8. Ray Browne, *Against Academia: The History of the Popular Culture Association / American Culture Association and Popular Culture Movement 1967–1988* (Bowling Green, OH: Bowling Green State University Popular Press, 1989), 1.

9. Howells, "Criticism and Fiction," 14.

10. Ibid., 87.

11. Ibid., 12.

12. Stephen King, "Hail to the Spoken Word," *Entertainment Weekly*, November 3, 2006, 86.

13. Stephen King, "Acceptance Speech," *National Book Award Acceptance Speech*, 2003, http://www. nationalbook. org/nbaacceptspeech_sking.html.

14. Howells, "Criticism and Fiction," 34.

15. Raymond Chandler, "The Simple Art of Murder," in *The Longman Anthology of Detective Fiction*, ed. Deane Mansfield-Kelley and Lois A. Marchino (New York: Pearson/Longman, 2005), 217.

16. King, "Acceptance Speech."

17. Ibid.

18. Howells, "Criticism and Fiction," 53.

19. Stephen King, "The Secret Gardiner," *Entertainment Weekly*, February 15, 2007, 84.

20. Stephen King, "Kick-Back Books." *Entertainment Weekly*, August 4, 2005, http://www.ew.com/ew/ article/commentary/ 0,6115,1089990_5.

21. King, "Goodbye, Harry," *Entertainment Weekly*, July 13, 2007. 76.

22. King, "Crying Wolfe," *Entertainment Weekly*, January 17, 2005, http://www. ew.com/ew/article/0,,1017 532,00. html.

23. Ibid.

24. Howells, "Criticism and Fiction," 29.

25. Ibid., 69.

26. Stephen King, "Potter Gold: Stephen King Takes a Shining to J. K. Rowling's Delightfully Dark *Harry Potter and the Order of the Phoenix*." *Entertainment Weekly*, July 11, 2003, http://www.ew.com/ ew/article/0,,462861,00.html.

27. Ibid.

28. Bloom, "Dumbing Down."

29. Ibid.

30. Howells, "Criticism and Fiction," 26.

31. Stephen King, "The Best Book You Can't Read," *Entertainment Weekly*, September 19, 2003, http:// www.ew.com/ew /article/0,,484759,0.html.

32. Howells, "Criticism and Fiction," 51.

33. Stephen King, "Personal Best," *Entertainment Weekly*, December 20, 2004, http://www.ew.com/ew/ article/0,,1008401,00.html.

34. Stephen King, "Do Movies Matter (Part 2)," *Entertainment Weekly*, November 19, 2003, http://www. ew.com/ew/article/0,,546828,00.html.

35. Ibid.

36. Howells, "Criticism and Fiction," 51.

37. Ibid., 31.

38. King, "Do Movies Matter (Part 2)."

39. Stephen King, "The Rating Game," *Entertainment Weekly*, March 5, 2004, http://www.ew.com/ew/ article/0,,595367,00.html.

40. Stephen King, "No Stars, Sorry," *Entertainment Weekly*, March 21, 2005, http://www.ew.com/ew/article/ 0,,1039066,00.html.

41. Stephen King, "Don't Go to Sleep," *Entertainment Weekly*, November 25, 2003, http://www.ew.com/ ew/article/0,,550 879,00.html.

42. Howells, "Criticism and Fiction," 47.

43. Stephen King, "Lights in a Box," *Entertainment Weekly*, November 11, 2005, http://www.ew.com/ ew/article/0,,1128488,00.html.

44. Ibid.

45. Stephen King, "Ready or Not," *Entertainment Weekly*, June 9, 2006, http://www.ew.com/ew/article/ 0,,1202235,00.html.

46. Ibid.

47. Bloom, "Dumbing Down."

48. King, "Ready or Not."

49. Stephen King, "Graceless and Tasteless," *Entertainment Weekly*, October 6, 2006, 78.

50. Ibid.

51. Ibid.

52. Stephen King, "Television Impaired," *Entertainment Weekly*, 22 January 22, 2007, http://www. ew.com/ew/article /0,,20008933,00.html.

53. Ibid.

54. Stephen King, "Scene It," *Entertainment Weekly*, November 9, 2005, http://www.ew.com/ew/ article/0,,1138886,00.html.

55. Stephen King, "No No No Easy Road," *Entertainment Weekly*, April 27, 2007, 148.

56. Howells, "Criticism and Fiction," 27.

57. King, "No No No Easy Road," 148.

58. Stephen King, "Uncle Stevie's Gotta Have It," *Entertainment Weekly*, June 22, 2007, 144.

59. Stephen King, "The Great Escape," *Entertainment Weekly*, October 5, 2007, http://www.ew.com/ew/ article/0,,20065612,00.html.

60. Howells, "Criticism and Fiction," 53.

61. Ibid., 53–54.

62. King, "The Great Escape."

The World at Large, America in Particular

Cultural Fears and Societal Mayhem in King's Fiction Since 1995

MARY FINDLEY

"*If all conscious thought,* all *memory,* all *ratiocinative ability were to be stripped from a human mind in a moment, what would remain would be pure and terrible.*"

—Stephen King, *Cell*

In his 1981 non-fiction book *Danse Macabre*, Stephen King asserts that the primary duty of literature is to "tell us the truth about ourselves by telling us lies about people who never existed."[1] King also asserts that "in an American society that has become more and more entranced by the cult of me-ism, it should not be surprising that the horror genre has turned more and more to trying to show us a reflection we won't like— our own."[2] While King has long been praised for his profound ability to weave horror tales that not only capture our imaginations, but also capture and comment on the political and social tensions that have shaped and continue to shape American life, most of the existing scholarship on King focuses on his novels and films pre 1995. While the leading issues King addresses within his canon remain largely the same—dysfunctional families in which children often pay the physical and emotional price of family discord, religion and its discontents, the oppression and marginalization of the social outcast, the fear of technology run amok, the loss of individual humanity and moral conscience in the face of seemingly insurmountable obstacles, and the fear that humankind and society as we know it will be unable to sustain itself within the larger context of a rapidly changing world—King's treatment of these issues has changed over the past three decades. The hopeful promise that a cruel world can and often does offer the possibility of redemption or resolution is replaced by the notion that the world is a dangerously cruel and terrible place.

Many of King's works after 1995 expose cultural fears "out straight with the bark still on" and societal ills are laid bare before us, oozing, festering, and bleeding.[3] Not that he hasn't exposed societal ills in his earlier works, but a marked increase in sheer brutality, violence and societal chaos rages supreme in his works post 1995. He makes no apology for this sometimes brutal picture of the world at large and America in particular, nor does he offer solutions. A departure from his earlier method of leading the reader to the dark closet, opening the door, shining the spotlight on the monster in the corner and saying, "There! Look at that!" before slaying the beast and returning the closet to its previously harmless state, King's later fiction leads the reader through dark literaryscapes where the contemporary monster is much more aloof, the world in which it is hiding is rarely safe, characters don't always experience growth, and life never quite returns to the harmless state it once was. In fact, in his later works, especially his most recent, the monster is no longer confined to some of its most popular hiding places: the closet, the schoolyard, the family, the home, the vehicle, the hotel, the community, the government lab, the prison or the self. Instead, it is nowhere and everywhere. It is undefined and indefinable. It exists, but isn't tangible. It lies in wait and waits in lies. It follows us, haunts us and taunts us. It *is* us. And King's new monster, the one that was lurking in the shadows as the dawn of the new millennium approached, has suddenly sprung to life ... and, more often than not, *this* monster wins.

Scholarship on King's works post 1995 is curiously lacking. As a result, his critical reputation and what we believe to be the so-called earmark features associated with King's fiction is seriously skewed. His earlier works, especially *Carrie, The Shining, The Stand, Christine* and *The Shawshank Redemption*, to name a few, have been analyzed, criticized, scrutinized and, as is indicated by the title of Heidi Strengell's 2005 book on King, "dissected." Suffice it to say, these early works have provided an enormous well for scholars to drink from. But little, if any, scholarship exists on King's works post 1995, and even some of the most recently published volumes on King's work, such as *Respecting The Stand:*

A Critical Analysis of Stephen King's Apocalpytic Novel by Jenifer Paquette, Tony Magistrale's 2008 edited collection of essays titled *The Films of Stephen King From* Carrie *to* Secret Window, and Lois Gresh and Robert Weinberg's 2007 study *The Science of Stephen King from* Carrie *to* Cell, focus primarily on the earlier works. Of the combined 30 films and novels discussed in these two works, only nine focus on works post 1995, and *The Green Mile* is represented twice. This is not to suggest that these scholars are in error, but it does posit an interesting dilemma regarding the way that King's reputation as a writer of contemporary horror fiction and chronicler of popular culture has been forged.

In her discussion regarding King as an interpreter of the postmodern condition, Strengell's assertion that he is "a man whose work suggests that conscious choices together with predestined inner quality determine a character's destiny and whose multiverse presents the moral message that dedication, determination, and willpower may sometimes overcome seemingly impossible odds"[4] mirrors the critical reputation that many scholars have ascribed to King's works. This belief has rarely been challenged by those who have studied King, but perhaps it should be. Do dedication, determination and willpower sometimes overcome seemingly impossible odds in King's later works? Is there a moral message in these works at all? Likewise, the idea that his works offer some semblance of resolution or resolve, or that his fictional landscape is ultimately a hopeful place where moral choices lead characters to positive ends, and good often wins out over evil, should also be challenged.

The world has changed since King first published *Carrie* in 1973. And King, forever a pop culture enthusiast, has kept pace with those changes, exploring them publically and in his fiction over the past 40 years. As the world has become more technologically advanced, as disease has continued to proliferate, as terrorism has emerged into the millennial lexicon, as the economy has reached a nadir, and as mere survival has become more and more difficult in a world where the middle class is dissolving, King's novels have ridden the crest of many of these waves, and later works reflect this emerging world of increased chaos. His works after 1995 often expose the dark underbelly of humanity and chronicle societal mayhem and cultural fear that are, perhaps, better kept in the closet. This dark underbelly, this monstrosity no longer seeks to "reaffirm the order we crave as human beings,"[5] but seeks, instead, to remind us of a nightmare we might not be able to wake up from.

King's most bold social and political commentary of the last 18 years clearly resides within the 2006 novel *Cell.* This novel truly is *The Stand,* rewritten for the new millennium without the benefit of spiritual or moral guidance, without clear lines between good and evil, and without the hope of a new tomorrow. *Cell* seems to run counter to King's earlier assertion that the core of the human condition: love, correct moral choices, kindness, and trust can save humanity from near extinction. Incorrectly advertised by reviewers and the media as a zombie novel, *Cell* chronicles the events that transpire after a mysterious pulse transmitted through cell phones wipes out the minds of most Americans, creating an apocalyptic world that the novel's protagonists, a small group of four survivors, must now navigate. Indeed, King's "phoners" are *not* zombies; they are worse. They are living, breathing humans who have been knocked down the evolutionary ladder to their base state, one of aggression and instinct. They are Americans laid bare—mindless slaves to their dependence on technology with a kill-or-be-killed mentality that has been honed on the road to capital gain. King sets this tone before page one when he quotes Konrad Lorenz in one of the three epigraphs of *Cell:* "Human aggression is instinctual. Humans have not evolved any ritualized aggression-inhibiting mechanisms to insure the survival of the species. For this reason man is considered a very dangerous animal."[6] King continues to explore this cynical, pessimistic, yet wholly realistic theme through the voice of Charles Ardai, the surviving Headmaster of Gaiten Academy, and the actions of not just the "phoners" but the "normals" as well. In fact, if we are to entertain the idea that King's early fiction "sounds a note to counter [our fears],"[7] and that the popularity of his fiction gives weight to the argument that King's message of hope and survival speaks directly to what people want to hear, as Deborah Notkin puts forth in her discussion about King and humanity in *Fear Itself: The Early Works of Stephen King*, then it stands to reason that the *lack* of popularity ascribed to his later works, and the lack of scholarship, are due to the fact that King's overriding message is now one we don't want to hear: one of political turmoil, never-ending societal chaos, excessive violence and hopelessness. King is doing exactly what he said: "showing us a reflection we won't like: our own."[8]

King's methodology here has not changed; the world and the people within it have. We had "sublimated the worst in us"[9] as Ardai states, but the sublimation has now lost its grip. To wit, the core of humankind has been exposed and King pulls no punches about what that core is: "At bottom, you see, we are not *Homo sapiens* at all. Our core is madness. The prime directive is murder. What Darwin was too polite to say, my friends, is that we came to rule the earth not because we were the smartest, or even the meanest, but because we have always been the craziest, most murderous motherfuckers in the jungle."[10] To blatantly make his point, perhaps the most jarring occurrence in *Cell* is the death of Alice Maxwell who is murdered by fellow pulse survivors who believed it was in their best interest to toss a cinder block at Alice rather than simply leave her (and her chosen companions) alone. This innocent teenager is akin to Carrie White, Fran Goldsmith, or even the younger female generation of Charlie McGee, Trisha McFarland or Bev Marsh, and, more importantly, with Alice, King gives us a character we know and love, places her in an impossible situation, watches her as she makes moral choices in the face of seemingly insurmountable obstacles, gives her a leadership role, and then, with little cause or provocation, brutally kills her with a ragged chunk of cinderblock. King doesn't afford either the reader or Alice the dignity of a quick death. She suffers for hours in a semi-conscious state before dying, and the reader is left trying to reconcile the brutal picture of humanity King has created. She was an innocent, strong, morally intact character who, in a world of decent people rather than "murderous motherfuckers," should have lived. In King's earlier works, one could argue that she would have lived. As the reader grapples with the unfairness of King's treatment of Alice and tries to rationalize her unfair death, only one line of reasoning becomes clear: life is often cruel and unfair, and the world is a dangerous place—even to those who make correct moral choices (just ask John Coffey).

Given the fact that there are no clear lines between good and evil, and that spiritual guidance and/or the presence of God is curiously missing from *Cell*, perhaps Alice's death should not have come as quite a shock. Unlike *The Stand*, where Mother Abigail clearly has the ear of God and leads her people to the Free Zone where they make a stand against Randall Flagg's dark army in Vegas, God seems to be on sabbatical in *Cell* and the lines between good and evil are blurred. The phoners are not necessarily the evil enemy, but the innocent victims of a pulse whose origins are unknown. Following suit, the normals are not necessarily good, as was proven by Gunnar, the delinquent that blindsided Alice with a cinderblock. The enemy, the monster, is a nefarious and invisible "they." Whoever *they* are is unknown, therefore *they* cannot be defeated. At best, the survivors can only deal with the fallout *they* created which bears a striking resemblance to current political and social issues affecting the world today. As Ardai states: "they may have thought they would unleash a destructive storm of terrorism. Instead they unleashed a tsunami of violence, and it's mutating. Horrible as the current days may now seem, we may later view them as a lull between one storm and the next. These days may also be our only chance to make a difference."[11] With no spiritual guidance to deal with the dark and invisible forces, the world of *Cell* is a dangerous and scary place. After all, without the help of God, Mother Abigail would be little more than a feeble old black woman living in a rundown hut in a cornfield and her followers would be lost sheep set out for the slaughter. And *Cell* is but just one example of King's recent texts in which a divine and benevolent guiding force, all but guaranteeing some sort of fortuitous resolution for King's cast of characters, is left off the stage so that the reader can witness the more important, horrific, and realistic, scenes of human folly.

Perhaps none of King's works speak to the idea that the world at large, and America in particular, is a hopeless and chaotic place as clearly and succinctly as his 2011 novel *11/22/63*. No longer requiring characters to navigate the world in which they live to find solutions to problems, King sends his protagonist, Jake Epping, to the past in an attempt to right the wrongs that have made American what it is today. As if stating that contemporary society is beyond the hope of finding a resolute and peaceful solution to the many ills that plague it, King turns his back on contemporary America completely and chooses to make Jake navigate back to a previous time, one of seeming innocence where the seeds of hope grow faster and taller than the seeds of hopelessness. Jake's moral obligation throughout the novel is to thwart the assassination of John F. Kennedy in an attempt to preserve the integrity and innocence of America: "If you ever wanted to change the world," Al Templeton tells Jake, "this is your chance. Save Kennedy, save his brother. Save Martin Luther King. Stop the race riots. Stop Vietnam, maybe. [...] Get rid of one wretched waif, buddy, and you could save millions of lives."[12] Jake needs to fix America, and the only way to do that, the only solution explored in this novel, is to go back to a time when, perhaps, the reflection we see is one we actually like.

What Jake ultimately discovers in the America of 1958, and what

King subsequently explores is a world that appears to be much more at peace with itself. Though a sanitized and Disneyized version of the reality of 1958, King's focus remains steadfast on all that is good about the idealized past, contrasting it with the problematic future as Jake navigates both worlds. In the America of 1958, comics cost a nickel, the paper is less than a dime, a new car costs about $315, crime is kept at bay, respect is a given, love is still innocent, and people always have time to stop and chat over a root beer at the local soda fountain. An evil and corrupt seed is being planted, in the form of Lee Harvey Oswald's assassination plot, but it's not too late to pull that weed and kill it before its roots spread and become unmanageable. There is hope here in the world of 1958, but King quickly makes it clear that the goodness and hope stay here. They are, quite literally, a world away from Jake's America of 2011, and that is how they will stay.

Even though Jake fulfills his moral obligation and kills Oswald, thus thwarting the assassination attempt on John F. Kennedy and insuring the betterment of the world, especially America, King sends an alternate message—*there is no hope*. Instead of offering Jake a better world to return to, one that he arguably deserves for his intrepid actions, he returns to a dystopian version of 2011 America. Because of his actions, crime now runs rampant, chaos rules supreme, an atomic holocaust has ravaged the American northeast, the civil rights reforms never happened, Maine has become part of Canada, electricity is scarce, Japanese islands have disappeared into the ocean, suicide rates have skyrocketed, the Middle East went up in flames, Russia collapsed, and more than a dozen American cities have been destroyed. No matter what, the world is a dangerously cruel and terrible place. And what's worse? There is no changing it. If the solution does not exist in the contemporary world, and returning to an idealized past to right the wrongs cannot fix the many problems inherent in contemporary society, wherein lies the hope? It could be argued that a degree of resolution is achieved since Jake returns to 1958, thus resetting and undoing everything completed on the previous trip, but the original problem—that of an America that clearly needs fixing—still exists. If, according to King, "The writer of horror fiction is neither more nor less than an agent of the status quo,"[13] then the underlying themes in his later works paint a bleak picture indeed.

The novels *Cell* and *11/22/63* are just two of many King novels post

1995 that explore a dark and sinister world that runs counter to King's current critical reputation as a writer of horror fiction that offers the promise of hope and survival in a cruel world, a reputation which is grounded and reinforced in scholarship based on his earlier works. Societal mayhem and cultural fears that expose a rather dark, hopeless and non-resolute world also run amok in *Desperation, The Regulators, Lisey's Story, Colorado Kid, Under the Dome* and many of the post–1995 *Dark Tower* novels. This is not to say that King, the writer, has become jaded in his golden years. Quite the contrary. King has remained constant, his goal clear: "to show us a reflection we might not like—our own."[14] King hasn't changed; the world has. And therein lies the difference.

Notes

1. Stephen King, *Danse Macabre* (New York: Berkley, 1981), 13.
2. Ibid., 282.
3. Ibid., 31.
4. Heidi Strengel, *Dissecting Stephen King: From the Gothic to Literary Naturalism* (Madison: University of Wisconsin Press, 2005), 17.
5. King, *Danse Macabre*, 39.
6. Stephen King, *Cell* (New York: Pocket, 2006).
7. Deborah Notkin, "Stephen King: Horror and Humanity for Our Time," in *Fear Itself: The Horror Fiction of Stephen King*, eds. Tim Underwood and Chuck Miller (New York: Plume, 1984), 160.
8. King, *Danse Macabre*, 282.
9. King, *Cell*, 206.
10. Ibid.
11. Ibid., 207.
12. Stephen King, *11/22/63* (New York: Gallery, 2012), 69.
13. King, *Danse Macabre*, 39.
14. Ibid., 282.

PART II

Spotlight on
The Dark Tower

Roland the Gunslinger's Generic Transformation

Michele Braun

> "I'll strike a thousand and then sev'n hundred strokes,
> Blood-red the steel of Durendal shall flow.
> Stout are the French, they will do battle bold,
> These men of Spain shall die and have no hope."
> —*Song of Roland*

> "His old self once more, a paragon of wisdom and manliness, Orlando also found himself cured of love: The damsel who had seemed hitherto so beautiful and good in his eyes, and whome he had so adored, he now dismissed as utterly worthless. His only concern, his only wish now was to recover all that Love had stolen from him."
> —Ludovico Ariosto, *Orlando Furioso*

> "There they stood, ranged along the hill-sides—met
> To view the last of me, a living frame
> For one more picture; in a sheet of flame
> I saw them and I knew them all. And yet
> Dauntless the slug-horn to my lips I set
> And blew. 'Childe Roland to the Dark Tower came.'"
> —Robert Browning, "Childe Roland
> to the DarkTower Came"

> "He was what he was and there he was, just that, no more than that, no more. He had no sense of humor and little imagination, but he was steadfast. He was a gunslinger. And in his heart, well-hidden, he still felt the bitter romance of the quest."
> —Stephen King, *The Dark Tower*

In the Afterword of *The Gunslinger*, Stephen King describes how Robert Browning's poem "Childe Roland to the Dark Tower Came" was

66

his inspiration for Roland the Gunslinger. But Browning's knight also had his predecessors, such as Orlando in the sixteenth century *Orlando Furioso* by Ludovico Ariosto or Charlemagne's knight in the eleventh century *Song of Roland*. The genre and heroic conventions change across these four texts but despite the different contexts, we can see similarities in the construction of the hero. Each of the Rolands that will be discussed in this essay undergoes a similar psychological trial, threatened with madness and its accompanying loss of self identity. With the narrative of each Roland's response to this threat of madness, we can trace the effects of changing genres and cultures on the hero.

In the *Dark Tower*, Roland's deeds are translated into a dark twentieth-century fantasy. Roland's metamorphosis reflects changes in genre, changing conventions of the hero, and changes in the attitudes, values and anxieties of the culture in which the book is written and received. The morally ambivalent gunslinger of King's tale reflects the complexity of the increasingly mechanized and globalized world of the twentieth century. Roland Deschain of Gilead is passionate and intensely loyal to his companions, a combination of pragmatism and instinct, and in his quest for Tower, he displays a sense of myopic single-mindedness so that when he needed to act, "he did not think, but it did not frighten him to operate on pure instinct"[1]; further "he was like something out of a fairytale or a myth, the last of his breed in a world that was writing the last page of its book."[2] The civilized elements in his world are disappearing and everything has changed; the world has "moved on" as we're continually told. Amidst this uncertainty, the contemporary reader finds parallels with our own rapidly-changing world.

Stephen King's Roland reflects twentieth century North American culture and the Rolands who precede him. The epigraphs at the beginning tell the story of these four Rolands. The first is a knight of Charlemagne's army. The story in the *Song of Roland* is an account of the last battle of the knight Roland, based on Charlemagne's retreat from Spain through the Pyrenees Mountains in AD 778 when his rearguard was decimated by a rival king. His story is recorded in a *chanson de geste*, or "song of heroic deeds," written down centuries later and named for him. Roland is surrounded by a host of noble companions, including a young knight named Oliver who is wise, unlike Roland who is proud, heedless and haughty. When the rearguard is first attacked, Oliver suggests Roland call for help, but the knight refuses, declaring that his proficiency with the sword is all they need. But they sustain multiple losses until Roland finally realizes they will need help to which Oliver responds: "'Companion, you got us in this mess. / There is wise valour, and there is recklessness: / Prudence is worth more than foolhardiness. / Through your o'erweening you have destroyed the French; / [...] Your prowess, Roland, is a curse on our heads."[3] Roland finally calls for help but by the time Charlemagne arrives, Roland's hubris has left no French survivors of the attack.

The second epigraph is drawn from a romance called *Orlando Furioso*, or *The Mad Roland*, written by Ludovico Ariosto in 1516. The story tells of Orlando "driven raving mad by love—and he a man who had been always esteemed for his great prudence. [...] Orlando, who had long been in love with the beautiful Angelica, and who [...] had now returned with her to the West, to where, at the foot of the lofty Pyrenees, King Charlemagne and the hosts of France and Germany were assembled."[4] Appropriate to a romance, the knight's madness is a form of love sickness, but both before and after his madness, he is a knight and warrior, tearing enemies apart with his bare hands.[5] The third Roland, the antecedent to King's Roland, is from Robert Browning's "Childe Roland to the Dark Tower Came." Browning claimed the poem came to him in a dream and he wrote it all down at once, an explanation and defense that accounts for the ambiguity within the poem as well as its speaker's intense emotional responses. The battle of the previous tales is replaced by a quest, which means that the character of the hero must also change. Excellence in the quest requires courage and loyalty, as it would in battle, but it also requires perseverance, patience and sensitivity to the nature of the quest. Childe Roland is a more complex hero who "is haunted by the question Browning's other simple-minded heroes never ask: when the crucial trial finally faces him, will he be fit?"[6] Browning's poem displays the Romantic ideal of the sensitive hero, who responds to the landscape and his memories by a kind of identification with them in which he reads the state of his own soul.

The generic conventions under which Roland operates vary, but elements of the epic and the romance dominate. The *Song of Roland*, which describes Charlemagne's knight is written as an epic, but its celebration as a *chanson de geste* suggests a romantic hero, thus it contains elements of both epic and romance. Similarly, the literary theorist Claudio Guillén notes that Ariosto's sixteenth century narrative, the *Orlando*

Furioso, created categorizing problems for its contemporary critics (was it epic or romance?) because a masterpiece like it requires the use of several genres in order to allow critics to get a grasp on it.[7] The madness of Orlando is part of its romance, since madness is a form of desire, but a similar desire also fuels the epic adventures of the knights in this tale.[8] As part epic, part romance, these stories reflect the changing cultural conventions of the period in which they are written. However, as E. D. Hirsch explains, genre "has a dimension of inexplicitness," because the reader does not hold the tale in mind as a whole. In storytelling, "everyone has noticed that [the storyteller] does not always tell the same story precisely the same way, for even though each telling might be controlled by the same generic conception, the sentences and meanings are usually not precisely the same."[9] So as time and genre change for these Rolands, that "same generic conception" changes, creating Rolands that vary in their characteristics. Despite the differing details, a unifying characteristic in these four texts is their allegiance to romance and its modes, in particular, its construction of the mythical hero. The gothic nature of Robert Browning's poem betrays its Romantic roots, and in the *Dark Tower* series, we are told Roland "was a romantic, he knew it, and he guarded the knowledge jealously."[10] Identifying Roland Deschain as a "romantic" differs from the earlier romances, because the notion of romance has evolved through changing conventions or topics.[11]

Roland the gunslinger's epic journey is filled out in a way that Childe Roland's cannot be, providing a finale that nonetheless leaves the door of the Tower booming shut behind Roland in much the same way as Browning leaves us with Childe Roland blowing his horn at the end of that poem. The cyclical nature of quest is reinforced in the circular Tower staircase and the reappearance of the endless desert as a voice in Roland's head whispering "*perhaps this time if you get there it will be different.*"[12] Bruce Beatie describes how in many mythic narratives, this journey-return pattern, most frequently found in medieval literature, is based upon the circular Addonis-Tammuz cycle where the god dies for a time, only to arise again. This "Tammuz-pattern" is associated with heroic epic and its pattern serves to affirm the listeners of their place within society through the repetition of the cycle.[13] Here, instead of the return of the god, we have the return of the hero, a return that reaffirms the enduring importance of Roland to the myth. In the older Roland stories—the *chanson de geste* and Ariosto's epic romance—characters are types, who fulfill particular narrative roles by performing particular actions. King's Roland, while firmly set in the late twentieth century, looks like those mythic and medieval heroes while still being individualized as a character. Like Charlemagne's Roland, he is a man of action and a triumph of pragmatism over idealism. In the opening page of *The Gunslinger*, we find that

> the gunslinger walked stolidly, not hurrying, not loafing. A hide waterbag was slung around his middle like a bloated sausage. It was almost full. He had progressed through the *khef* over many years, and had reached the fifth level. At the seventh or eighth, he would not have been thirsty; he could have watched his own body dehydrate with clinical, detached attention […] He was not seventh or eighth. He was fifth. So he was thirsty, although he had no particular urge to drink. In a vague way, all this pleased him. It was romantic.[14]

In a story that spans thousands of pages, the first thing we are told is that Roland has only achieved the fifth level of *khef*. Right away, we know that Roland's journey has only just begun and as the story unfolds, we understand that he has not reached the Tower either. With this beginning, one is led to suspect that these two facts are interrelated in the gunslinger's story. Of course at the end, as Roland steps through the final door at the top of the Tower, he cycles back to the desert in which he began. As a nexus in space and time,[15] the Tower reinforces the cyclical nature of Roland's mythic quest, introducing a psychological and metaphysical interpretation of it.

This is not a mindless merry go round that Roland is forced to traverse; things change, just as one would assume when an individual achieves a higher level of *khef*. As Roland approaches the Tower, he hears a horn and regrets not having picked up Cuthbert's horn as he left the battlefield. In the final coda, as Roland emerges into the heat and sun of the desert on the other side of the Tower, he pats Cuthbert's horn that hangs at his side.[16] In this incarnation of his quest (the sixth?), he will have the horn to sound as he approaches the Tower, just as his predecessor Childe Roland had.

In tracking these Rolands, I am not attempting to claim that the Roland in each of these stories is the same figure simply rewritten for a new audience, but I do suggest this knight named Roland reflects changing generic and cultural conventions of these various texts. In the novel, the newest of these genres, the character is realistic because the novel is "distinguished from other genres and from previous forms of fiction by the amount of attention it habitually accords both the individualization of its characters and to the detailed presentation of their environment."[17] These kind of detailed realistic characters are the kind Virginia Woolf meant when she said great novels have a character that has "the power to make you think not merely of it itself, but of all sorts of things through its eyes—of religion, of love, of war, of peace, of family life,"[18] all things that look different at different times in history. Stephen King's Roland looks and acts like someone we would recognize: Roland's unflinching devotion to his quest for the Tower draws our admiration, while his morally ambiguous actions make us uncomfortable. He is simultaneously hero and anti-hero, an indeterminate position characteristic of a postmodern sensibility.

In discussing genre, we note that the *Song of Roland* assumes the audience's familiarity with the story, and its epic nature means its characters have little or no psychological depth. As editor Dorothy Sayers notes, what clues we do have about a character's inner state are reported, "but for the most part we have to watch and listen and work out for ourselves the motives which prompt characters and the relationship between them."[19] We are told that Roland is "high of heart and stubborn," but also valiant, and fierce,[20] but we do not understand the extent of his pride until we see the results on the battlefield. In Ariosto's later romance, *Orlando Furioso*, the battle found in the *chanson* still exists, but it is overshadowed by the adventures of the individual knights as they pursue the objects of their desire, whether those are other knights, magical horns or practical objects like weapons.

In newer forms of narrative, desire is revealed through internal thought so that the reader begins to gain a sense of psychological depth in those characters. Orlando's thoughts drive his actions and we are privy to those thoughts. Upon hearing the story of a damsel in distress, we are told: "Orlando could scarcely wait for the end of the story before he swore he would be the first at that enterprise, like a person who cannot endure to listen to an account of some wicked, loathsome deed."[21] His emotions and thoughts mark him as a psychologically deeper character than the earlier eleventh-century Roland. This psychological depth of character reaches its apogee in Robert Browning's nineteenth-century poem "Childe Roland to the Dark Tower Came," a poem that provides an excellent example of the Romantic conceit in which the landscape mirrors the emotional state of the speaker who beholds it. Readings of the poem generally recognize the importance of the knight's thoughts and feelings so that his repugnance at the landscape, "I think I never saw / Such starved ignoble nature; nothing throve,"[22] and its inhabitants, "I never saw a brute I hated so—/ He must be wicked to deserve such pain"[23] are typical responses of the Romantic hero to the world around him. Childe Roland's responses to the Tower are primarily psychological, which has led critics to read the poem as a dying man's last thoughts, a dead man's memories, a dream, or a metaphysical or spiritual quest.[24] The gunslinger's Tower is even more personal since when he actually ascends the Tower, each level represents some element of his life: an event, a memory, or a token of a developmental milestone, and the final door leads him back through to an earlier stage of his quest.

As a hero, Roland is part of the functional machinery of mythology. The hero embodies the values of a society, which change in each time and place, as well as its vision of masculinity so that "heroism is always a difficult kind of masculinity: times change, and what cultures demand of their heroes change with the times."[25] The changes in the heroic character perform a pedagogical or illustrative function where the hero embodies the values of that culture, modeling them within the pages of the story. Joseph Campbell describes how "every mythology has to do with the wisdom of life as related to a specific culture at a specific time. It integrates the individual into his society,"[26] and Frederic Jameson identifies this function as ideological; the romance, *chanson de geste*, and American Western all position good and evil in opposition, which is a characteristic of "those historical periods sometimes designated as the 'times of troubles,' in which central authority disappears and marauding bands of robbers and brigands range geographical immensities with impunity."[27] These four Rolands share the kinship identified by Jameson.

In addition to Browning's poem, Stephen King also credits the spaghetti Westerns of Sergio Leone for influencing his writing of this epic. In fact, within the series, the character Stephen King tells Roland, "As the Man With No Name—a fantasy version of Clint Eastwood—you were okay. A lot of fun to partner up with. [...] But then you changed. Right under my hand. It got so I couldn't tell if you were the hero, the antihero, or no hero at all. When you let the kid drop, that was the capper."[28] This tension between hero and anti-hero is identified by Maurice

Yacowar as the hallmark of the late twentieth century Western hero where "the culture espouses law, order, peace, individualism, but continually calls upon the outlaw, the chaos of war, and suppressive restraints, all for the communal good [...] The virtuous gunman doesn't die, then, but is recycled, recast for every new age, as an archetype to validate the use of the gun."[29] King's Roland, who exhibits both "idealism and pragmatism," is clearly a product of the culture which created him.

As Stephen King has said, he was heavily influenced by the spaghetti Western and Clint Eastwood in creating the character. But as I hope is becoming evident, Roland Deschain also displays characteristics that can also only be described as medieval. Whether this is intentional on the part of the author is not clear, nor is it necessarily important. Roland begins the tale resembling Eastwood's lone hero, but by the end of the story, he is transformed into someone who can identify with, and value, his companions. Nearing the Tower, Roland speaks harshly to Oy, the billy-bumbler accompanying his party, and we are told: "He felt angry and ill at ease with himself, feelings he had never suffered before hauling Eddie, Susannah, and Jake from America-side into his life. Before they'd come he'd felt almost nothing, and while that was a narrow way to live, in some ways it wasn't so bad; at least you didn't waste time wondering if you should apologize to animals for taking a high tone to them, by gods."[30]

The Roland before Eddie, Susannah and Jake enter his world, the one that kills an entire town in the first book, and lets Jake, who he comes to think of as a son, die, would never feel remorse for his actions but by the end of the series, Roland has developed an emotional life, which may have been the purpose of his rotation through this cycle of his Tower quest.[31] In the Tower, Roland's developing interior life takes on Freudian terms that disturb him. Within the room of the Tower that corresponds to his coming of age, he recalls a long suppressed memory of conflicted desire for his mother and this peel into the id of his soul terrifies him.[32] This psychological distress is a far cry from the stoic gunslinger several thousand pages and several decades earlier.

One way to understand the changes in the character of Roland is to examine a unique feature of this hero: his madness. All four Rolands find their sanity challenged at some point of their journey or quest. Charlemagne's Roland succumbs to a kind of battle madness, caused in part by his pride, while Orlando's madness is caused by love. Browning's

Roland is ambiguously mad, potentially traversing a landscape found only in his imagination. King's Roland is convinced at one point that he is going mad, but unlike some of his predecessors, he embraces his madness as just one more challenge to surmount on the way to the Tower. The difference in type of madness, effect on the hero, and resolution for each Roland, reflect different generic and cultural conventions.

Madness erodes identity by distorting reality; madness is extreme (thus heroic); madness is connected to an excess of emotion beyond what the character can handle; madness is exotic; and madness requires sane companions. In literature, madness is either a stereotypical behavior that reveals the internal immorality of the character, or a trial which the hero must undergo. For our heroes, madness acts as an internal antagonist that the character must fight instead of an ogre or another knight. Madness also represents the excessive nature of the hero—Charlemagne's Roland slashes indiscriminately with his sword, then tries to damage it on a rock to prevent the enemy from obtaining it, while Orlando, in his madness, strips off all his armour and weaponry and flings them about after reading of Angelica's love for another knight. In these larger than life characters, their madness expresses their individual character. Since the madness of a hero is temporary because the hero must regain his wits before he is needed to act heroically, narrative's ability to establish the individual and serial identity of the character allows a reader to understand that madness is not typical of the hero.[33] The hero must recover from the madness before he is needed to perform the next heroic action: Charlemagne's Roland recovers his senses in time to blow the horn summoning help; Orlando recovers his senses just in time for the big battle at Bizerta; Childe Roland recovers in time to see the Tower before him; and the gunslinger recovers his wits in time to save Jake from the muties of Lud.

In *Madness and Civilization*, Michel Foucault identifies madness as an extreme state of existence in which there is a "plenitude of death" for which there is no physical cure, only the possibility of "divine mercy."[34] In Roland Deschain's madness, this "plenitude of death" is literalized through Roland's conflicting memories of both Jake's death and his nonexistence. His sensitivity to the paradox of these two conflicting timelines is characteristic of the larger quest he is on. His journey to the Dark Tower is physical, but Roland's confrontation with Marten, witnessing of Susan's death, or choice to let Jake drop, are psychological challenges as well. In this, he resembles Samuel Coleridge's categorization of madness as "a disease of the will, of reason, of the feelings, and of the sensory organs."[35] Only in King's tale, Roland's confused senses would seem also to stem from his unrelenting commitment to the Tower. Even as he promises Jake that he will not allow him to die a second time, the narrator tells us, "yet his heart, that silent, watchful, lifelong prisoner of *ka*, received the words of this promise not just with wonder but with doubt."[36] The conflict between Roland's quest for the Tower and his love of the boy Jake causes his original madness.[37] But by the time of Jake's second death, Roland has accepted the effect of *ka* on his life and although he grieves, he does not become mad as he did the first time.

The madness of heroes is often intimately connected to their companions, as either cause or as healer. This connection between the hero and his companions is a medieval characteristic that Jeffrey Jerome Cohen describes in "Medieval Masculinities": "heroes often have close friends for whom they felt a passionate, sometimes even an eroticised or sadomasochistic attachment: this pairing is the 'heroes and their buddies' topos. At times the friend seems to exist only to die or disappear, precipitating a fall into the kind of madness or mourning an absent female beloved might trigger."[38] Cohen's medieval 'heroes and their buddies' seems to be a prerequisite for the Roland hero through all its incarnations. Charlemagne's Roland is accompanied by his stalwart friend Oliver, whose death shocks Roland into recognition of his responsibility for the decimation of the rearguard. Orlando is part of a huge cast of characters, including Astolpho, who is willing to risk his own life to help Orlando regain his wits. Childe Roland also had companions though by the time he reaches the Dark Tower, they have all died or been disgraced. But Roland of Gilead has many companions who are critical to his quest, and the Dark Tower series chronicles his acquisition of a new *ka-tet*, replacing the childhood companions with whom he began the quest. The deaths of his initial companions weigh heavily on the quest, and part of Roland's progress toward the Tower lies in redeeming his humanity by developing an emotional attachment to his new companions that he'd never had before. When Susannah leaves him during the final stage of the Tower quest, the narrator tells us: "It occurred to him that if he had never loved them, he would never have felt so alone as this. Yet of all his many regrets, the re-opening of his heart was not among them, even now."[39] His newfound affection for his companions motivates him to save Jake a second time, even if in the end, his *ka-tet* is again sacrificed for the Tower.

Roland Deschain's companions are the salve for his madness, but like his predecessors, his madness is connected to magic through objects or the landscape. Charlemagne's Roland is able to blow a horn note loud enough that Charlemagne's army, several leagues away, can hear it, and his sword seems to possess a power that makes it indestructible. For Orlando, his wits are restored to him magically when Astolpho travels to the moon, to collect and bring the vial containing his wits back to earth, restoring Orlando's senses. Although Orlando's loss of wits arises from the common convention of love madness, their restoration is magical. The trip to the moon is one of several fantastic elements Sergio Zatti identifies as a metaphor for "the relationship between the poem itself and chivalric mythology" of the romance genre.[40] Here epic and romance collude to produce the fantastical elements of madness and magic. In Browning's poem, the magic resides in the landscape that surrounds the knight. The "hoary cripple with malicious eye," the "sudden little river" and the "stiff blind horse, his every bone a-stare"[41] seem to suddenly emerge out of the landscape, just as at the end of the day, when Childe Roland is losing hope, the landscape suddenly shifts to reveal the Dark Tower before him: "For looking up, aware I somehow grew, / 'Spite the dusk, and plain had given place / All round to mountains."[42] Browning's poem suggests that the magic in the unearthly landscape corresponds to the knight's frame of mind.

For Roland Deschain, the magic in his madness is metaphysical but it also incorporates magic talismans like Charlemagne's Roland, the mental anguish of Childe Roland, and even a sort of love madness like Orlando. Childe Roland's mental anguish results from reacting to the ugly landscape around him with its grass "scant as hair / In leprosy," its river that "might have been a bath / For the fiend's glowing hoof" and its suicidal willows.[43] Roland Deschain's mental anguish emerges from a more twentieth century dilemma, the paradox of time, or alternate universes.

The lack of agent in Roland's madness reveals his difference from his predecessors. When the antagonist ceases to be a villain, this "distinguishes the romance narrative from those of *chanson de geste* and the Western at the same time that it raises a new and productive dilemma" because the experience of evil is no longer associated with a human agent but becomes "a free-floating and disembodied element, a baleful optical illusion, in its own right: that 'realm' of sorcery and magical forces which constitutes the semic organization of the 'world' of romance."[44] No evil human agent threatens Roland's (and Jake's) sanity; rather it is time itself that threatens to snap Roland's mind. By entering Jack Mort and preventing Jake's death in his own world (the "Keystone" world that we recognize as ours), Roland prevents Jake from entering the world of the Tower. This splits Roland's mind: one half insists the boy existed, the other denies it. When Susannah asks him to tell her what's wrong, we are told:

> He had never been a man who understood himself deeply or cared to; the concept of self-consciousness (let alone self-analysis) was alien to him. His way was to act.... Of them all, he had been the most perfectly made, a man whose deeply romantic core was encased in a brutally simple box which consisted of instinct and pragmatism. He took one of those quick looks inside now and decided to tell her everything. There was something wrong with him, oh yes. Yes indeed. Something wrong with his mind, something as simple as his nature and as strange as the weird, wandering life into which that nature had impelled him.
>
> He opened his mouth to say *"I'll tell you what's wrong, Susannah, and I'll do it in just three words. I'm going insane.*[45]

The simplicity of Roland's nature and his ability to act on instinct alone—we're told at another point in the story that he was a man "whose tendency had been to shoot first and ask questions later"[46]—make him dangerous. He gives up his guns to Eddie and Susannah, who think "he looked so strange without his guns. So *wrong.*"[47]

Jake, the boy who Roland remembers as both alive and dead is also experiencing the same kind of insanity, knowing he is dead in one world and alive in another. Unlike the stoic Roland, Jake's split mind manifests as voices arguing in his head: *"You died. I didn't though. I'm right here, safe in my own bed. That doesn't matter. You died, and you know it.* The hell of it was, he knew both things. *I don't know which voice is true, but I know I can't go on like this. So just quit it, both of you. Stop arguing and leave me alone. Okay? Please?"*[48] Through Jake's emotional distress, we understand what Roland, the Clint Eastwood-esque hero, cannot articulate, and the tension between two opposing versions of reality is threatening to tear apart both their minds. The magical talismans in this story are a set of keys, one which Jake finds in the abandoned lot next to the rose, and the key that Eddie is carving. Jake's experience of the split timeline bothers him so much he feels physically ill till he grasps the key, and Roland weeps with relief (something that amazes and frightens his companions) when Eddie's key causes the voices to stop.[49] The keys provide both relief from the building madness, and open the doorway between Jake's and Roland's world, so Jake can enter and solve the sanity-threatening temporal paradox. Unlike his predecessors, Roland Deschain's madness is both mystical and metaphysical, based on the twentieth-century notion that time is not linear.

Frederic Jameson, in *Postmodernism, or the Cultural Logic of Late Capitalism*, claims that postmodern cultural producers "have nowhere to turn but the past: the imitation of dead styles, speech through all the masks and voices stored up in the imaginary museum of a now global culture."[50] But this explanation does not sufficiently account for the character of Roland Deschain. King's Roland is not simply the last resort of a desperate writer, plumbing earlier writing for material. Roland Deschain shares traits with many other Rolands—Charlemagne's Roland, the love-sick Orlando, Browning's knight—as well as cultural icons such as Clint Eastwood and the Western. But Roland Deschain of Gilead is more than just an inheritor of the romance tradition in literature and the Western film genre. In his quest and his madness, he exhibits uniquely contemporary characteristics of the hero whose ambiguous morality reflect the turmoil of his twentieth century readers. It is not surprising that it requires the several thousand pages of *The Dark Tower* just to explore all the complexities of this uniquely contemporary hero.

Notes

1. Stephen King, *The Gunslinger* (New York: Plume, 1988), 122.
2. Ibid., 42.
3. *Song of Roland*, ed. Dorothy Sayers (New York: Penguin, 1957), 131.1723–26, 1731.
4. Ludovico Ariosto, *Orlando Furioso*, trans. Guido Waldman (Oxford: Oxford University Press, 1983), 1. 2, 5.
5. Ibid., 24.5.
6. J.W. Harper, Introduction to *Men and Women and other Poems*, edited by Colin Graham (London: Everyman, 1993): xxiii.
7. Claudio Guillén, *Literature as System: Essays toward the Theory of Literary History*. (New Brunswick, NJ: Princeton University Press, 1971), 121–22. C.S. Lewis, *Studies in Medieval and Renaissance Literature* (Cambridge: Cambridge University Press, 1966), 111–12, describes the greatness of Ariosto's narrative as emerging out of this very problem of categorization, or merging of categories. The hero Orlando exhibits both public and private virtues, reflecting the values of epic heroes

(public virtue) and romance heroes, or heroes of the comedy or burlesque (private virtue).

8. Eugenio Donato, "'Per Selve E Boscherecci Labirint'": Desire and Narrative Structure in Ariosto's *OrlandoFurioso*," in *Literary Theory/Renaissance Texts*, eds. Patricia Parker and David Quint (Baltimore: Johns Hopkins University Press, 1986), 33.

9. E.D. Hirsch, *Validity in Interpretation* (New Haven, CT: Yale University Press, 1967), 79–80.

10. King, *The Gunslinger*, 66.

11. See, for example, Alastair Fowler, *Kinds of Literature*.

12. Stephen King, *The Dark Tower* (Hampton Falls, NH: Donald M. Grant, 2004), 828.

13. Bruce Beatie, "Patterns of Myth in Medieval Narrative," *Symposium* 25, no. 2 (1971): 108–114.

14. King, *The Gunslinger*, 11.

15. Ibid., 209.

16. King, *The Dark Tower*, 829.

17. Ian Watt, "From The Rise of the Novel: Studies in Defoe, Richardson, and Fielding," in *Theory of the Novel: A Historical Approach*, ed. by M. McKeon (Baltimore: Johns Hopkins University Press, 2000), 369.

18. Virginia Woolf, "Mr. Bennett and Mrs. Brown," in *Theory of the Novel: A Historical Approach*, ed. by M. McKeon. (Baltimore: Johns Hopkins University Press, 2000) 750.

19. *Song of Roland*, 10–11.

20. *Song of Roland*, 18.256, 41.545, 87.1093.

21. Ludovico Ariosto, *Orlando Furioso*, 9.14–15.

22. Robert Browning, "Childe Roland to the Dark Tower Came," in *Men and Women and other Poems*, edited by Colin Graham (London: Everyman, 1993) X. 55–56.

23. Ibid., XIV. 83–4.

24. For examples of these readings, see Anne Williams' "Browning's 'Childe Roland,' Apprentice for Night" (*Victorian Poetry* 21:1 [1983], 27–42), John McComb's "Beyond the Dark Tower: Childe Roland's Painful Memories" (*ELH* 42 [1975]: 460–470), or Frederick Glaysher's "At The Dark Tower" (*Studies in Browning and his Circle* 12 [1984]: 34–40). Joyce S. Meyers in "'Childe Roland to the Dark Tower Came': A Nightmare Confrontation with Death" (*Victorian Poetry* 8, no. 4 [1970]: 335–339) describes the poem as a "dream or metaphysical journey" which means that a revelation or confrontation will be its natural end. Roland's sense of impending doom, and identification with the creatures and landscape he encounters all suggest the action of the poem is all in his mind. The presence of all his dead companions as he approaches the tower further suggest that the revelation at the end of the poem will be his own death and blowing his horn is a defiance of that fate.

25. Jeffrey Jerome Cohen, "Medieval Masculinities: Heroism, Sanctity, and Gender," last updated April 1995, http://www.georgetown.edu/labyrinth/e-center/interscripta/mm.html, par 21.

26. Joseph Campbell, *The Power of Myth* (New York: Random House, 1988), 66.

27. Frederic Jameson, *The Political Unconscious: Narrative as a Socially Symbolic Act* (Ithaca, NY: Cornell UP, 1981), 118.

28. Stephen King, *Song of Susannah* (Hampton Falls, NH: Donald M. Grant, 2004), 285.

29. Maurice Yacowar, "Negotiating the Loner," *Queen's Quarterly* 105. 4 (1998): 549–551.

30. King, *The Dark Tower*, 758.

31. This change may also reflect the changing cultural expectations of both the author and the audience of the text. A strictly synchronic exploration of generic transformation (from the Western film to popular fantasy epic), or an exploration of intra-generic transformation over the lifetime of the series might well yield interesting results regarding the character of Roland the gunslinger, but such an exploration extends beyond the scope of this essay.

32. King, *The Dark Tower*, 824

33. Robin Downie, "Madness in Literature: Device and Understanding," in *Madness and Creativity in Literature and Culture*, ed. Corinne Saunders and Jane Macnaughton (New York: Palgrave Macmillan, 2005), 57.

34. Michel Foucault, *Madness and Civilization: A History of Insanity in the Age of Reason* (New York: Pantheon, 1965), 31.

35. Frederick Burwick, "Romantic Supernaturalism: The Case Study as Gothic Tale," *Wordsworth Circle* 34, no.2 (2003): 77.

36. Stephen King, *The Waste Lands,* 213.

37. The fact that Jake's second exit from the series is gentler than the first takes the sting out of his death for the reader as well as for Roland. Immediately after Jake's death, Susannah dreams both he and Eddie are alive and later we learn that he does pass on to a world where he is no longer tied to the Tower. But the distance between the writing of its episode and the earlier one beneath the mountains is several years, during which time, the writer grew older with Roland, and perhaps also grew a bit more reluctant to dispatch any more additional members of the ka-tet in as brutal a manner as he did in earlier years.

38. Jeffrey Jerome Cohen "Medieval Masculinities: Heroism, Sanctity, and Gender," last updated April 1995, http://www.georgetown.edu/labyrinth/e-center/interscripta/mm.html," par 18.

39. King, *The Dark Tower*, 749.

40. Sergio Zatti, *The Quest for Epic: From Ariosto to Tasso*, trans. Sally Hill and Dennis Looney (Toronto: University of Toronto Press, 2006), 13.

41. Browning, "Childe Roland," 2, 109, 76.

42. Ibid., 163–5.

43. Ibid., 73–74, 112–13,118.

44. Jameson, *Political Unconscious*, 119.

45. Stephen King, *The Waste Lands* (New York: Plume, 1991), 18.

46. King, *The Dark Tower*, 503.

47. King, *The Waste Lands*, 83.

48. Ibid.,108.

49. Ibid., 146, 152.

50. Frederic Jameson, "From *Postmodernism, or the Cultural Logic of Late Capitalism*," in *A Critical and Cultural Theory Reader*, ed. Anthony Easthope and Kate McGowan (Toronto: University of Toronto Press, 1994), 197.

"Childe Roland to the Dark Tower Came"

The Heroic Aspects of the Gunslinger

T. Gilchrist White

"The man in black fled across the desert, and the gunslinger fol-lowed."[1] Thus opens *The Gunslinger*, the first volume of Stephen King's *The Dark Tower* series. In the story of Roland Deschain of Gilead, "The Gunslinger," King has created a complex narrative which blends many literary forms and influences. King himself states in his "Introduction" to *The Gunslinger* "what I wanted to write was a novel that contained [J. R. R.] Tolkien's sense of quest and magic but set against [Sergio] Leone's almost absurdly majestic Western backdrop."[2] King also notes, "I'm just saying that I wanted to write an epic, and in some ways, I succeeded."[3] King didn't just succeed "in some ways"; he has created a story that is fundamentally a modern epic journey of a hero's quest, the quest of Roland Deschain of Gilead for the Dark Tower.

An epic can evolve from a culture's folk tales and history handed down orally from story-teller to story-teller, like the Sumerian *The Epic of Gilgamesh*, Homer's *The Odyssey*, or the Indian *The Ramayana*, or an epic can be imaginatively written like Virgil's *Aeneid*, Dante's *Divine Comedy*, or John Milton's *Paradise Lost*. Literary critics use a set of char-acteristics, or conventions, to describe epics. These conventions include: beginning *in medias res*, or "in the middle of things"; a series of flash-backs to tell the hero's history; vast settings that cover many nations, the world, or the universe; supernatural forces that interfere with the affairs of humans; action that consists of deeds of great valor or supernatural courage; a hero who embodies the values of his culture; and, an invocation to a muse and an opening statement of theme. Epics may also have catalogs or lists of objects, places, military armaments, and the like; epithets or stock phrases are often used to describe characters and places. However, literary works do not have to have all of these conventions to be considered epics. While *The Odyssey*, *The Aeneid*, *Paradise Lost*, and *The Divine Comedy* have these conventions, others such as *The Epic of Gilgamesh* and *The Ramayana* only have some of them.

King's imaginative epic, *The Dark Tower*, though, follows in the tradition of the world's great epics, incorporating many of the conventions that literary critics have long recognized. In *The Gunslinger*, the first book of the epic, the reader is thrown into the middle of the story, with Roland already on his quest, following a man in black across a seemingly endless desert. In epics, the hero recounts his initiation into his journey and his adventures usually through a series of flashbacks. The first of many flashbacks occurs early in *The Gunslinger* when Roland tells a desert-dweller named Brown of his stay in the town Tull.[4] However, it is not until *Wizard and Glass*, book four of *The Dark Tower*, that Roland tells most of his story to the members of his travelling band, or *ka-tet* (Eddie, Susannah, Jake, and Oy). Another characteristic of epics is a vast setting, and *The Dark Tower*'s setting spans several different interconnected universes, including the fictional Mid-World and several versions of Earth. Moreover, time is unfixed in Roland's world so it acts not only as part of the vast setting but also as part of the supernatural forces that interfere with an epic hero's journey. Other supernatural forces that intervene in Roland's journey are the man in black, who can appear and disappear at will and change forms; the Crimson King, who has orchestrated the destruction of The Dark Tower; and, the spirit Mia, who uses Susannah's body to carry and give birth to the monster child Mordred. Like Rama, Odysseus, and Aeneas before him, Roland is arguably a hero who embodies the values of twenty-first–century America: Roland is self-serving, arrogant, and focused on attaining the object of his quest at any cost. But he also re-learns compassion, grief, and the value of friendship. And while King's story fulfills the definition of a literary epic with its beginning *in medias res*, flashbacks, hero, vast settings, supernatural forces, heroic deeds, and a universal theme, King's *The Dark Tower* goes beyond the basic elements of a literary epic: King has created a story that taps into the mythological depths of humankind's psyche.

As Joseph Campbell argues in *The Hero with a Thousand Faces* and elsewhere, mythological heroes exist in every culture and in many different forms. For Campbell, the mythological hero "ventures forth from the world of common day into a region of supernatural wonder: fabulous forces are there encountered and a decisive victory is won: the hero comes back from this mysterious adventure with the power to bestow boons on his fellow man."[5] In Campbell's model, the hero sets off on a journey because he is ready to be tested, and his journey involves a quest, often a search for a place or an object. The journey also includes physical and spiritual deeds through which the hero's consciousness is transformed into something greater than himself. Growing out of the journey is a moral objective that requires the hero to save a people, an individual person, or an idea. The mythological hero sacrifices himself, and his non-heroic, immature self, for a new way of being or becoming. In the physical deed, the hero "performs a courageous act in battle or saves a life," and in the spiritual deed, the hero "learns to experience the supernormal range of human spiritual life and then comes back with a message."[6] According to Campbell, the trials of the hero "are designed to see to it that the intending hero should be really a hero. [...] Does he have the courage, the knowledge, the capacity, to enable him to serve?"[7]

Roland of Gilead fits Campbell's definition of a mythological hero. As hero, Roland does venture out from his everyday world into worlds of supernatural wonder, and he encounters and defeats many forces. Roland is ready to be tested as he sets off on his quest for the Dark Tower, he experiences physical and spiritual deeds, and he saves an idea and a people from total destruction. Because Gilead, his home, falls to rebel forces, Roland begins his quest to save the Dark Tower and the world he has known. Roland reveals the object of his quest to Jake at the Way Station. Almost offhandedly, Roland tells Jake that the man in black "may have to ... take me someplace [...] to find a tower."[8] Roland's journey includes physical and spiritual deeds that demonstrate he has "the courage, the knowledge, [and] the capacity" to serve as hero.[9] He also has the courage to enter the speaking ring to gain knowledge about his quest (*The Gunslinger*), and he proves himself over and over in defeating forces that stand in his way like the Tick-Tock Man and his minions in the city of Lud or the wolves of the Calla. Like all proto-heroes who must lose themselves in order to become real heroes, Roland has given himself up for his quest; in fact, he's obsessed with the Tower—

nothing will prevent him from seeking it, and he will kill, or attempt to kill, anything or anyone that stands in his way. In *The Gunslinger*, Roland sacrifices Jake to catch up with the man in black. When he finally palavers with the man in black, who asks the gunslinger what he thinks his purpose is regarding his quest, Roland says "My purpose? You know that. To find the Tower. I'm sworn."[10]

As to the quest to which Roland is sworn, or obsessed, Campbell asserts that the mythological hero's journey has three stages: departure, initiation, and the return and the reintegration with society. The first stage of the journey, departure or separation, has several possible phases: "the call to adventure"; "refusal of the call"; "supernatural aid"; "the crossing of the first threshold"; and, "the belly of the whale."[11] The second stage, initiation, has six possible phases: "the road of trials"; "the meeting with the goddess"; "woman as the temptress"; "atonement with the father"; "apotheosis"; and, "the ultimate boon."[12] The third and final stage also has six possible phases: "refusal of the return"; "the magic flight"; "rescue from without"; "the crossing of the return threshold or the return to the world of common day"; "master of two worlds"; and, "freedom to live, the nature and function of the ultimate boon."[13] A mythological hero's journey does not have to include each of these phases or aspects of each of the stages; it is a general outline that most of these heroic stories follow. While Joseph Campbell's writings focus on the singular nature of the heroic journey, Stephen King's narrative follows two journeys that overlap. The first journey is that of Roland alone; the early part of his journey is essentially solitary and the end of his quest is essentially alone. The second is the journey that Eddie, Susannah, Jake, and Oy take with Roland, and like the journey of Roland alone, this second journey follows the pattern that Campbell describes.

The first stage of Roland's journey encompasses four of the five steps that Campbell describes: "the call to adventure," "supernatural aid," "the crossing of the first threshold," and, "the belly of the whale." Roland does not refuse his call to adventure. In the call to adventure, the hero may receive a summons to a high historical undertaking.[14] Roland's adventure is of historical importance to his fictional world—he is called to save his and all other worlds from the Crimson King, the force that is destroying the Dark Tower. According to Campbell, "The herald or announcer of the adventure[...] is often dark, loathly, or terrifying, judged evil by the world,"[15] and often there is "an atmosphere of irresistible fascination about the figure that appears suddenly as guide, marking a new period, a new stage, in the biography."[16] To that end, Roland's father Stephen first tells his son that his duty as a gunslinger is to protect the Tower. This knowledge comes the morning after Roland has won his right to wear the guns of an adult gunslinger. At the time, Roland doesn't understand that this duty will also be his call to adventure, his quest to find the Tower. In Mejis, after he, Cuthbert, and Alain have slain Jonas and his men, Roland gazes into the wizard's glass and sees bits of his future including his first glimpse of The Dark Tower: "a dusty gray-black pillar rearing on the horizon: the Dark Tower, the place where all Beams, all lines of force, converge."[17] In the wizard's glass, Roland accepts the quest: "I will enter you [the Dark Tower], me and my friends, if *ka* wills it so; we will enter you and we will conquer the wrongness within you. It may be years yet, but I swear by bird and bear and hare and fish, by all I love that– " and the glass carries him off in mid-thought.[18] Campbell states that the herald who announces the call to the quest is often dark and terrifying. For Roland, it is the magical presence within the glass that both calls Roland and warns him off. When Cuthbert and Alain force him out of the glass's influence, Roland tells his friends that they will return home to Gilead for a short time, and then they will turn west, "In search of the Dark Tower."[19]

The other phases of the call to adventure—supernatural aid, crossing the first threshold, and the belly of the whale in which the hero "is swallowed into the unknown"[20]—are certainly part of Roland's journey, but Roland never gives all of the details. It is only hinted at through Roland's allusions to the battles and deaths of his friends Cuthbert and Alain. Although for Campbell supernatural aid is a positive force, for Roland it is mixed since he is propelled into his journey both by the pink glass and by Rhea of Cöos's magic. The narrator never tells us of Roland's crossing the first threshold of adventure. Roland reveals part of that threshold to Eddie, Susannah, Jake, and Oy as he relates his return to Gilead from Mejis in *Wizard and Glass*. He shows them what happens in Gilead before he began his quest. Through the magic of the glass, Roland's ka-tet sees Roland kill his mother through trickery. The ka-tet of Eddie, Susannah, Jake, and Oy believe that Rhea of Cöos is the magical force behind Roland's act of murder. Roland states, "A man doesn't get past such a thing [...]No, I don't think so. Not ever. [...] Some responsibilities can't be shirked. Some *sins* can't be shirked. Yes, Rhea was there—in a way, at least—but I can't shift it all to the Cöos, much as I might like to."[21] His act of murder not only forces Roland to begin his adventure, it also pushes him into the unknown, "the belly of the whale."

The second stage of the hero's journey is marked by trials and victories of initiation.[22] As Campbell states, the road of trials is a succession of tests and ordeals, in which "the hero is covertly aided by the advice, amulets, and secret agents of the supernatural helper whom he met before his entrance into this region. Or it may be that he here discovers for the first time that there is a benign power everywhere supporting him in his superhuman passage."[23] Campbell identifies six possible divisions of the trials stage: "the road of trials"; "the meeting with the goddess"; "woman as temptress"; "atonement with the father"; "apotheosis"; and, "the ultimate boon."[24] Like other epic works, this stage comprises the bulk of King's narrative. In *The Gunslinger*, the reader learns about Tull and the fate of its people at Roland's hands, and the reader joins Roland as he continues following the man in black and finds Jake Chambers at the way station. After crossing the desert, Roland and Jake face the next trial: the darkness under the mountains. Roland and Jake fight off the Slow Mutants, a race of mutated humans, who attack them. Then, as Roland is about to catch him, the man in black gives Roland a choice: death for Jake and himself or palaver with the man in black. Roland chooses the man in black and Jake falls between railroad ties into the dark, bottomless chasm.

In *The Drawing of the Three*, the second book of the series, Roland acquires two of his four companions who will aid him on his journey. The remaining two companions join Roland in *The Waste Lands*. For Campbell, companions are important agents of support for the hero and his quest. After his palaver with the man in black, Roland travels West to the sea where he falls asleep on the beach. When he wakes up, he is attacked by lobstrosities and loses two fingers of his right hand. Growing increasingly sick from infection, he walks northward on the beach until he comes to a door. Through this door, he is able to draw Eddie, a heroin addict. In Eddie's world, Roland and Eddie fight a mobster named Balazar and his henchmen. Eddie also gets antibiotics for Roland before both men pass through the door to Roland's world and it shuts. The second door that he and Eddie reach leads to the world of Odetta Holmes/Detta Walker, a woman with two personalities. Before drawing Odetta/Detta, Eddie kicks his heroin addiction and Roland seems to get well from infection. The third door through which Roland intends to draw his third companion is really a trap. Instead of drawing a third member for his ka-tet, Roland ends up inside Jack Mort, a man who is responsible for Odetta/Detta's split personality and her amputated legs. While inside Mort, Roland acquires an abundant supply of ammunition and antibiotics, and he causes Mort to jump in front of a train to force Odetta and Detta together. He also saves Jake from dying in his world (Mort is the one who pushes Jake in *The Gunslinger*). Because Jake doesn't die, both Roland and Jake experience a division of memories, one true and one false, which slowly drives them toward madness. This plot line is developed and resolved in *The Waste Lands*. When they pull Jake through a door in the earth that connects to a haunted mansion in Jake's world, Roland, Eddie, and Susannah draw the last human member of their ka-tet as they travel along the path of the Beam. When Jake enters Roland's world for a second time, both Jake's and Roland's minds and memories are cleared and they are released from insanity. Four days later, a billy-bumbler, whom Jake names Oy, adopts him and becomes the last member of the ka-tet.

Symbolically, Roland's illness in *The Drawing of the Three* signals a transformation in his role as mythic hero. As he regains his health, Roland remains a mythic hero, but he is transformed into an agent of the call to adventure, and psychologically, Roland accepts his dual role as hero and agent of the call to adventure for Eddie, Susannah, and eventually, Jake. In fact, Roland gains renewed energy for the journey as he recovers and begins teaching Eddie and Susannah to be gunslingers: "Soon the Tower would fill him again, but now he only blessed what gods there were that his aim was still true. "[25] Indeed, while Roland is the principal mythological hero, Eddie, Susannah, and Jake become mythological heroes with their own hero's journey—departure, initiation, return and reintegration into society. The first stage, departure, in Campbell's model, comes through the agency of Roland. Eddie and Susannah receive a call to adventure when Roland pulls them from their New York City "whens" into his Mid-World. For Eddie, the refusal begins as he is drawn into Roland's world and continues until he meets and falls in love with Odetta Holmes. Odetta herself refuses to recognize that there is a call to adventure at all as she insists to Eddie that he is a dream brought on by concussion.[26] Detta also refuses the call, but she only wishes to return to her world. Only when Odetta/Detta are forced to recognize each other and unite to form one, whole individual, Susannah, does Susannah willingly accept the call as she blasts the lobstrosities to prevent them from devouring Eddie and Roland.[27]

Before Jake is drawn into Roland's world, he is issued a call to adventure. In *The Waste Lands* as he is trying to make sense of his memories of Roland's world and a distant feeling that he should have died, Jake feels the pull of The Manhattan Restaurant of the Mind, where he discovers two books, *Charlie the Choo-Choo* and a riddle book. Although he does not know the significance of these children's books, Jake instinctively knows they are important. The lot where Tom and Gerry's Artistic Deli stood also draws Jake. Surrounded by fencing and filled with trash and broken glass, the vacant lot protects the rose, which is connected to the Dark Tower, and yields up a key that Jake needs to cross between worlds. In a dream, Jake receives information from Eddie about the house on Dutch Hill which is the doorway between Jake's world of New York City and Roland's world of decay. Because he is slowly going mad by his conflicting memories, Jake willingly accepts his call to adventure even though it leads him into the haunted house on Dutch Hill. The house itself is a guardian of the doorway through which Jake must pass, and it almost eats Jake alive.

As with Roland's mythological journey, the other phases of the departure stage for Eddie, Susannah, and Jake include crossing the first threshold and the belly of the whale. A first threshold occurs for Eddie and Susannah when the bear, Shardik, attacks their camp in the Old Woods. As preparation for the adventure, Roland teaches Eddie and Susannah how to be gunslingers. As Roland tests Susannah's shooting, Eddie is attacked by Shardik, and Susannah kills it. Then, Roland tells Eddie and Susannah the story of the Twelve Guardians, who were made by the Old Ones. Roland believes that Shardik is one of those Guardians. Originally, the Old Ones made the Guardians to protect the Beams that support the multiple worlds spinning from the Dark Tower. As they begin to follow Shardik's backtrail to his lair, Eddie thinks, "This is where the quest for Roland's Dark Tower really begins, at least for us."[28] Shardik's lair does indeed guard a portal of one of the Beams, and from Shardik's home, the way the leaves on the trees lean and the direction in which the clouds move clearly point out the path of the Beam. Jake crosses the first threshold of adventure when he is pulled through the doorway in the house on Dutch Hill into Roland's world. The physical illnesses of Roland, Susannah, and Eddie coupled with the amputations of Roland and Susannah, signal inner, spiritual transformations in the characters. As the characters get well and heal, they move toward the next stage of the adventure. Jake, too, undergoes a spiritual transformation as he is literally reborn into Roland's world through the earthen doorway in the mansion, a symbolic grave. All of the characters join Roland in the belly of the whale once crossing the first threshold. For Roland, Eddie, Susannah, and Jake (and Oy), the belly of the whale—the unknown—is the territory they must cross, or adventure that they must navigate, to reach the Dark Tower.

Part of the adventure stage, for Campbell, is an encounter with a goddess figure. Unlike other mythological heroes, Roland doesn't encounter a goddess. Instead, Roland meets a female demon in the speaking ring in *The Gunslinger*. Susannah encounters the same demon in masculine form in *The Waste Lands* as Roland, Susannah, and Eddie draw Jake into their world. Campbell argues that the meeting with the goddess is a marriage and represents "the hero's total mastery of life" since woman is symbolic of the life force. In a perverse way, Roland's and Susannah's encounter with the demon is a marriage. Instead of a benign encounter, however, Roland's and Susannah's experience leads to Susannah's pregnancy and possession by Mia, a maternal supernatural force. Through Susannah, Mia is able to carry and give birth to a monster child, half-human (Roland's son) and half-spider (the Crimson King's son). Before Susannah/Mia gives birth, the followers of the Crimson King force the separation of the two women into their physical forms. Thus, Susannah becomes herself again, and Mia becomes a woman in labor. However, the baby that Mia carries is part human and part spider, and when the baby is born, the spider Mordred sucks the life out of his mother, Mia, almost as soon as he is born. Transforming between human and spider, Mordred follows Roland until Roland kills him on the Tower road.[29]

For Roland, the phase in which the hero meets his father and transcends the earthly world occurs as he enters the Tower and climbs its stairs: "the sense that he had entered the body of Gan himself" grows stronger.[30] Literally, Roland enters the body of his father, the creator god, Gan. Instead of divinity or atonement, however, Roland meets a rebirth into his quest at the top of the Tower. The ultimate boon is the saving of the beams and the multiple worlds, which Roland accomplishes with his reaching the Tower. Paradoxically, it is also the beginning of his journey—again. Unlike Roland, Eddie, Susannah, Jake, and Oy do not meet their fathers or transcend the earthly world. However, they do play an important part in saving the beams which support the multiple universes of their fictional worlds.

The third and final stage of the hero's journey, according to Campbell, is return and reintegration into society, and includes several possible phases: "refusal of the return"; "the magic flight"; "rescue from without"; "the crossing of the return threshold or the return to the world of common day"; "master of two worlds"; and, "freedom to live, the nature and function of the ultimate boon."[31] For Roland, his return and reintegration should come when he saves the Dark Tower. However, when he finds the Tower and climbs the stairs to the top room and opens the door, Roland finds himself in the desert again, following the man in black. This time, however, Roland has the horn of Arthur Eld, his ancestor. Roland serves the Tower and his quest. Though he saves the Tower and the worlds from destruction (and the implication is that he has done this act many times before), he hasn't escaped his own life. He is caught up in *samsara*, the Hindu cycle of birth, death, and rebirth, but for Roland it is seeking, finding, and rebirth into the seeking again. There is a haunting sense that he just hasn't gotten it quite right. Roland's return into the world isn't the usual return for a mythological hero. Instead of a reintegration into society, Roland's is a rebirth into the journey. The narrator says, as Roland opens the door at the top of the Dark Tower,

> He [Roland] saw and understood at once, the knowledge falling upon him as a hammerblow, hot as the sun of the desert that was the apotheosis of all deserts. How many times had he climbed these stairs only to find himself peeled back, curved back, turned back? Not to the beginning (when things might have been changed and time's curse lifted), but to that moment in the Mohaine Desert when he had finally understood that his thoughtless, questionless quest would ultimately succeed? How many times had he traveled a loop like the one in the clip that had once pinched off his navel, his own tet-ka can Gan? How many times *would* he travel it?
>
> "*Oh, no!*" he screamed. "*Please, not again! Have pity! Have mercy!*"
>
> The hands pulled him forward regardless. The hands of the Tower knew no mercy.
>
> They were the hands of Gan, the hands of ka, and they knew no mercy.[32]

At the point he opens and steps through the door at the top of the Tower, Roland simultaneously crosses the return threshold, masters two worlds and all worlds of the Tower, and begins his journey again, whereas Eddie, Susannah, Jake, and Oy are all reintegrated into society. They choose to meet in a version of New York City where all of them can live and be happy together. Despite their deaths, Eddie and Jake live again through the magic of the doors between worlds. By prior arrangement, all four meet in the same year, at the same time, in New York.

Campbell views the hero's journey as a parallel to the rite of passage in human society. In human societies, each child undergoes a similar journey and transformation as he or she is initiated into the rights and responsibilities of adulthood. Therefore, everyone has a symbolic, heroic journey within them. In *The Dark Tower* series, Eddie, Susannah, and Jake each makes this rite of passage from dependency to adulthood. Eddie's personal journey brings him through his heroin addiction and dependency on his brother to the state of a functioning adult, capable of heroic deeds. Likewise, Susannah's split personalities (Odetta and Detta) are immature beings, trapped by their single natures until Roland forces them to become one being, Susannah. After the two sides of her personality are joined, Susannah also becomes a functioning adult, capable of heroic deeds. Because Jake really is an adolescent, his rite of passage from childhood into adulthood is genuine. For Campbell, the hero's psychological growth and development emerges as he undertakes the mythic journey.

Fundamentally, Roland Deschain of Gilead's journey is a quest for the Dark Tower. *The Dark Tower* series is structured like a literary epic blended with many different genres. More broadly, it is a search for understanding and meaning in the modern world through the mythological hero's journey. As in some of King's other fiction, *The Dark Tower* explores the implications of technology gone wrong and humankind's response to it. The very ending of the narrative carries Roland, and the reader, back to the beginning, a kind of *samsara*, the Hindu cycle of birth, life, death, and rebirth, suggesting that we like Roland haven't gotten it quite right.

Notes

1. Stephen King, *The Gunslinger* (New York: Signet, 2003), 3.
2. King, introduction to *The Gunslinger* (New York: Signet, 2003), xiv.
3. Ibid., xv.
4. King, *The Gunslinger*, 22–87.

5. Joseph Campbell, *The Hero With a Thousand Faces* (Princeton, NJ: Princeton University Press, 1973), 30.

6. Joseph Campbell with Bill Moyers, *The Power of Myth* (New York: Anchor, 1991), 152.

7. Ibid., 154.

8. King, *The Gunslinger*, 118–119.

9. Campbell, *The Power of Myth*, 154.

10. King, *The Gunslinger*, 295.

11. Campbell, *A Hero With a Thousand Faces*, 36.

12. Ibid.

13. Ibid., 37.

14. Ibid., 51.

15. Ibid., 53.

16. Ibid., 55.

17. Stephen King, *Wizard and Glass* (New York: Signet, 1998), 596.

18. Ibid.

19. Ibid., 601.

20. Campbell, *The Hero with a Thousand Faces*, 90.

21. King, *Wizard and Glass*, 688.

22. Campbell, *The Hero With a Thousand Faces*, 36.

23. Ibid., 97.

24. Ibid., 36.

25. Stephen King, *The Drawing of the Three* (New York: Signet, 1990), 455.

26. Ibid., 267–268.

27. Ibid., 450–451.

28. Stephen King, *The Waste Lands* (New York: Signet, 1991), 84.

29. Stephen King, *The Dark Tower* (New York: Scribner, 2004), 770.

30. Ibid., 822.

31. Campbell, *The Hero With a Thousand Faces*, 37.

32. Ibid., 827.

Riddles Wrapped in Mystery Inside Enigmas

Anglo-Saxon Literature as the Key to Unlocking the Ending of The Dark Tower *Series*

JENNIFER D. LOMAN

Stephen King's *The Dark Tower* series is an amalgamation of genres, incorporating tropes from science fiction, poetry, and films of the American West. Yet, a background in Anglo-Saxon riddling traditions suggests yet another genre as *The Dark Tower* series is an extended riddle for both the reader and for the series' protagonist, Roland Deschain of Gilead. Riddling is both a form of entertainment and education in Anglo-Saxon culture—and the same holds true for King's work. It is invigorating for King's "Constant Reader" to reread the text and put together the clues to solve the riddles. Despite Roland's circular quest that allows him to relive his world and quest, the gunslinger, however, never manages to adeptly read the clues. Daniel Tiffany notes that the etymological root of both "riddle" and "read" is the Old English verb, *raedan*, meaning "to give or take counsel, to advise, to deliberate."[1] Roland's pursuit of the Dark Tower will prove cyclically endless because he does not apply *raedan*. A close reading of King's *The Dark Tower* series and an examination its similarities to Anglo-Saxon literature demonstrate that an awareness of Anglo-Saxon concepts is the key to unlocking the riddlic ending of King's magnum opus in which Roland's ka-tet ultimately succeeds, but Roland does not.

Attempting to completely unlock the ending of *The Dark Tower* series may be mildly quixotic, and may result in rather subjective conclusions, but the discoveries are nonetheless quite telling. Part of the difficulty, though, resides within any given reader's attempt to interpret the numerous vague and unclear symbols, meanings, and metaphors within the story of Roland Deschain. As to deciphering ambiguous metaphor, Craig Williamson says "We wander a riddlic landscape, dimly chartered, haunted by unknown or shifting shapes, full of disguised characters, until we reach a kenning, a metaphoric way of knowing that carries us beyond categories of perceptions, beyond the dead world of literal truth."[2]

Notice the use of the word *kenning* here; Kevin Crossley-Holland states that "the whole body of Old English literature is packed out with many riddles; they are known as kennings and are in fact condensed metaphor."[3] King's *The Dark Tower* series reveals striking similarity with Anglo-Saxon kenning and riddle traditions. King uses the word *ken* to mean "know" in the dialect he creates for the Calla Bryn Sturgis.[4] Further, "ken," from the Anglo-Saxon *cennan*, means "to make known, declare, confess, acknowledge," and "kenning" suggests both "understanding and paraphrastic naming."[5] Moreover, King's invented word, *ka-tet*, is a kenning combining metaphorically both the concepts of fate and a group of people with shared goals: "Each member of the ka-tet is a piece of a puzzle. Each individual piece is a mystery … put together, the collective pieces form a greater picture."[6] The members of a ka-tet have telepathic understanding, and the naming of their group brings with it a sense of belonging to the members of Roland's ka-tet as all are outsiders, or Others, in their home worlds. Roland, however, is an Other at times within his own ka-tet. He realizes he stands outside of the American culture of his group of gunslingers, stating "I'll always be an outsider... I can't even say aspirin. Every time I try, the word comes out wrong."[7] In addition, he chooses a destiny that is "different from those of his companions."[8]

To wit, Williamson's description of the riddlic landscape reminds us of both Roland's "isolated" journey and the Anglo-Saxon elegy *The Wanderer*. Both share a theme of exile characterized by Stephen Pollington as "of having outlived one's companions […] with only *sorg to gefaren* 'sorrow as a companion.'"[9] Just as the speaker of *The Wanderer* lives a life of constant sorrow, so does Roland as King uses Ralph Stanley's song, "Man of Constant Sorrow," in the series, suggesting a link to the often dispirited Roland.[10] Regarding Roland's destitution and myopic persona, we look back to the term *sorg* as "relating to 'a deep inward state'" which acts as a "gray veil over man's entire existence."[11] As such, from the gunslinger's lack of "understanding of the ideograms" in his campfire in *The Gunslinger*[12] to his inability in the final book to realize that Susannah's dream of Eddie in Central Park is not a "trick and a glammer [...] into todash space" but a vision of redemptive reunion with the ka-tet he loves,[13] Roland continually misreads the signs that could lead him to salvation. Roland's *sorg* blinds him.

Eddie, a member of Roland's ka-tet, is able to beat Blaine the Mono because Eddie learns to see not only the weakness of Others, but also the strength within himself. In the end of *The Waste Lands*, the ka-tet have agreed to participate in a neck riddle—a classification Williamson describes as when "the speaker saves his neck by the riddle, for the judge or executioner has promised release in exchange for a riddle that cannot be guessed."[14] Roland follows a formal and traditional protocol for riddling with Blaine similar to rules found within many Anglo-Saxon riddling games. And in this particular case, Roland is the key player in this contest because of his training in Gilead, yet he fails miserably. He feels as if he is disappearing like the rest of his world, and he cannot remember all the riddles he once knew: "It's not like forgetting. It's as if they were never there in the first place."[15]

Relegated to the sidelines because he's seen as the group's weakest link, Eddie, meanwhile, falls into deep concentration. Just as the Old English riddles "challenge their audience to deeper thought,"[16] Eddie quietly takes on a similar challenge. Furthermore, Eddie exhibits heroic qualities as he solves Blaine's riddle, aligning with Williamson's suggestion that the riddle solver moves through the traditional phases of the questing hero:

1. Departure from the dead world of reified categories.
2a. Confrontation with the metaphoric world of unknown monsters and shifting shapes.
2b. Recognition [...] of the Other and its relation to the Self
3. Return to the old world with rejuvenated eyes.[17]

Eddie engages in all these stages. Formerly, he allowed the mocking voice of his dead older brother to eat away at his self-esteem, but now he recognizes that "Henry's voice [has] changed; it now sound[s] sober and clear-minded... like a friend instead of an enemy."[18] Eddie also senses "what was underneath" Roland's earlier dismissive comment about how Eddie's dead-baby-crossing-the-road riddle was "silly" and therefore unacceptable,[19] recognizing "the contempt with which it had been laced. [And] Contempt had always been one of Henry's favorite weapons."[20] Williams notes that the "present meaning" of the word *silly* is "almost opposite to the original one [...] descend[ing] from Old English *saelig* 'blessed, happy, fortunate' downward to its present day 'foolish, stupid.'"[21] However, the occurrences of Old English *saelig* "sometimes include references to temporal blessings and personal endowments."[22] Indeed, Eddie confronts Blaine and thwarts the robotic monster train who intends to kill them all in a suicidal crash because Eddie recognizes the same contempt in Blaine's voice for his silly riddles.[23] Eddie knows that silliness will provoke Blaine, and the train will lose the contest by losing control. As Gwendolyn A. Morgan notes, "to engage in riddling is to become involved in a verbal contest on its most primal level: to confound an adversary [...] is to gain power."[24] Here, Eddie gains self-worth and recognition from his ka-tet, especially as Roland, who admits that he "held [Eddie's] jokes in contempt," apologizes to Eddie, saying: "there is a kind of blindness in me. An arrogant blindness."[25]

Unlike Eddie, Roland never gets past Williamson's first stage of the hero: "departure from the dead world of reified categories."[26] In the riddling contest with Blaine, Roland simply, and arrogantly, enters the contest and defers to riddles he learned in his youth, failing to recognize that Blaine has been programmed with a stock of riddles that were undoubtedly old when Roland was young. Moreover, Williamson lists thirteen different categories of Anglo-Saxon riddles, noting "that there are no Old English riddles in this category whatsoever—the Tricky Question Group," and Williamson describes this anomalous group as mere "joking questions."[27] Eddie, who is silly in the blessed, happy way of Old English *saelig*, has to "hold back laughter" as he riddles Blaine with joking riddles, and his blessed happiness fills Jake with "hope" that feels like "a rose in the full fever of its summer."[28] Roland, in contrast, is blind; he doesn't recognize the paradox that, although Blaine is an Other, the train has similar riddling tendencies to him, absent of tricky questions. As Pollington states that with Anglo-Saxon riddles, "it is the paradox which gives us the important clue—the insight which helps resolve the contradiction."[29] Roland's nature, including a high level of hubris, holds him "captive" and blinds him, whereas Eddie's *saelig* nature allows him to deliberate, and therefore riddle like that of Old English *raedan*.

Like Eddie, the Anglo-Saxon riddles contemplate the concept of the non-human Other. Williamson states that in "half of the riddles" of the Anglo-Saxon *The Exeter Book* "the reader identifies with the 'I' of the human riddler; in half, the 'I' of the creature. [...] Meaning depends upon our manipulation in images of the Other."[30] A metaphorical duality can be found in the imagery of both the Anglo-Saxon riddles and *The Dark Tower Series*. For example, the "the heart" of the supernatural Rose, the center of love and life in the *Dark Tower* universe, "open[s] for [Jake], exposing a dazzle of light [...] It was a sun" while, simultaneously, this same Rose possesses a "worm [...] beating like a sick and dirty heart,"[31] denoting the duality of the universe, or how evil is toxic to good. Similarly, Anglo-Saxon riddles juxtapose opposites as clues to create a paradoxical tension to be resolved by the answer. To explore this notion further, let's consider the Anglo-Saxon Riddle 76:

> I am a prince's property and joy,/ Sometimes his shoulder-companion,/ Close comrade in arms, king's servant,/ Lord's treasure. Sometimes my lady,/ A bright-haired beauty, lays serving/ Hands on my body, though she is noble/ And the daughter of an earl. I bear/ In my belly what blooms in the wood,/ The bee's delight. Sometimes I ride/ A proud horse in the rush of battle—/ Harsh is my voice, hard is my tongue./ I bear the scop's meed when his song is done./ My gift is good, my way winning,/ My color dark. Say what I'm called.[32]

Here a non-human object becomes multiple others with human connotations: a body, a poet, a tongue, a shoulder-companion. Anglo-Saxon scholars agree that the answer to this riddle is horn, and Williamson interprets line twelve to mean that the horn is used to drink beer presumably during a feast in the Anglo-Saxon great hall. "Drinking horns" were associated in Anglo-Saxon times with "a royal burial,"[33] and Morgan associates the horn with loss of life, viewing the horn as a "harbinger of death" as well as a companion to "fierce warriors," but also as a symbol "of life" because of its "association with growth."[34] Further, Morgan interprets, or translates, line eight as "having in my bosom that which grew in groves," suggesting "not only the wooden parts of the horn itself, but also a cornucopia, in which rest the fruits of the earth," denoting fertility and growth.[35] Morgan concludes: "It may strike fear into any enemy with a battle charge or soothe with music," expressing "both strife and harmony."[36] Thus, in this riddle, the horn has an "equal capacity for good and evil."[37]

Morgan's conclusions about the horn's associations with life and death/strife and harmony bear a striking similarity to the variants of the "Commala Song" sung in the Calla and in Gilead. The word, *come*, derives from the Anglo-Saxon *cuman* meaning "come, approach, be born, come to oneself, recover, become, come together, and assemble."[38] Like the horn from Anglo-Saxon Riddle 76, "Commala, The Rice Song" suggests both growth and fertility; indeed, Eddie Dean understands it to be a song for the "planting of both rice and children."[39] "The Rice Song" takes on the connotations of the horn's battle charge, especially when the townspeople chant "Come … Come … Come …" as Roland dances to the "Commala" in preparation for battle with the robotic wolves. Roland, smiling, dances "faster and faster" for a prolonged period of time, "yet his eyes didn't smile, not those blue bombardier's eyes; they were as cold as ever,"[40] and through this fast-paced and intense dancing, Roland becomes a horn, calling the "Calla *folken*" to come to battle, to come fight to the death. As part of his elaborate riddle, King weaves the concept of sorrow into Roland's warrior dance to the "Commala" song. Susannah sings a version of Stanley's "Man of Constant Sorrow" during the festivities that precede Roland's Commala Dance, and while singing she substitutes the word "maid" for "man."[41] Susannah, whose name means "lily" or "rose" in Hebrew, appears to sing on behalf of the Rose here, expressing its sorrow that Roland's warrior dance has led the Calla *folken* to chose violence. Violence can be a gray veil over human existence; even violence in the name of good leaves victims, as Eddie notes when he spoke about the dead following the battle: "No one seemed to feel that the losses were in any way equal to the gains," which is true "if it wasn't your wife or your son who'd fallen."[42]

As we navigate the many correlations between riddling and *The Dark Tower* series, we now look towards additional issues of interpretation and duality, and one critical point of examination is concerned with when we identify with the "I" of the human and then sometimes identify with the inanimate subject or non-human creature. In other words, as Williamson says, "meaning depends upon our manipulation in images of the Other,"[43] and as such, the non-human horn can transform into a body part, a companion, a poet, and more in Anglo-Saxon riddle-songs. Such transformations are "metaphoric because each riddlic creature takes on the guise of another [...] And [are] metamorphic because in the natural flow all creatures shift shapes [...] [like] horn to battle-singer or mead-belly."[44] Like Anglo-Saxon riddling, King creates a metamorphic shift in shape by having Jake and his pseudo-dog, the bumbler creature, Oy, switch bodies in the seventh book of the series. And in this instance, to understand this riddling process we must look at the sequence of clues. In the final book of *The Dark Tower* series, Jake asks Oy to change places with him because Jake, with his gift of the touch, has accidentally envisioned dinosaurs in his head, and these dinosaurs pose an actual danger to him. The dinosaurs are manifestations of his greatest fear brought about by a technological marvel, and in order to escape his now very-real imaginings, he switches minds with Oy because the creature is from a different world and has no concept of dinosaurs. Unsurprisingly, they both struggle in their new bodily forms.[45] Bev Vincent concludes that this is "an amusing scene, but ultimately irrelevant,"[46] missing the riddlic clue. This scene is the first indication of their metamorphic shape-shifting, suggesting a riddle is indeed at hand and that the scene King has crafted is not a haphazard or whimsical construction. Another clue comes when Eddie is on his deathbed, and Jake makes a realization that Roland never does: "the loss of Eddie [is] too great a price to pay" for any goal.[47] Jake prays to "God, to Gan, and to the Man Jesus" for "a miracle" to save Eddie's life, finally, and unknowingly, offering his own life in sacrifice.[48] Jake prays, "Save my friend's life, and I will save yours, he pray[s] to Stephen King, a man he'd never seen. Save Eddie, and we won't let that van hit you. I swear it."[49] Ultimately, Jake realizes that the death of a friend is too costly. Here, King establishes Jake's willingness to act on behalf of an Other, namely the character, Stephen King.

Building upon the human-to-creature shape-shifting he has already created in Roland's son Mordred, who is able to change shapes from human form into that of a large spider, as well as the shape-shifting relationship between Jake and Oy, King emphasizes the duality of Jake and Eddie as Eddie is on his deathbed. King establishes the connection between the two characters throughout the series, with but one example being that they share a keen telepathy as shown during their riddling duel with Blaine the Mono in *Wizard and Glass*.[50] They also both call Roland "father," so they are both pseudo-sons of Roland. In addition, they both have the gift of visions, which is important to note as Lapdige, et al. note

> Visions were a genre of literature [...] as a vehicle for contemplation on the achievements of the present life, on a terrifying threat of the Day of Judgment, and on the need for immediate and significant repentance is the Judgment is to be faced.[51]

The threat of the "Day of Judgment" is apparent in Sheemie's prophetic vision of the Beam which holds the universe together; his vision involves the image of Beam as an Other: a boy who looks like Jake and has one of his eyes put out.[52] Thus, the image of the boy in the dream has duality, connoting both Jake and Eddie because Eddie's fatal injury is a gunshot over his right eye.[53] As Sheemie speaks of his vision, "Jake realiz[es] he knew this tale," and Eddie finishes one of Sheemie's sentences as if he too knows the tale.[54] Their subconscious awareness of this tale is an indication of their connection to the Beam and therefore to God, or Gan.

To say the least, riddles are the juxtaposition of opposite images, and Jake is Eddie's mirror opposite. Before he is fatally wounded, Eddie never achieves Jake's realization about the death of a loved one being too costly. Indeed, Eddie is entranced in Roland's warrior dance, placing the quest for the Tower above his love for his wife, Susannah. He had, though, vowed not to get caught up in the game of "bullets [...] do[ing] the talking [...] a replay of [the] same old shitstorm" in the second book of the series, also stating "I've been dirty, man. If I found out anything, it's that I don't want to die dirty."[55] Yet he does in fact "die dirty" by showing no mercy in shooting Pimli Prentiss. Eddie shoots Pimli because he didn't like "his contempt," and he does so even though Pimli was "shot in the chest, bleeding heavily, and clearly dying fast."[56] Eddie, following Roland's lead, stops deliberating as in Old English *raedan*, drifting away from the *saelig* nature which allowed him to out-riddle Blaine. King indicates Eddie's folly during Eddie's fatal shot in which Eddie slaps a hand over the wound "like a man who'd remembered something of vital importance just a little too late."[57] Eddie's "dirty death" is the opposite of Jake's deaths on behalf of saving others.

Just as Eddie "dies dirty," Roland continues to, in essence, live a "dirty life," serving as but another example of mirroring throughout *The Dark Tower* series, and we are reminded of this as we recall that Roland is an accomplice in the eventual murder of Oy/Jake. Roland's axel is the violence he brings to others: "the showdown" that "always came [is] the central fact of his life and the axel upon which his own ka revolved."[58] The Anglo-Saxon King Alfred in his adaptation of Boethius' *The Consolation of Philosophy* writes that fate is "the consequence of the risk one takes by increasing the distance between himself (or his will) and the divine axel. The farther one is from the right mindedness of God, the more mobile or mutable or unstable he is, the more subject to disaster."[59] In *The Dark Tower* series, Roland incorrectly thinks that the Tower is "a central linchpin that holds all of existence together,"[60] and that his sole reason for existence is to save and protect the Tower—at *all* costs, including the loss of life to his friends and companions. He retains that belief even though it has been suggested to him that "life and love" are "reason" and "purpose" for his existence and quest.[61] Additionally, when Marian Carver of the Tet Corporation tells him that his "quest to defeat the forces of the Crimson King has been successful," he admits to Marian that he has "sacrificed many friends […] and [his] own soul" simply to reach the Tower.[62] He is blinded by his quest because his axel is misplaced. Just as John M. Hill notes J.R.R. Tolkien's depiction of the angst of Germanic heroes "caught in the chains of circumstance of their own character,"[63] so too does Roland Deschain— whose name is pronounced by King as "des-chain"— put the chain of events in motion that eventually lead to the *murðor*, meaning "heinous or secret murder" in Anglo Saxon, of his adopted son, Jake.

As Jake fatally injures himself to save Stephen King, fulfilling a promise to Eddie to save both the character *and* "real" writer Stephen King, Roland damns himself further by concerning himself with King as Jake dies on the side of the road, leaving Jake to the care of a stranger and his faithful friend Oy. Except Jake doesn't die; he once again takes on the shape of Oy, exchanging minds with the bumbler so that he can leave critical information for the gunslinger in the mind of the small creature. Consequently, the bumbler stops doing his trademark echo of the last thing he hears,[64] and when Roland asks Oy to say goodbye to Jake during the burial, the bumbler says, "I, Ake"[65] as an attempt to identify his presence in the Oy's body. When Roland later puts his forehead against the bumbler's forehead, it is Jake's voice he telepathically hears passing along Eddie's warning of the dangerous Dandelo. But Roland, who states that he was never very good at riddling,[66] fails to read the clues in the tradition of the Old English *raedan*.

Similarly, Roland fails to "take counsel"—another aspect of the Old English *raedan*. He not only dismisses, or fails to heed, the advice of Jake via Oy, but he also brushes aside the visions that Susannah has of Eddie and Jake awaiting them in a parallel American world because Roland refuses to give up his quest. He tells Susannah that her vision of a portal door into a world where their loved ones await them is "a trick," asking her "What if you roll right through and into todash space?"[67] Robin Furth describes the word "todash" as a verb, rather than an adjective, to mean "body and mind travel" between the spaces of parallel worlds, and to "todash" has inherent risks because "monsters live in the crevices between realities."[68] King's kenning of "todash space" suggests two Anglo-Saxon words: *todon*, meaning "to open, unbind," and *todal*, meaning "partition, division."[69] Susannah chooses to unbind herself from the ka-tet because "Roland's way was the way of the gun. Roland's way was death."[70] She chooses the path of the Rose, of faith and love, answering Roland's question about todash space by saying "Then I will light the darkness with thoughts of those I love."[71] Roland refuses to do the same, and his refusal brings continued violence to Others: Oy/Jake, Patrick Danville, and even his son, Mordred.

As death surrounds Roland, mainly because of his short-sighted obsession, we can easily conclude that he is doomed. And as Pollington says, "if a man is doomed then not even his courage can help him against the course of events."[72] Roland may enter the Dark Tower due to his courage, but he is friendless soul with no virtue left but courage. Roland's Tower is revealed as a metaphorical representation of obsession, blindness, and violent folly—a "place of death" because Roland's "life had made it so."[73] So, Roland is denied death because he denied the strength of love by sacrificing others, despite any "courage" he exhibits. Roland is forced through the door at the top of the tower, and he comes full circle, returning to the purgatorial desert at the beginning of his quest.[74]

At the conclusion of *The Dark Tower*, King hints that Roland may, on this new incarnation of his quest, finally have the peace of mortality when Roland "touch[es] the horn" on his belt.[75] The horn, as suggested by Anglo-Saxon Riddle 76, denotes both good and evil, life and death. If Roland has the requisite strength of character (and not just courage), he can choose a path that is in keeping with the horn's Anglo-Saxon function as a "symbol of the oaths of loyalty and mutual support."[76] He can deny the "Come … come … come …" chant of the darkness of his soul represented metaphorically by his Tower, and live instead by the Anglo-Saxon *cuman* "to recover." He can start by examining the maxims in his life, maxims that are passed down by oral tradition, remembering that he, like the Anglo-Saxon scribes, is an Other, trying to make sense of words from another time. If Roland's does so, than he may recover the original meaning. The Gunslinger's Litany that Roland uses to train his warriors to kill without mercy is in fact a riddlic prayer requiring deliberation:

> I do not aim with my hand; he who aims with his hand has forgotten the face of his father. I aim with my eye. I do not shoot with my hand; he who shoots with his hand has forgotten the face of his father. I shoot with my mind. I do not kill with my gun; he who kills with his gun has forgotten the face of his father. I kill with my heart.[77]

The others of Roland's ka-tet ultimately solve the riddle of this dualistic prayer. Eddie Dean, who remembers nearly too late that the path of the gun is the path to ruin, aims with his eye, his vision, to help Jake fulfill his Christ-like duty. Susannah Dean, who realizes that the way of the gun is the way of death, shoots with her mind and deliberates, solving the riddle of how to return to those she loves. Jake Chambers, whose last name connotes both the chambers of a gun and a heart, ultimately chooses to love with his heart, enough to die to save another. Thus, on his "day of judgment" this twin of Eddie of the silly *saelig* nature is resurrected to another world; Jake is like the Anglo-Saxon sacred terms *gesaelig, ofersaelig,* and *gesaeligost*: "He shall be blessed, exceedingly blessed, the most blessed of creatures world without end."[78] When Susannah meets Eddie and Jake in Central Park with the clue of the Christmas song "What Child is This?" playing in the background, she learns that their last name is now "Toren," which bears quite the obvious similarity to the word "tower." In short, unlike the lone gunslinger, Roland, who chooses the path of death and ends up a suspended soul, the "Toren" family constructs a tower of love, a magical, protected circle of love, and "there was happiness."[79]

Just as the whole body of Anglo-Saxon literature is filled with riddles and kennings, so is the whole body of King's seven-volume *The Dark Tower Series.* An understanding of Anglo-Saxon conventions provides a key to unlocking King's riddlic landscape. King suggests that his "Constant Readers" and Roland of Gilead wander another riddlic landscape: human existence. At the heart of both Anglo-Saxon literature and

King's magnum opus is the fundamental riddle: What is life? Like the riddler of the Anglo-Saxon Horn Riddle 76, King suggests that the truth of life is found in the paradox, in the juxtaposition of dualistic meaning, in the tension between good and evil, between the Rose and the Tower.

Notes

1. Daniel Tiffany, "Lyric Substance: On Riddles, Materialism, and Poetic Obscurity," *Critical Inquiry* 28, no. 1 (2001): 78.

2. Craig Williamson, *Feast of Creatures: Anglo Saxon Riddle-Songs* (Philadelphia: University of Pennsylvania Press, 1982), 36.

3. Kevin Crossley-Holland, *The Anglo-Saxon World: An Anthology* (Oxford: Oxford University Press, 1982), 236.

4. Robin Furth, *Stephen King's The Dark Tower: The Complete Concordance* (New York: Scribner, 2006), 527.

5. Williamson, *Feast of Creatures*, 36.

6. Furth, *Stephen King's The Dark Tower*, 461.

7. Stephen King, *The Wolves of the Calla* (Hampton Falls, NH: Donald M. Grant, 2003), 173.

8. Furth, *Stephen King's The Dark Tower*, 461.

9. Stephen Pollington, *The Mead Hall: Feasting in Anglo-Saxon England* (Norfolk, VA: Anglo Saxon, 2003), 224.

10. King *The Wolves of the Calla*, 238; Stephen King, *The Dark Tower* (New York: Pocket, 2006), 464 and 488.

11. Emily Doris Grübl, "Abschliessende Zusammenfassung," Studien zu den Angelsdchsischen Elegien (Marburg: Elwert-Grafe und Umzer, 1948), pp. 178–87, quoted in Edith Whitehurst Williams, "The Anglo-Saxon Theme of Exile in Renaissance Lyrics: A Perspective on Two Sonnets of Sir Walter Raleigh," *Journal of English Literary History* 42, no. 2 (1975): 176.

12. Stephen King, *The Gunslinger* (New York: Signet, 2003), 14.

13. King, *The Dark Tower*, 928.

14. Williamson, *Feast of Creatures*, 21.

15. Stephen King, *Wizard and Glass* (New York: Signet, 2003), 36–7.

16. Michael Lapidge, et al., *The Blackwell Encyclopedia of Anglo Saxon England* (Oxford: Blackwell, 1999), 210.

17. Williamson, *Feast of Creatures*, 37.

18. King, *Wizard and Glass*, 50.

19. Stephen King, *The Waste Lands* (New York: Signet, 2003), 390.

20. Ibid., 51.

21. Edith Whitehurst Williams, "Auden, Yeats, and the Word 'Silly': A Study in Semantic Change, *South Atlantic Review* 46, no. 4 (1981): 18.

22. Ibid., 19.

23. King, *Wizard and Glass*, 51–3.

24. Gwendolyn A. Morgan, "Dualism and Mirror Imagery in Anglo-Saxon Riddles," *Journal of the Fantastic in the Arts* 5, no. 1 (1992): 82.

25. King, *Wizard and Glass*, 60.

26. Williamson, *Feast of Creatures*, 37.

27. Ibid., 22.

28. King, *Wizard and Glass*, 9–50.

29. Pollington, *The Mead Hall*, 212.

30. Williamson, *Feast of Creatures*, 25.

31. King, *The Waste Lands*, 180.

32. "Riddle 76," Swarthmore College-English Department (Old English Riddles), last modified 2004, http:// www.swarthmore.edu/Humanities/english/oldenglish/ 76.html.

33. Pollington, *The Mead Hall*, 149.

34. Morgan, "Dualism," 78.

35. Ibid., 78–9.

36. Ibid., 78.

37. Ibid., 78.

38. J.R. Clark Hall, *A Concise Anglo-Saxon Dictionary* (Toronto: University of Toronto Press), 76.

39. King, *Wolves of the Calla*, 233.

40. Ibid., 238.

41. Ibid., 234.

42. Ibid., 693.

43. Williamson, *Feast of Creatures*, 25.

44. Ibid., 3.

45. King, *The Dark Tower*, 121–123.

46. Bev Vincent, *The Road to the Dark Tower: Exploring Stephen King's Magnum Opus* (New York: New American Library, 2004), 162.

47. King, The Dark Tower, 480.

48. Ibid.

49. Ibid.

50. King, *Wizard and Glass*, 49–50.

51. Lapdige, et al., *The Blackwell Encyclopedia*, 462.

52. King, *The Dark Tower*, 411.

53. Ibid., 477.

54. Ibid., 411.

55. Stephen King, *The Drawing of the Three* (New York: Signet, 2003), 462.

56. King, *The Dark Tower*, 477.

57. Ibid.

58. King, *The Waste Lands*, 581.

59. Milton McC. Gatch, *Loyalties and Traditions: Man and his World in Old English Literature* (New York: Pegasus, 1971), 108.

60. King, *The Gunslinger*, 179.

61. King, *Wolves of the Calla*, 188.

62. King, *The Dark Tower*, 627–628.

63. John M. Hill, *The Anglo-Saxon Warrior Ethic: Restructuring Lordship in Early English Literature* (Gainesville: University Press of Florida, 2000), 81.

64. King, *The Dark Tower*, 579. Recall that Oy's speech is typically a matter of mimicry, as he usually attempts to repeat the last thing he hears and rarely speaks autonomously.

65. Ibid., 587.

66. King, *The Waste Lands*, 391.

67. King, *The Dark Tower*, 928.

68. Furth, *Stephen King's The Dark Tower*, 465.

69. Hall, *A Concise Anglo-Saxon Dictionary*, 343.

70. King, *The Dark Tower*, 929.

71. Ibid., 928.

72. Stephen Pollington, *The English Warrior from Earliest Times to 1066* (Norfolk, VA: Anglo Saxon, 1996), 167.

73. King, *The Dark Tower*, 1026.

74. Ibid., 1029.

75. Ibid., 1030.

76. Pollington, *The English Warrior*, 149.

77. Stephen King, *The Song of Susannah* (New York: Signet, 2006), 252.

78. Williams, "Auden, Yeats, and the Word 'Silly,'" 19.

79. King, *The Dark Tower*, 1010.

A Rose, a Stone, an Unfound Door

Metaphor and Intertextuality in The Dark Tower Series

GEORGIANNA O. MILLER

It has been said that "a (literary) text is, by definition, a dialogue with other texts."[1] Stephen King, the infamous pop horror writer, admits that he has often borrowed situations, ideas, or themes from other authors and incorporated them into his own work. And despite the fact that King has won literary prizes such as the O. Henry and the National Book Award's Medal of Distinguished Contribution to American Letters, many of Stephen King's "sources" are of a higher literary quality than his critics might suspect. For example, his magnum opus series *The Dark Tower* was originally inspired by the poem "Childe Roland to the Dark Tower Came" by Robert Browning.[2] This poem was also inspired by another work—in fact, "Browning subtitles his poem with a reference to Edgar's song in *King Lear*" by William Shakespeare.[3] Some scholars even suggest that it is possible that Shakespeare drew his inspiration from the Norman poet Turold's *La Chanson de Roland*, written c. 1100.[4]

King makes no mention of the Modernist poet T.S. Eliot in any of the "arguments" preceding his *Dark Tower* books. However, there are enough similarities between *The Dark Tower* and Eliot's work, not only "The Waste Land," but also certain themes and symbols from "Ash Wednesday" and "The Four Quartets," to justify an intertextual reading. However, the intertextuality of King's masterwork does not stop there. T.S. Eliot was also heavily influenced by Dante. In 1949 Eliot said during an interview, "No one has had a greater influence on me than Dante."[5]

Indeed, "The Waste Land" is often regarded as Eliot's equivalent of the *Inferno*, while "Ash Wednesday" and "The Four Quartets" have been believed to correspond with *Purgatorio* and *Paradiso* respectively.

This suggests that an intertextual reading of Eliot and King's work can be productively expanded to include Dantean influences on King. In fact, *The Dark Tower* bears certain similarities to *The Divine Comedy* that are not present throughout Eliot's poetry. Thus, Dante's and King's works could be read intertextually in their own right. For simplicity's sake, however, this paper will be divided into two sections. The first section, Eliot's influence on King, will address the independent influence of the Modernist author. The latter section, Dante's influence on Eliot and King, will explore similarities common to both Eliot's and King's work and Dante's *Divine Comedy*.

Eliot's Influence on King: The Sibyl

The epigraph to "The Waste Land" by T.S. Eliot comes from Petronius' story of the Sibyl in his *Satyricon*: "For I saw with my own eyes the Sibyl hanging in the jar at Cumae, and when the acolytes said, 'Sibyl, what do you wish?' she replied, 'I wish to die.'"[6] This is in reference to the story of the Sibyl who wished for eternal life but not eternal youth. When her wish was granted, she was forced to waste away becoming ever more frail and ugly. Before Eliot's poem even begins, the reader is presented with an image of the feminine being powerless in a male-dominated society despite her "wisdom and prophetic powers."[7] The images of death and destruction throughout Eliot's "The Waste Land" are not seen as natural and indicative of rebirth. Rather, they are symptoms of a diseased and corrupted society, one that is sick at its heart.

Similarly, in Stephen King's *Dark Tower* series, we are presented with a world that has, as the novels' characters put it, "moved on." A revolution has toppled the main character Roland's "world of light." As a result, anarchy and destruction have rendered government and technology useless—and often dangerous. In the first installment, *The Gunslinger*, we are introduced to Roland, who is chasing a man in black for reasons of which he is not entirely sure. The parallel to Eliot's Sibyl can be seen midway through this volume. Roland visits a ring of stones in which a succubus with the power of prophesy is imprisoned: an Oracle.

Against his better judgment, Roland knows he must seek her wisdom because he needs information regarding the nature of his quest. Like the Sibyl, King's Oracle is trapped—the Sibyl by a bottle, the Oracle by a circle of stones. Roland forces the Oracle to prophesy by promising to cater to her weakness, which, as in many portrayals of the feminine throughout history, is sex. He teases her with the promise of sex, but withholds until she tells his future. Once he has what he wants, Roland gives in to her sexual desires until his disgust overcomes him, at which time he abandons her to her stones. Eliot's poem can, in a sense, be seen as a prophecy that was fulfilled because no one would listen to the Sibyl. However, there is "no reference to her knowledge or to the force of life which is eternally hers, only to her desire for death."[8] King's Oracle also has a gift, but unlike the Sibyl's gift which is ignored, the Oracle is used and then forgotten. She has power, but no leverage, so she must wield her power at the whim of men. Thus, both of these figures are the "abandoned and ignored voice of feminine spirituality" in their respective worlds.[9]

Throughout Eliot's "The Waste Land," all feminine figures "are sterile, physically repulsive, or falsely seductive. Their sexuality is dangerous, deadly, or dead."[10] In the fallen world of *The Dark Tower*, the feminine will often receive a similar treatment. Even the land, traditionally a feminine image, is barren due to what seems to have been a nuclear disaster of some kind. The children the land bears (both plants and animals) are deformed, sterile "muties" that have been tainted by the poison of war. Eliot's "The Waste Land" was also written in response to a disordering of the world by war, in his case World War I. Like the Sibyl, however, Eliot's poetic masterpiece comes too late to avert the disaster which has already struck. The best we can hope for are the "Lilacs out of the dead land."[11] The nuclear disaster of King's world is perhaps meant to serve as a prophecy of what *could* happen in his reader's world, but has not yet. Fiction as Oracle, perhaps.

Eliot's Influence on King: The Tarot Reading

Near the end of the first section of "The Waste Land," The Burial of the Dead, the Sibyl is associated with Madame Sosostris who is portrayed as a famous clairvoyant, "a false diviner whose reading of the ancient form of wisdom, the Tarot, gives no hope."[12] In Eliot's poem, the fortune teller gives an unnamed character a reading, turning over the following cards: the drowned Phoenician Sailor, the Belladonna, the man with three staves, the Wheel, and the one-eyed merchant with something on his back. The Hanged Man is significant in his absence, and Madame Sosostris' client is warned to "Fear death by water."[13]

In traditional Tarot decks, the figure of the Hanged Man is not a negative image. In fact, "Spiritual awareness is the message of this card. Wherever it appears in the pack it shows a need to reevaluate the current situation ... [it] symbolizes death and rebirth."[14] By mentioning the lack of the card in her reading, Madame Sosostris is suggesting to her unnamed patron that modern society, and especially World War I, has had a negative effect on the spirituality of the world. Recovery or spiritual healing will be difficult, if not impossible, to achieve.

Near the end of *The Gunslinger*, the first book or section within King's longer work, the man in black also gives Roland a Tarot reading. Both close ties and significant differences exist between the two readings. Unlike Madame Sosostris's reading from which the Hanged Man is missing, in the man in black's reading the Hanged Man is the first card turned over. In fact, the man in black identifies this trump card from the Major Arcana with Roland. In addition to spiritual awareness, the Hanged Man indicates that "other people find the seeker hard to understand and solitary in his or her actions."[15] This is certainly true of Roland, a sort of knight referred to as a gunslinger. Roland is in fact the *last* gunslinger, and he is questing for a way to heal his world. If Roland is the Hanged Man, he is the "regenerative power"[16] capable of healing the rift. Thus King's reading begins on a more hopeful note than Eliot's does.

The next card the man in black turns over is the Sailor. The man in black says, "He drowns, gunslinger, and no one throws out the line."[17] In Eliot's reading, the drowned sailor is identified as the clairvoyant's patron. In the man in black's reading, however, the Sailor represents those whom the gunslinger is charged with saving. What is especially interesting about the presence of a drowned sailor in both readings is the fact that the Sailor is not an actual figure in the Tarot deck. The man in black follows this card with "The Prisoner," portrayed as a young man with a baboon on his back. Roland is not told what the character is imprisoned by. This card corresponds neatly with Eliot's "one-eyed merchant, and this card,/Which is blank, is something he carries on his back,/Which I am forbidden to see."[18] The next card to be turned is "The Lady of the Shadows," who is portrayed as two-faced, possessing good and evil. The Lady that Madame Sosostris turns over is Belladonna, a plant in the Nightshade family that, while poisonous, also has medicinal properties. Thus Belladonna, like the Lady of the Shadows, is two-faced. Like the Drowned Sailor, the Belladonna is not an actual card in the Tarot deck. Perhaps the closest approximation is The High Priestess, who is the number two card in the Major Arcana and who "symbolizes duality; creativity and destruction, light and dark."[19]

King's man in black also turns over Death, The Tower, and Life; no mention is made of Eliot's man with three staves or the Wheel, although the eastern philosophy picturing *ka*, or fate, as a wheel figures heavily throughout *The Dark Tower* series. Other, more subtle connections also exist: the man in black refers to The Lady of the Shadows as "a veritable Janus,"[20] and it is the Roman god Janus who rules the Wheel of Fortune turned over in Madame Sosostris' reading.[21] The Tower card is not turned over in Eliot's reading. However, tower imagery appears in the later sections of his poem The Fire Sermon and What the Thunder Said.[22]

Structurally, both Tarot readings serve similar functions in *The Dark Tower* and in "The Waste Land." They end the first section of the longer works of which they are a part. They also provide a frame. The second book in *The Dark Tower*, called *The Drawing of the Three*, is loosely structured around the man in black's reading. The sections include: Prologue: the Sailor; The Prisoner; Shuffle; The Lady of Shadows; Reshuffle; The Pusher; and Final Shuffle. As mentioned previously, the sections in Eliot's "The Waste Land" that follow Madame Sosostris' reading can be seen as the content of her prophesy. The Belladonna, or Priestess on a throne, and the Drowned Phoenician Sailor in particular reappear throughout the long poem.

The structure of the third book in King's series, *The Waste Lands*, owes perhaps the clearest debt to Eliot. The first of three epigraphs in the novel is the following quote from the first section of Eliot's "The Waste Land," The Burial of the Dead:

> A heap of broken images, where the sun beats,
> And the dead tree gives no shelter, the cricket no relief,
> And the dry stone no sound of water. Only
> There is shadow under this red rock,

(Come in under the shadow of this red rock),
And I will show you something different from either
Your shadow in the morning striding behind you
Or your shadow at evening rising to meet you;
I will show you fear in a handful of dust.[23]

King's book is organized into two major sections: Fear in a Handful of Dust and A Heap of Broken Images. While previous connections might only be obvious to the widely read, "The Waste Land" is arguably Eliot's most well-known work. By naming his book after the poem, King begs an intertextual reading of the two pieces. He reinforces that desire by including the epigraph for those readers who have not recognized previous similarities and who may be unfamiliar with the Modernist work.

Dante's Influence on Eliot and King: The Pilgrim

Eliot's poetry lacks a unified voice or narrator; indeed, it is rare for a narrator to remain consistent for the length of a single poem. However, both Dante and King's multi-volume epics follow the journeys of a pilgrim. In *The Divine Comedy*, the speaker/narrator is Dante himself. While a distinction is clearly made between Dante the Pilgrim and Dante the Poet earlier in the *Comedy*, once the cycle is almost complete the difference between the two becomes negligible. Dante's initial guide is Virgil, although he is replaced at the end of the *Purgatorio* with Beatrice, who is the guide during the ultimate work in the series, *Paradiso*.

In *The Dark Tower* the pilgrim is the gunslinger Roland, who is accompanied by fellow pilgrims which he "draws" from our world. Because his fellow pilgrims are not from Roland's reality and need his expertise of the world in which they find themselves, Roland ultimately serves as both pilgrim and guide. As suggested by Indick, "because [*The Dark Tower*] is epic by its very nature, [King] is for once willing to deal with archetypes and larger-than-life figures."[24] The unique similarity in structure between Dante's and King's multivolume works is relatively rare. More often than not, Dantean influences bear a direct correspondence to the work of both Eliot and King. For example, Dante's *Inferno* begins "midway along the journey of our life."[25] Dante began writing the epic work c. 1307, but it takes place in 1300, when the Pilgrim was thirty-five—literally "one-half of man's Biblical life span of seventy years."[26] This age becomes a time of questioning for Dante, a time to reevaluate the things upon which he had previously placed value. Throughout the *Comedy*, the Pilgrim learns that his choices have been lacking. His various guides help illuminate what he should place value on. The work marks a turning point from Dante's career as a largely romantic poet to more serious subject matter.[27]

Similarly, Eliot's "The Waste Land" was published in 1922, just before he was thirty-five,[28] and "signaled a new kind of art that would express life in the twentieth century."[29] While chapters had been previously published elsewhere, King's first installment of *The Dark Tower* was published in its entirety in 1982, also the year he turned thirty-five.[30] Like the other works mentioned here, *The Gunslinger* was also a major departure from its author's previous works. For example, it was published in an extremely small print run and marketed as fantasy. In fact, King fans did not find out about the book's existence until his next "horror" book was released and *The Gunslinger* was listed in the frontmatter. Because he felt it was so different from his previous work and that his main audience wouldn't enjoy it, King only consented to have *The Gunslinger* reprinted after large amounts of reader pressure.

Not only were the three works begun or published at almost exactly the same point in each writer's lives, their beginnings are astonishingly similar. Canto I of *Inferno* finds the Pilgrim "in a dark wood,"[31] which we discover later in the canto is actually a "gran diserto."[32] One translation of "gran diserto" is "great desert," which introduces the theme of Exodus that will continue throughout the *Comedy*. Another interpretation of "gran diserto" employed by numerous translators is wasteland.[33] This idea of the wasteland goes on to become the title of Eliot's poem, which begins "April is the cruelest month, breeding/Lilacs out of the dead land."[34] What land is deader than a desert? The theme of Exodus runs throughout Eliot's "The Waste Land" as well, although the Promised Land is never reached (there are stronger hints of the Promised Land in "Ash Wednesday" and "Four Quartets"). King's *Dark Tower* series begins as follows:

> The man in black fled across the desert, and the gunslinger followed.
>
> The desert was the apotheosis of all deserts, huge, standing to the sky for what might have been parsecs in all directions. White; blinding; waterless; without feature save for the faint, cloudy haze of the mountains.[35]

Thus in the first two paragraphs the theme of Exodus in the desert, as well as the hint of purification or insight in the mountains, are introduced. This purification will occur at the Mount of Purgatory in Dante's *Comedy* and on the stairwell in Eliot's "Ash Wednesday."

However, purification can only take place after the wasteland has been crossed. In the works of all three authors, we learn that we must descend before we can ascend. In *Inferno* we take a path downward through Hell where the ultimate sinner waits at the nadir: Satan. He is described thus:

> Beneath each face two mighty wings stretched out,
> the size you might expect of this huge bird
> (I never saw a ship with larger sails):
> not feathered wings but rather like the ones
> a bat would have. He flapped them constantly,
> keeping three winds continuously in motion
> to lock Cocytus eternally in ice.[36]

Yet that same Canto, where Dante has literally hit bottom, ends with "I saw the lovely things the heavens hold,/and we came out to see once more the stars."[37]

If "The Waste Land" is Eliot's equivalent to the *Inferno*, then the phrase "These fragments I have shored against my ruins," followed by the repetition of the word "shantih," which means peace that surpasses understanding, is a conscious imitation of Dante.[38] We will be reminded again of Satan in the first section of "Ash Wednesday," when the narrator tells us "Because these wings are no longer wings to fly/But merely vans to beat the air."[39] The section ends with lines from the Hail Mary, wherein the poet/speaker is asking for the very intercession granted to Dante in the *Comedy*.

Also similar to the *Comedy*, the last paragraph of King's *The Gunslinger* begins, "There the gunslinger sat, his face turned up into the fading light. He dreamed his dreams and watched as the stars came out."[40] So although the longest, and arguably the hardest portions of the journey lay ahead, all three of these "first" works end on a hopeful note. In addition to their structure, key images resonate throughout the works of the three authors. These images hold much the same symbolic meaning in all the works discussed: the city, the bridge, and—most importantly—the rose.

Dante's Influence on Eliot and King: City and Bridge

In Canto III of *Inferno*, Virgil and Dante are preparing to enter Hell proper. They pass through a gate that reads:

> I Am The Way Into The Doleful City
> I Am The Way Into Eternal Grief
> I Am The Way To A Forsaken Race.[41]

Although later a Heavenly City will be reached, the first image of a city that we are given is a negative one. Dante and Virgil bridge the gap between the vestibule and Hell when Charon reluctantly agrees to ferry them across the river Acheron.

The river in Eliot's case is the Thames, and the city is London. Manganiello points out that "for Eliot […] the city and the desert converge, but in 'The Waste Land' both are barren."[42] Compare Dante's lines above to "The Burial of the Dead":

> Unreal City,
> Under the brown fog of a winter dawn,
> A crowd flowed over London Bridge, so many,
> I had not thought death had undone so many.
> Sighs, short and frequent, were exhaled,
> And each man fixed his eyes before his feet.[43]

In fact, Eliot admits that the line "sighs, short and frequent" is a modification of a line from Canto IV:

> there were no wails but just the sounds of sighs
> rising and trembling through the timeless air,
> the sounds of sighs of untormented grief
> burdening these groups, diverse and teeming,
> made up of men and women and of infants.[44]

The city is unreal—that is, spiritually dead like the city in *Inferno*. Had he lived in the twentieth century, Dante could easily have written the lines above.

It is not until the third volume of the *Dark Tower* series that we will see King's City, but it will be just as bleak as those of Dante and Eliot are. In the section of *The Waste Lands* entitled "A Heap of Broken Images," we find a subsection called Bridge and City. It is here that we make a crossing into the city of Lud, which is next to the river Send. The pilgrims must cross a "bridge [...] that looked anything but solid and eternal. The vertical hangers on the left sagged slackly; the ones remaining on the right almost screamed with tension."[45] On the other side of the bridge, the city itself "appeared to have been either burned or blasted. The skyline reminded him of a diseased jaw from which many teeth have already fallen."[46] When King's pilgrims enter the city, they find it is a place where two factions are constantly at war. In another subtle connection to the Eliot's Tarot reading, faction members routinely kill those within their own bands by hanging them. Beyond Eliot, King scholar Tony Magistrale points out that "[t]he most loathsome monsters in King's canon, as is the case as well in Dante's *Inferno*, are always partially human; they represent the twisting of human tendencies and desires until these desires become bestial, connected by only a remote resemblance to the rest of humanity."[47] In other words, Roland and his band had hoped the city would retain the vestiges of light and knowledge, but they find only violence and despair.

Dante's Influence on Eliot and King: The Rose

The hopes of all three authors to overcome violence and despair lay in a single redemptive symbol: the Rose. In *Paradise*, the arena in which the Elect contemplate God takes the form of a white rose. The white rose is symbolic of "innocence, virginity, spiritual unfolding."[48] Dante's rose is also called "this beautiful Rose of joy."[49] Beauty and joy are connotations of the red rose, but it can also symbolize the blood of Christ, suggesting the union of opposites.[50] In Dante's description we seem to get the opposites of flower and flame:

> So now, appearing to me in the form
> of a white rose was Heaven's sacred host,
> those whom with His own blood Christ made His bride, [...]
> Their faces showed the glow of living flame[51]

This parallel is strong between this Canto and Eliot's "Ash Wednesday," where the lady of silences is referred to as a Rose: "The single Rose/Is now the Garden/Where all loves end/Terminate torment."[52]

Eliot's Lady, who appears in the beginning of the second section of "Ash Wednesday," is equated with Dante's Beatrice. Indeed, she appears to be the intercessor Eliot was searching for in the first section of the poem which, as previously mentioned, ends with the Hail Mary. This parallel becomes even stronger throughout "The Four Quartets." The last section, "Little Gidding," ends with an image almost identical to Dante's:

> And all shall be well and
> All manner of things shall be well
> When the tongues of flame are in-folded
> Into the crowned knot of fire
> And the fire and the rose are one.[53]

Eliot's synthesis of the fire and the rose reflects the "HIGHEST WISDOM JOINED WITH PRIMAL LOVE" alluded to on the doorway to Hell in Canto III of *Inferno*.[54] The circle becomes complete with this union. Both the flame, symbolizing punishment and purification, and the rose, signifying the Beatific Vision, are necessary facets of God.

These visions are extremely telling within the context of King's work, where the Tower is revealed in a dream as a place where "[t]he field was a deep scarlet, as if some titanic battle had been fought here[...] then he realized that it was not blood he was looking at, but roses."[55] The Tower itself is described throughout the series as the center of all Time and Size, and the tone used in conjunction with it is often more sinister than comforting. However, the Rose is always a positive image, such as in a vision Eddie, one of Roland's fellow pilgrims, sees:

> Then the shape in the flames changed again [...] For a moment Eddie saw a rose—a triumphant rose that might have bloomed in the dawn of this world's first day, a thing of depthless, timeless beauty [...] it was there in the fire, burning out in triumph and some wonderful, inchoate defiance, declaring that despair was a mirage and death a dream.[56]

King's rose also seems similar to the rose in Hebrew mysticism, where the center of the rose is the sun.[57] In the vision of another of the pilgrims, "the rose began to open before his eyes. It disclosed a dark scarlet furnace [...] *It was a sun*: a vast forge burning at the center of this rose."[58] In the Hebrew interpretation, the petals of the rose are the "harmonious diversities of nature."[59] In King's epic work, the pilgrims are questing because that harmony has been disrupted, and they are attempting to set it right.

Conclusion

In his *Divine Comedy,* Dante attempted to "remove those living in this life from their state of misery and lead them to the state of felicity."[60] In order to best accomplish this goal, he felt that his poetry had to be accessible to the common citizen of his day. Thus, as the *De vulgarie loquentia* posits, his use of the vernacular language is an appropriate choice.[61] In addition to the vernacular language, Dante also used "pop culture" figures and references throughout the *Comedy*—people and stories the readers of his day would immediately recognize and relate to. Dante had the additional advantage of a unified system of belief in his society. He did not have to explain or defend his choice of subject matter, and instead could concentrate his every effort on the message he was attempting to get across to his reader.

Eliot did not have the advantage of a unified system of belief. He found himself not only attempting to get across his message, the quest for enlightenment in a shattered world, but also defending his use of religious references. Indeed, poems like "The Waste Land" both bemoan and reflect the fragmented society in which he found himself. Yet part of Eliot's failure is quite possibly his own fault. His verse is so dense as to put off many of his potential modern readers. Although this is partly due to the fact that, like Dante, many of Eliot's ideas were simply dense and intricate, he does not couch these ideas in "low" language in order to give the reader an advantage. The Constant Reader certainly has that advantage in King's work. He has written over fifty books, and all of them have been worldwide number-one bestsellers. His use of the vernacular in these works, combined with a writing style steeped in pop culture references and tributes to other authors are both the reason for his unprecedented popularity and the reason for the negative critical response to his writing.

The fact that he is extremely prolific is not unique to King. Dante, Eliot, and countless numbers of other writers have a large body of work to their credit. The idea of the palimpsest, of layers of historical and literary meaning, in writing is also not unique to King. In fact, many of the concepts he uses to structure his *Dark Tower* series and other works, and many of the symbols he uses to invest that work with meaning, are drawn from canonical sources of which Dante and Eliot are only two examples. A definitive critical analysis of *The Dark Tower* would not be complete without fully exploring King's acknowledged debt to authors such as Browning, and there are certainly other authors not discussed here. But an intertextual reading of the works of these three authors alone yields significant thematic and structural similarities.

Notes

1. Cyrena N. Pondrom, "*Trilogy* and *Four Quartets*: Contrapuntal Visions of Spiritual Quest," *Agenda* 25, no. 3–4 (1987–88): 155.

2. Stephen King, *The Gunslinger*. rev. ed. (New York: Signet, 2003), 221.

3. Ben P. Indick, "Stephen King as an Epic Writer," in *Discovering Modern Horror Fiction*, ed. Darrell Schweitzer (Mercer Island: Starmont House, 1985), 62.

4. "Chanson de Roland, La," *Merriam Webster's Encyclopedia of Literature*, 1995 ed. (Springfield: Merriam-Webster, 1995), 227.

5. Qtd. in Dominic Manganiello. *T.S. Eliot and Dante* (New York: St. Martin's, 1989), 1.

6. Melody M. Zajdel, "'I See Her Differently': H.D.'s *Trilogy* as Feminist Response to Masculine Modernism," in *Sagetrieb: A Journal Devoted to Poets in the Pound-H.D.-Williams Tradition*, 5, no. 1 (1986): 9.

7. Ibid.

8. Ibid.

9. Ibid.

10. Ibid.

11. Eliot, T.S. *T.S. Eliot: Collected Poems 1909–1962* (New York: Harcourt Brace, 1963), 53.

12. Zajdel, "'I See Her Differently,'" 10.

13. Eliot, *Collected,,* 54.

14. Adam Fronteras, *The Tarot: The Traditional Tarot Reinterpreted for the Modern World* (New York: Stewart, Tabori, & Chang: 1996), 54–55.

15. Ibid., 55.

16. Zajdel, "'I See Her Differently,'" 10.

17. King, *The Gunslinger*, 200.

18. Eliot, *Collected*, 54.

19. Fronteras, *The Tarot*, 34.

20. King, *The Gunslinger*, 201.

21. Fronteras, *The Tarot*, 50.

22. Eliot, *Collected*, 64, 67.

23. Ibid., 53–54.

24. Indick, "Stephen King," 61.

25. Dante, *The Divine Comedy Volume I: Inferno*, trans. Mark Musa (New York: Penguin,1971), 67.

26. Dante, *Inferno*, 72.

27. Ibid., 25.

28. Manganiello, *T.S. Eliot*, 40.

29. Nancy K. Gish, *The Waste Land: A Poem of Memory and Desire* (Boston: Twayne, 1988), 4.

30. Stephen King, *On Writing: A Memoir of the Craft* (New York: Pocket, 2000), 34.

31. Dante, *Inferno*, 67.

32. Manganiello, *T.S. Eliot*, 40.

33. Dante, *Inferno,* 69, and Robert Pinsky, trans., *The Inferno of Dante*, by Dante (New York: Farrar, Straus, and Giroux,1994), 5.

34. Eliot, *Collected*, 53.

35. King, *The Gunslinger*, 11.

36. Dante, *Inferno*, 381.

37. Ibid., 383.

38. Eliot, *Collected*, 69.

39. Ibid., 86.

40. King, *The Gunslinger*, 216.

41. Dante, *Inferno*, 89.

42. Manganiello, *T.S. Eliot*, 42.

43. Eliot, *Collected*, 55.

44. Dante, *Inferno*, 98.

45. Stephen King, *The Waste Lands* (New York: Signet, 2003), 289.

46. Ibid.

47. Tony Magistrale, *Landscape of Fear: Stephen King's American Gothic* (Bowling Green, OH: Bowling Green State University Popular Press, 1988), 72.

48. G. Schiffhorst, "The Rose." Class Handout. LIT 6426: Dante and Eliot. UCF Colbourn Hall, Orlando. 2 April 2002.

49. Dante, *Paradise*, 380.

50. Schiffhorst, "The Rose."

51. Dante, *The Divine Comedy Volume III: Paradise*, trans. Mark Musa (New York: Penguin, 1984), 365.

52. Eliot, *Collected*, 88.

53. Ibid., 209.

54. Dante, *Inferno*, 89.

55. King, *The Waste Lands*, 52.

56. Ibid., 49.

57. Schiffhorst, "The Rose"

58. King, *The Waste Lands*, 125.

59. Schiffhorst, "The Rose."

60. Qtd. in Dante, *Inferno*, 43.

61. Dante, *Inferno*, 37.

PART III

Writing into the Millennium

Survival of the Sweetest

Little Miss Bosox and
the Saving Grace of Baseball in
The Girl Who Loved Tom Gordon

ABIGAIL L. BOWERS *and*
LOWELL MICK WHITE

Baseball literature is nearly as old as the game itself, stretching well back into the nineteenth century. For most of that time, though, baseball fictions were aimed at children. According to Debra A. Dagavarian, these juvenile books were written to be more than entertainment: they were designed with a goal of socializing young people, to instill traditional American values such as honesty, hard work, and fair play.[1] Baseball was present—mentioned, at least—in adult literatures of the early twentieth century (several characters in Hemingway's stories talk about baseball, for example, and the mysterious Meyer Wolfsheim, fixer of the 1919 World Series, appears in Fitzgerald's *The Great Gatsby*), but it wasn't until the 1950s that writers began producing serious, adult novels and stories about baseball. Today, the literature of baseball is enormous; Timothy Morris, a professor at the University of Texas at Arlington, maintains a massive online directory, *Guide to Baseball Fiction*, an ever-expanding annotated bibliography of novels, short stories, movies, and criticism.[2]

However, if the juvenile baseball books of the nineteenth and early twentieth centuries were written to be about more than baseball, to be works that would help mold the character of young people, so also the later adult baseball fictions transcend the sport, as authors used baseball to examine the psychology of the individual and his or her (usually *his,*

122

for baseball books are mostly masculine in their orientation) relationship to society. Ralph S. Graber notes, "The quality of baseball fiction for adults continued to improve in the 1930s and 40's."[3] Bernard Malamud's *The Natural*, the first important work of adult baseball literature, portrays the inability of an individual to learn from his mistakes.[4] Philip Roth's *The Great American Novel* chronicles the worst team in baseball history, but is also a wicked spoof of McCarthyism and witch-hunting.[5] W. P. Kinsella's *Shoeless Joe* is about the reconciliation of a ruptured father-son relationship.[6] Baseball, in the hands of these and many, many other writers, becomes a tool to achieve their larger literary goals, showing that, as Ralph S. Graber says, "baseball literature has moved from the story told for the juvenile to the fiction which attracts the intellectual to examine the game in literature for the light it sheds on American life and the paradoxes of modern existence."[7]

It is no accident, then, that Stephen King structures *The Girl Who Loved Tom Gordon* in the manner of a baseball game. King's love of baseball and the macabre come together in *The Girl Who Loved Tom Gordon*, wherein the author's touching and tender understanding for the world around him, along with his description of this seemingly safe world as something frightening, provides a backdrop for his own preoccupation with and love for the game of baseball and allows something seemingly simple to take on the aura of a saving grace in the text. The text is composed so that readers feel they are watching and participating in a Boston Red Sox game. Each chapter represents a certain aspect of a game, including the "pregame," which sets up the story; a "seventh inning stretch"; a "save situation"; and a "postgame." Just as the sport itself progresses through nine innings, so, too, does Trisha McFarland's nine-day misadventure through the forests of Maine and New Hampshire.

As she becomes increasingly lost, the chapters—where innings represents days—take on a progressively dark and more dangerous tone, thus creating the paradox of modern existence by portraying a twentieth century girl trapped in a rustic nightmare. In an interview about the novel, King states,

> My idea was to write a kind of fairy-tale, "Hansel and Gretel" without Hansel. My heroine (Trisha) would be a child of divorce living with her mother and maintaining a meaningful connection with her father mostly through their mutual love of baseball and the Boston Red Sox. Lost in the woods, she'd find herself imagining that he favorite Red Sox player was with her, keeping

her company and guiding her through the terrible situation in which she found herself. Tom Gordon, #36, would be that player. Gordon is a real pitcher for the Red Sox; without his consent I wouldn't have wanted to publish the book. He did give it, for which I am deeply grateful.[8]

The participation of the real Tom Gordon, allowing the use of his name as both character and title, is central here, lending an air of verisimilitude and even charm (although in an interview with Tyler Kepner for *The New York Times*, the real Tom Gordon notes while he admires King, the author did not quite capture his character).[9] His presence guides Trisha from the beginning of her journey through to the end, where she meets the seemingly inscrutable "God of the Lost" right before she is, as she will predict, "saved" in the same way that Gordon tends to "save" games.

At the onset of the novel—and the game—Trisha outfits herself in BoSox gear, including "her blue Red Sox batting practice jersey (the one with 36 GORDON on the back)."[10] In order to escape her mother and brother's constant bickering, Trisha "open[s] the door to her favorite fantasy. She t[akes] off her Red Sox cap and look[s] at the signature written across the brim in broad black felt-tip strokes," and pretends that she has met Tom Gordon at a hotdog wagon in Sanford. When Trisha leaves the Appalachian Trail, she is "with Tom Gordon, 36, and he [is] offering to buy her a hotdog."[11] This imagining of her relationship with Tom Gordon distracts her from the "literally unimaginable" perils awaiting her when she strays off the path to take a pee, unwittingly plunging herself into the deep, dark dangers of the woods. According to Rebecca S. Kraus, a policy analyst for the U.S. Immigration and Naturalization Service, as well as a baseball sociologist and author of *Minor League Baseball: Community Building through Hometown Sports*, "Baseball provide[s] an emotional release, a sense of hope, and a place [...]. to gather in [...] time[s] of need, thus fulfilling its role as the national pastime."[12] For Trisha, baseball provides the emotional release to escape the fights between her parents, the fact that her father is an alcoholic, and that her brother Pete is caught in the throes of teen angst. Survival is not just a question of pluck and determination; for Trisha, it is also the presence of Tom Gordon and the Boston Red Sox in her life that help accomplish this goal. In fact, her first night in the woods is alleviated by the sound of the Red Sox playing, particularly when Tom Gordon is brought in as the relief pitcher. Her survival begins to depend solely on baseball, becoming her place to, as Kraus put it, "gather" in her own time of need; that is, the thought of baseball provides Trisha with an emotional release and a sense of hope that she will be rescued. Trisha, afraid of "other sounds in the dark" of the woods, listens to the ballgame, believing that "*If we win, if Tom gets the save,* I'll *be saved* ... It was stupid, of course ... but as the dark drew deeper ... it also seemed irrefutable ... if Tom Gordon got the save, *she* would get the save."[13] When the Boston Red Sox win the game—and Tom Gordon does indeed get the save—Trisha believes that she, too, will win, and be saved.

Baseball, in many literary works, often seems coated with a patina of nostalgia and depicted as a province for memory, of longing, and as the connection between generations (particularly between fathers and sons). It is a game whose fans often look to its past at the exclusion of the present, finding in baseball history a source of innocence and strength. Baseball, in spite of the way the game works—someone must win, another must lose, and no one knows which team will do what— creates a space where time seems suspended. In the game of baseball, time is arbitrary, allowing for an appealing retreat into a past world where the hectic pace of everyday life stops, and where "we can just slow things down for a moment and bring what is behind us into focus."[14]

Certainly that is the case in W. P. Kinsella's novel *Shoeless Joe*, and the movie based on it, *Field of Dreams*. The characters in the book and the movie find healing and solace as they watch the ghosts of long-dead ballplayers on the seemingly sacred field. The dead ballplayers, preserved in their youthful prime, magically reflect the hopes and affections of the living people who watch them play—both the character viewers in the story, and the actual viewers and readers of the fictional works. Over and over again, memory and childhood are cited as important aspects of baseball. In the movie, the character Terrance Mann, played by James Earl Jones, says of the magic diamond that the memories of the past become so thick, spectators will feel the need to "brush them away from their faces." Mann continues, "America has rolled by like an army of steamrollers. It's been erased like a blackboard, rebuilt, and erased again. But baseball has marked the time... [I]t reminds us of all that once was good. And that could be again."[15] The America represented by the game of baseball is one of innocence, of a time that has passed, but could— potentially—be resurrected, if only people would stop and remember what "once was good."

In *The Girl Who Loved Tom Gordon*, King uses the nostalgic context of baseball as a rhetorical appeal, urging readers to evoke their own memories of grace and connectedness—their own nostalgia. King's character, though, experiences no happy feelings of baseball nostalgia. For Trisha MacFarland, baseball is the *Now*. It is her present. It is the part of her life that gives her joy and completeness—and order, and rules. It gives her something to believe in, and the presence of Tom Gordon, whether real or imagined, helps cement this somewhat safe feeling in spite of the danger and disorder with which she is surrounded. Baseball, for Trisha, is a wondrous game. The thrill of watching or listening to her beloved Red Sox brings back memories of a happier time in her life, and convinces her that she will get out. The rules and regulations of the sport, along with the touch of superstition it always seems to bring, help Trisha cope with the very real nightmare in which she finds herself.

Baseball is a game of order and rules. Trisha's world, however, is unruly. The divorce of her parents, her dad's alcoholism, her mom's bitchiness, her brother's teenaged sullenness—together these often unremarkable elements of everyday life combine to create a world where a little girl can be forgotten and left to stray in the woods, a world where boundaries are diffuse and easily transgressed. Other than Trisha, the world surrounding her is filled with one reliable element: the continual and never-ending unpleasantness of the people who inhabit it. In fact, even in the woods, she is unable to escape this unpleasantness; as Christopher Lehmann-Haupt notes in *The New York Times Book Review* of the novel: "Along with a threatening natural world, what oppresses the reader is the knowledge that as the god of his fictional universe, Mr. King is perfectly capable of destroying a child; in his past fiction children have often not been guaranteed survival. To make matters worse, the world that Trisha is struggling to return to is not that much better than the one she is lost in."[16] In fact, Lehmann-Haupt notes that King uses simple things about the forest that would upset most readers lost in the woods, including insects, thirst, snakes, hunger, swamps, cliffs, thick foliage with thorns, extreme weather, noises in the dark, and what some consider his or her own worst enemy—imagination.[17] However, along with this unruly world she has left behind, and the one she has recently entered, Trisha is being stalking by something big and frightening and capable of killing large animals—as well as taming wild hornets and wasps.

Unlike the world Trisha has left behind—and the one she is currently inhabiting—baseball provides a universe where order is not just necessary, but triumphant. This orderliness does not exist merely between the white lines of the field, or within the friendly confines of the ball park, but is able, through powers of technology—the television and the radio—to radiate out everywhere, even to a little girl, tall for her age, lost in the woods. While it has become somewhat of an ironic cliché to refer to baseball as "The National Pastime"—particularly in light of the fact that baseball has become bogged down with doping scandals and locked into contemporary competition with football, basketball, and even NASCAR—it is also common to refer to baseball as a religion. As a religious metaphor, baseball can be seen as a transcendent force, something that through elegance, cleanliness, and orderliness, can elevate the fan above the humdrum concerns of the everyday world.

In *Bull Durham,* Annie Savoy notes, "I believe in the church of baseball." She adds, "I've tried all the major religions and most of the minor ones...I've tried them all, I really have, and the only church that truly feeds the soul, day in, day out, is the church of baseball."[18] In the same film, character Crash Davis compares ballparks to cathedrals. Critic Allen E. Hye, in *The Great God Baseball: Religion in Modern Baseball Fiction,* agrees: "The game itself possesses religious character in its familiar ritual of sense and sacred space."[19] In *Tom Gordon,* King underscores this religious character by referencing "the Fenway Faithful" and the "Boston Church of baseball."[20] In *Faithful: Two Diehard Boston Red Sox Fans Chronicle the Historic 2004 Season,* a non-fiction memoir King co-authored with Stewart O'Nan, King adds, "Baseball's a wonderful game. There's no greater thrill than when your team pulls one out. [...] [T]here's really nothing on God's earth like being at the ballpark...If Heaven's that good, I guess I wanna go." King adds, "Born Again in New England."[21] Hye points out the "mystical attractions of baseball ... the pastoral amid the urban, cool green grass as an oasis in the hot, granite desert."[22] In *Shoeless Joe,* character Ray Kinsella states, "a ballpark at night is more like a church than a church,"[23] and this religious feeling continues as the ghostly players who appear at Kinsella's sacred field look around and wonder if they are, in fact, in heaven.

Trisha in *Tom Gordon,* however, is denied the visual cues that metaphorically transform a ballpark into a church—though that may work to her advantage. She is connected to the game, to the worship services, through radio, a medium that privileges the imagination. She is able to take part in the services in her mind. In *Faithful*, King writes, "Listening to a baseball game on the radio may be outmoded in this age of computers and satellite television, but it hath its own particular pleasures; with each inning you build your own Fenway of the mind from scrap-heap memories and pure imagination."[24] Hye notes that the religious dimension in fictionalized baseball stories draws readers into encounters with "the wonders of life—our society, our national pastime, our imagination, and our sense of spiritual awareness."[25] This is precisely what Trish encounters, via the radio, in the Maine woods—though, this being a King novel, "the wonder of life" is somewhat dark.

In a flashback, which comes on the evening of her first night alone in the woods, Trisha asks her beer-soaked father about the existence of God. Her father explains that he believes in "the Subaudible," a more-or-less benign power operating in the background of life, just below the apprehension of most people. Dad's Subaudible is mostly a force for good, preventing, for example, nuclear wars or (most) airplane crashes despite the frailties of temperament and ability of the folks who have their fingers on The Button or who sit at the controls of an airliner. When Trisha presses her father to be more specific, he ponders a moment (through his desire for a beer), then tells Trisha, "'I believe that your heartthrob Tom Gordon can save 40 games this year,' he said. 'I believe that right now he's the best closer in the major leagues—that if he stays healthy and the Sox hitting holds up, he could be pitching in the World Series come October. Is that enough for you?'"[26] For Trisha, sitting on a broken tree in the woods, there is no "Subaudible" for her to pray to; in fact, there is not even Tom Gordon to pray to—"that would be ludicrous," she thinks.[27] However, Trisha can listen to him pitch, and this gives her a sense of safety—and more, a sense of spiritual comfort.

The woods themselves are often seen as a place to find spiritual comfort. Native American shamans believed in the concept of animism, which suggests that

> the world is profoundly alive and that all natural objects and phenomena—the trees and rocks, wind, rain, snow, birds, insects and fish, as well as humans—are all alive and have vital essence; everything that exists lives and has consciousness… For the Native Americans, each wind is the breath of some being that lives in the direction from which the wind blows. The wind talks with the voice of its spirit as it roars, moans, sighs or whistles.[28]

The Appalachian Mountains themselves are old, even by geological standards, and once rivaled the height and majesty of the Himalayas. Today, the Appalachian Mountains are about one-third of the size they had been when first formed—almost 470 million years ago.[29] While scientists previously believed that the first humans had inhabited North America as little as 25,000 years ago, new excavations in South Carolina suggest that the first human settlement actually occurred 50,000 years ago.[30] Early Americans used shamans to connect to the spiritual world— and prehistoric humans have left evidence that clearly indicates they believed that they were connected to the world of nature. Ancient mountain ranges like Appalachia indicate that spirits dwelled there before Christianity was brought to the New World by the Europeans. If this is the case, then it certainly seems plausible that Trisha's God of the Lost could be an incarnation of an ancient religion that existed long before humans had the language to name it. Furthermore, the Appalachian Mountains became the site of various conflicts, including the removal of the Cherokee Nation (the largest Native American population of the Appalachian Mountains), as well as battles between the French and the Dutch over settlement rights.[31] Those who worship nature believe that places retain the spirit of what happened to them; as a result, Trisha's God of the Lost could be a remnant of the violent wars that occurred during the European occupation of the New England area.

Michael Pollan, author of *The Botany of Desire*, suggests that there are three stories about Man and Nature, told in order to make sense the human relationship to the natural world. Nature represents, Pollan notes, awe, mystery, and shame, because humans seem to believe that they stand apart from nature.[32] He also notes that nature is "a moral and spiritual space,"[33] and indeed, Henry David Thoreau, in *Walden*, claims that he went to the woods because he "wished to live deliberately, to front only the essential facts of life"; in short, to "simplify,"[34] erasing the rift between the natural world and the divine. Close attention to nature would allow for an understanding of the latter—nature provides a spiritual catharsis, and creates an other-worldly space where the natural world, even at its wildest, never falls away or distracts from the spiritual one.[35] However, nature's beneficent and beautiful face can also dissolve bonds of civilization,[36] creating a terrifying experience that may draw a negative spiritual force, instead of a positive one. Lost in the unforgiving woods, Trisha is forced to fend for herself, despite an as-yet unproven gift for learning and adapting and a lack of experience in navigating the woods.

Bill Bryson, writing of hiking the Appalachian Trail, has said, "The woods were full of peril [and] [...] [l]iterally unimaginable things could happen to you out there."[37] In fact, for Bryson, the Appalachian Trail possesses an other-worldly feeling, because they truly seem quite menacing due to their remoteness; at the same time, this remoteness can be very intimate and almost caressing. The woods can also be hostile and aggressive, and "[y]ou do feel very small out there. And you find yourself vulnerable to it, kind of at its mercy."[38] King addresses the vulnerability people feel in the woods. Trisha finds the woods unfriendly, a deep, dark Northern forest that stretches off, and off, perhaps forever. Ralph Waldo Emerson writes that once entering the New England woods, "you leave far behind all human relations ... and live only with the savages—water, air, light, carbon, lime, and granite."[39] And yet even these basic, natural elements are structured unexpectedly: according to Trish's received knowledge, running water—a river, a stream—should lead to some place civilized. In her case, the stream leads her deeper into the woods and ends in a lonely and mosquito-ridden bog. Emerson writes of the woods at night: "Frogs pipe, waters far off tinkle, dry leaves hiss, grass bends and rustles, and I have died out of the human world."[40] For Trish, like countless humans before her, the woods do not make sense, making her feel "muddled and without bearings ... small and confused and vulnerable."[41] Bryson notes, "[W]oods are spooky." He adds that there is something "innately sinister" about the woods, "some ineffable thing that makes you sense an atmosphere of pregnant doom" that "leaves you profoundly aware that you are out of your element [...] Though you tell yourself it's preposterous, you can't quite shake the feeling that you are being watched."[42] While Trisha hopes that she is being watched by her idol Tom Gordon, she feels overwhelming suspicion and fear that the God of Lost is the one tracking her. The fear she feels grows with each step she takes off the path of civilization, delving her deeper into the unknown of the forest.

The spiritual worship of nature, coupled with Trisha's fervent adoration of Tom Gordon, provides her with a sense of salvation. In fact, baseball thus becomes Trisha's salvation. Tom Gordon becomes her personal fireman, rescuing her—her hero, and her saint. Trisha's Walkman becomes crucial to the story, too. The tape she has been listening to, along with her best friend Pepsi, is Chumbawumba's *Tubthumping*. In *The Girl Who Loved Tom Gordon*, technology, in the form of Trisha's Walkman, becomes her only link to the world of "civilization," and acts as a force for good, a source of comfort and hope. In many King works—for example, in *Christine, The Tommyknockers*, and *Cell*—technology is an ominous, sinister force that exploits human weakness and leads almost inevitably to death or dismemberment or madness. *The Girl Who Loved Tom Gordon*, though, is an exception to King's anti-technology archetype. Technology here leads to consolation. Trisha McFarland's explicit reliance on her Walkman to keep her tied to the outside world offers both emotional and physical salvation. It may be important here to mark the generational distinction between Trisha and King's other technologically anxious characters: perhaps King's creation of Trisha indicates approval towards those who can navigate the Nowscape against those who cannot.

It is through her machine that Trisha can listen to the Red Sox, can root for Tom Gordon, can repeat the idea that, while she gets knocked down, she can still get up again, and where she can keep her faith and hope alive. She can imagine the stadium and thus transport herself out of the woods, even if for a moment. By the time the batteries wear out, the machine will give Trisha the strength to survive—though even then, the Walkman retains its power as a talisman and weapon. She clings to the Walkman as a link to the civilization she has become separated from. Instead of the technological Nowscape that King's characters usually find themselves in, Trisha finds herself in the forest—a natural place, untouched by human hands—and it is the forest that is unknown and mysterious and filled with anxiety and fear.

The American woods, notes Bryson, have been unnerving hikers for 300 years. In fact, Bryson points out that Thoreau, on a visit to Katahdin in 1846, found the wilderness to be "a forbidding, oppressive, primeval country that was 'grim and wild [...] savage and dreary,' fit only for 'men nearer of kin to the rocks and wild animals.'"[43] While the woods of wild Appalachia may have unnerved Thoreau, Trisha calmly accepts the fact that there are places in the forest that are grim, wild, savage, and dangerous. In a crucial scene in the woods at night, Trisha is threatened by the stalking—*thing*—and knows that "It was very close, whatever it was, and it was deciding. Either it would come and tear her apart, or it would move on. It wasn't a joke and it wasn't a dream. It was death and madness standing or crouching or perhaps perching just beyond the edge of the clearing."[44] She accepts, the way children do, that there is obviously a monster in the woods, and she is unsurprised that this creature is hunting her. She is frightened but resolute in spite of it.

Trisha responds in the form of a prayer: she thinks of Tom Gordon and wills him to appear. She sees him to the right of her, and begins to question him about the monster in the woods. He responds with indifference, but his presence—angelic and almost glowing in his white uniform—brings her comfort, so she continues to question the Tom Gordon she has conjured. Trisha presses him to reveal the secret of closing—thinking that Gordon will respond with an answer of "God," or something like it—he instead surprises her. Gordon tells her, "*You have to try to get ahead of the first hitter, was what he said. You have to challenge him with that first pitch, throw a strike he can't hit. He comes to the plate thinking, I'm better than this guy. You have to take that idea away from him, and it's best not to wait. It's best to do it right away. Establishing that it's you who's better, that's the secret of closing.*"[45] This idea becomes Trisha's mantra, a chorus in her hymn of Tom Gordon. She knows that she must establish that it is she who is better, and this opens her up to an almost transcendental moment of self-sufficiency.

The end of the novel, the last inning, shows how important the field of play is to the sport. The baseball diamond where Trisha plays out her last "game" against The God of the Lost is important when considering the context of what, exactly, a diamond is, as well as how it pertains to the forests of New England. The Appalachian Mountains hold vast treasures, including various habitats for flora and fauna. In fact, the antiquity of the mountains, coupled with the topographic diversity, has created huge coal deposits. Coal is a fossil fuel, forming from the remains of vegetation that grew over 400 million years ago, though most of the coal found in the Appalachia region was formed 300 million years ago.[46] In the world of Appalachian coal mining, coal itself is referred to as a "black diamond"—most likely due to the cruelty and desperation seen and felt by the miners of the fossil fuel. Much of Appalachia is not a kind place, and Trisha experiences this first hand, though her "diamond" is something a little different than the "black diamonds" the miners are risking their lives for.

In the 1953 film *Gentlemen Prefer Blondes*, Marilyn Monroe sings the iconic song "Diamonds Are a Girl's Best Friend." Diamonds are considered the ultimate gemstones, and they are the hardest natural substance.[47] They are considered precious by many, and considered to be an indicator of wealth and taste. Diamonds are "the perfect consumer good: always in demand, attached to a stable social relation, durable, and [...] help [to] fill [a] void" when all alone.[48] However, although considered the hardest mineral, diamonds are not the toughest. As Robert N. Proctor, a Stanford professor who specializes in twentieth century science, technology, and medicine points out, "Diamonds are very hard, but they are not very tough. Toughness is quite different from hardness: hardness indicates how easily a stone may be *scratched*, toughness how easily it may be *broken*. Diamonds are brittle, which means they can easily be ground into a powder."[49] Although the gemstones are brittle, the "diamond" that is a girl's best friend—in this case—has nothing whatsoever to do with the actual gemstone, and everything to do with the legends and myths behind them. For Trisha McFarland, diamonds *are* indicative of toughness and hardness, and should, in fact, be considered a girl's best friend. For young Trisha, lost in the woods, the baseball diamond becomes the reigning figure that saves her, and in this case, the appropriation of the myth behind diamonds—that they are forever, that they help to fill a void—fits perfectly. The baseball diamond, and everything associated with it, helps to save her life.

Mediated through the Walkman, baseball and the person (real and imagined) of Tom Gordon give Trisha the strength to believe in herself. As Trisha moves through the wilderness, the conjured specter of Tom Gordon walks with her. When Trisha finally confronts the thing, the dark spirit of the woods, she is fading rapidly from hunger and exhaustion. Yet she seizes the chance to at least *try* to establish that she is better. Using the now-dead but still-powerful Walkman as a weapon, she settles back in a pitching stance, as she has seen Tom Gordon do so many times in crucial situations. She winds up, and—*Closes.*[50]

The novels of Stephen King are eerie, macabre, and often morbid, and children do not always fare well in his texts. In fact, many times, children become both the unwitting harbinger of horrors to come (Gage in *Pet Sematary*, for example), or perhaps the mouthpiece of an inscrutable evil (Danny in *The Shining*). However, the little girls in two of Stephen King's later novels, Kyra Devore in *Bag of Bones* and Trisha in *The Girl Who Loved Tom Gordon*, find a safe refuge. Trisha McFarland, wearing a Boston Red Sox practice jersey and a signed ball cap, avoids death from various perils, including wasps, parasitic water, and the god of lost through her love of baseball and her imaginings related to Tom Gordon, #36, the relief pitcher for the team in 1998. King states, "*The Girl Who Loved Tom Gordon* isn't about Tom Gordon or baseball, and not really about love, either. It's about survival, and God, and it's about God's opposite as well." He explains, "Trisha isn't alone in her wanderings. There is something else in the woods—the God of the Lost is how she comes to think of it—and in time she'll have to face it."[51] However, it is obvious that without baseball, and the guiding angelic hallucination of Tom Gordon, Trisha would have succumbed to her fears, and to death. In this novel, King examines hope and faith, and shows how people truly can live or die with their favorite team—that sheer survival can be linked to the game of baseball.

Notes

1. Debra A. Dagavarian, *Saying it Ain't So: American Values as Revealed in Children's Baseball Stories, 1880–1950* (New York: Peter Lang, 1987).

2. Timothy Morris, *Guide to Baseball Fiction*, accessed October 6, 2013, http:// www.uta.edu/ English/tim/ baseball.

3. Ralph S. Graber, "Baseball in American Fiction," *English Journal* 56, no.8 (1967): 1107–1114.

4. Bernard Malamud, *The Natural* (New York: Farrar, Straus and Giroux, 1952).

5. Philip Roth, *The Great American Novel* (New York: Holt, 1973).

6. W.P. Kinsella, *Shoeless Joe* (Boston: Houghton Mifflin, 1982).

7. Graber, "Baseball," 1114.

8. "King Winds Real Life into Latest Fiction," CNN.com, http://www.cnn.com/ books/ news.

9. Tyler Kepner, "The Emotional, Excitable Tom Gordon," *The New York Times*, last modified April 2 2005, http://www.nytimes.com/2005/04/02/sports/baseball/ 02gordon.html?_r=0.

10. Stephen King, *The Girl Who Loved Tom Gordon* (New York: Pocket Books, 1999), 3.

11. Ibid., 10–13.

12. Rebecca Kraus, "A Shelter in the Storm: Baseball Responds to September 11," *NINE: A Journal of Baseball History and Culture* 12, no.1 (2003): 88–101.

13. King, *Tom Gordon*, 77, 79.

14. Ann Marlowe, *How to Stop Time: Heroin from A to Z* (New York: Anchor, 1999), 10, 49.

15. *Field of Dreams*, directed by Phil Alden Robinson (1989; Universal City, CA: Universal Pictures, 1998) DVD.

16. Christopher Lehmann-Haupt, "Books of the Times; A Modern Fairy Tale of the Dark North Woods," last modified April 15, 1999, http://www.nytimes.com/1999/ 04/15/books/ books-of-the-times-a-modern-fairy-tale-of-the-dark-north-woods. html.

17. Ibid.

18. *Bull Durham*, directed by Ron Shelton (1988; Culver City, CA: MGM, 2002) DVD.

19. Allen E. Hye, *The Great God Baseball: Religion in Modern Baseball Fiction* (Macon, GA: Mercer University Press, 2004), 8.

20. King, *Tom Gordon*, 248.

21. Stewart O'Nan and Stephen King, *Faithful* (New York: Scribner, 2004), 103.

22. Hye, *The Great God*, 10.

23. Kinsella, *Shoeless Joe*, 94.

24. O'Nan and King, *Faithful*, 138.

25. Hye, *The Great God*, 12.

26. Ibid., 73.

27. Ibid., 74.

28. Susan Greenwood and Raje Airey, *The Complete Illustrated Encyclopedia of Witchcraft & Practical Magic* (London: Hermes House, 2006), 15.

29. Bill Bryson, *A Walk in the Woods* (New York: Broadway, 1998), 190–191.

30. Marsha Walton and Michael Coren, "Scientist: Man in Americas Earlier than Thought," *Science and Space*, CNN, http://www.cnn.com/2004/TECH/science/11/17/carlina.dig/index.html.

31. "Appalachian Mountains," *Destination 360*, accessed October 6, 2013, http://www.destination360.com/ north-america/us/north-carolina/Appalachian-mountains.php.

32. Michael Pollan, *The Botany of Desire* (New York: Random House, 2001), xxv.

33. Michael Pollan, *Second Nature: A Gardener's Education* (New York: Grove, 1991), 41.

34. Henry David Thoreau, *Walden* (New York: Signet, 2004), 67.

35. Pollan, *Botany*, 34–35.

36. Ibid., 36.

37. Bryson, *A Walk*, 5.

38. Ibid., 5.

39. Ralph Waldo Emerson, *Selections from Ralph Waldo Emerson*, ed. Stephen E. Whicher (Boston: Houghton Mifflin, 1957), 88.

40. Ibid., 88.

41. Bryson, *A Walk*, 44.

42. Ibid., 44.

43. Ibid., 45.

44. King, *Tom Gordon*, 101, emphasis original.

45. Ibid., 103–104.

46. "How Coal Is Formed," *COAL: Ancient Gift Serving Modern Man*, accessed October 6, 2013. http:// www.ket.org/Trips/Coal/AGSMM/agsmmhow.html.

47. "Diamond," *Minerals Education Coalition*, accessed October 6, 2013, http://www.misneralseducation coalition.org/minerals/diamond.

48. Robert N. Proctor, "Anti-Agate: The Great Diamond Hoax and the Semi-Precious Stone Scam," *Configurations* 9 (2001): 381–412.

49. Ibid., n 398.

50. King, *Tom Gordon*, 244–256.

51. "King Winds Real Life into Latest Fiction," CNN.*com*, last modified April 5, 1999, http://www.cnn.com/ books/news/9904/05/Stephen.King/.

More Than Just Ghost Lore in a Bad Place

Mikael Håfström's Cinematographic Translation of 1408[1]

ALEXANDRA REUBER

At first, Mikael Håfström's movie *1408* seems to be just another typical ghost story: typical in the sense that it aims "to scare its readers"[2] through a confrontation with the inexplicable that finds manifestation in the restless souls of the dead re-entering the world of the living. This analysis, however, shows that Håfström's film goes beyond the features of a typical ghost story portraying ghosts seeking revenge, demanding retribution, requiring the completion of unfinished business, or correcting an injustice. Moreover, this analysis illustrates that the film, which is loosely based on Stephen King's short story of the same title published in 2002, even goes beyond the author's unidentifiable textual gore expressed in the original text. It moves away from the domineering "feelings of revulsion, disgust, and loathing"[3] expressed in King's text. Håfström's individual use of the folkloric, spiritual, and literary perception of ghosts, together with his personal interpretation of King's literary text, leads to a ghost story that, despite some similarities with other ghost stories, is very different in its focus.

From Folklore to Fiction

In Håfström's film, the appearances of ghosts/supernatural beings fulfil two functions: on the one hand, they are a symptomatic expression of the main character's pathological mourning and melancholy provoked by his daughter's fatal illness; on the other hand, they function as a personification of the main character's personal desire for as well as fear of death. In this sense, Håfström's adaptation of ghost lore and of the literary source is a product of "mixture of repetition and difference, of familiarity and novelty."[4] Only through the interplay between the past and present understanding of ghosts does Håfström actualize his own perception of the invisible world of the dead in film, concretize his personal interpretation of King's horror tale, and visualize his psychological understanding of a modern ghost story.

In contrast to Stephen King's short story "1408," which plunges the reader right into the horrifying events of room 1408 without ever specifying the origins of the supernatural "happenings" or linguistically defining the strange phenomena, Mikael Håfström's cinematographic adaptation of the textual source offers an independent understanding of the text's bewildering "voice of the room,"[5] the "whiff of burning sulphur,"[6] the intense light "filling the room with that yellow-orange glow,"[7] and the "rips in the wallpaper [and] black pores that quickly [grow] to become mouths."[8] Similar to Algernon Blackwood's ghost stories, in which "trees, bushes, earth, snow, even the wind"[9] function as ghosts, Håfström's adaptation of King's text lets everything come to life: the hotel room, the walls, the furniture, and, first and foremost, the human mind. Moreover, the film's director creates a full story-line around "the intruder" of this particular hotel room, and thus adds to and reinterprets King's dominating "gross-out level."[10]

Even though both text and film stress the fact that the story's main character—Mike Enslin—is searching for different places to be, and another life, Stephen King's manuscript differs from its filmic adaptation also in the sense that it neither provides the reader with any insight into Mike Enslin's emotional and mental state nor offers a possible answer to the question why he desires to enter a forbidden universe that has been locked away since 1978 and that is characterized by the hotel manager, Olin, as evil. Moreover, King's short story does not elaborate on why a fiction writer who specializes in the investigation and depiction of so-called paranormal occurrences demands to enter a room that is not even "listed on any of the websites dealing with paranormal locations or psychic hotspots"[11] other than to prove to the hotel manager and to himself that there "are no ghosts in room 1408 and never have been."[12]

Even though Stephen King, on more than one occasion, has stated explicitly that Mike Enslin does not believe in any paranormal phenomena, the king of horror fiction never grants the reader any explanation why Enslin continues describing his ghostly encounters. The reader of King's text gets the impression that Mike Enslin, like the once-prolific ghost story writer M. R. James, only writes about ghostly encounters because it gives pleasure "of a certain sort to [the] readers."[13] Mike Enslin's disbelief in the supernatural and even in the natural finds a much stronger articulation in Håfström's filmic adaptation of the material. Through an "extended intertextual engagement"[14] with the source text, the director actually uses horror fiction's conventional "theme of the nuclear family in crisis"[15] as departure point for everything that follows.

According to Håfström's adaptation, Mike Enslin's strong disbelief and negative outlook on life—his cynicism regarding death, religion and the existence of the afterlife—is a symptomatic expression of his anger and non-acceptance of "the limitations of the physical world."[16] He cannot come to terms with the fact that neither modern medicine nor he himself was able to heal his daughter and to prevent her from dying. Thus, he unconsciously seeks consolation in his unfruitful investigations of apparently haunted dwellings whose individual stories he publishes in his books: *Ten Nights in Ten Haunted Houses, Ten Nights in Ten Haunted Graveyards*, or *Ten Nights in Ten Haunted Castles*.[17] Enslin's true motivation to investigate and to hopefully experience what King calls "phobic pressure points"[18] results from something other than his apparent interest in paranormal activity and writing: it follows from an unresolved trauma that still rules his mental and emotional life leading him back to the emotionally charged city of New York, the city of pain, mourning and death.

It is in the city of New York, on the thirteenth floor of the Dolphin Hotel, that he faces the real horrors of his life: his melancholic desire for a complete family life, his still unprocessed mourning for his daughter Katie, and his guilty conscience over not having tried harder to save his daughter's life and his marriage. In order to succeed in his unconscious attempt to detach himself from his still too dominant nostalgia for the past, he has to test reality in the seclusion of "a poisoned room,"[19] in which internal psychological processes take the form of ghostly apparitions and become external dangers stimulating the desire for, as well as provoking the fear of, death. Even though Mike Enslin does "have visions and epiphanies which change everything"[20] around him, the ghosts in Håfström's film differ from those described by Sheridan Le Fanu, M. R. James, Walter de la Mare, or Henry James, as they are more than a spiritual power, an evil force, or "a traditional medium of communication between the past and the present, the dead and the living."[21]

Moving Towards and Into the Room 1408

Similar to the Overlook Hotel in *The Shining* (1977), Sara Laughs in *Bag of Bones* (1998), the summer cabin in *Secret Window, Secret Garden* (1990), or the pink villa in *Duma Key* (2008), the hotel room 1408 is another "Bad Place"[22] within King's fictional world. Like many haunted houses in ghost stories, gothic novels, or horror films, room 1408 "stands for the unknown, for ignorance that threatens the safety of the occupants"[23] by absorbing, transforming and setting free "the emotions that had been spent there."[24] As such, it is a personalized space that somehow holds all of its occupants' hopes, fears, and desires. In regard to Mike Enslin, it is a space that he unconsciously fills and fuels with re-occurring thoughts and emotions from the past provoking weeping or laughing fits and extreme changes in his mental and physical condition. Therefore, as a Bad Place, room 1408 imposes a mental, a physical and an emotional threat to Enslin's being.

The room becomes "a protagonist in its own right."[25] It becomes Enslin's main antagonist. Whereas King's manuscript ends without defining the antagonistic evil of room 1408, Håfström's film provides (at least) suggestions of how to understand these evil forces. Håfström turns away from King's original text in which nothing is familiar and moves toward the re-occurrence of the repressed that now reappears in an unfamiliar disguise. In other words, Håfström exchanges King's unidentifiable textual gore with a cinematographic representation of Enslin's repressed past—the true ghost of the "room on the thirteenth floor."[26] By doing so, Håfström achieves three things: first, he challenges the viewer's understanding of ghosts in a film of the twenty-first century; second, he alludes to the possible meanings of King's text depending "upon a complex invocation of ideas of similarity [with] and difference [from]"[27] the textual source; third, he creates an independent work of art.

Regardless whether King's choice of floor and room number alludes to the superstitious fears stemming from ancient Scandinavian folklore,[28] from ancient Egyptian beliefs,[29] or from M.R. James' short story "Number 13," what matters is that Håfström's filmic adaptation differs from King's text in the sense that the adaptation alludes to everything that is associated with the number 13 and King's text does not. The illustration of the room's hostile energy and supernatural forces that continuously decrease its size, transform its layout from a regular room to a stormy sea, to a field of ice, and finally to a room on fire, helps viewers visualize Enslin's fear of destruction, of great suffering, and of approaching death. At the same time, these happenings represent Enslin's conflicting emotions including not only the fear of but also the desire for death, a desire that has been nourished by his extremely guilty and melancholic conscience.

Furthermore, Håfström's film illustrates that Enslin's obsession with death is set into motion through what Sigmund Freud once called "hyperremembering" and is defined as "a process of obsessive recollection during which the survivor resuscitates the existence of the lost other in the space of the psyche, replacing an actual absence with an imaginary presence."[30] In other words, Enslin's profound mourning of the death of his daughter does hinder him "to adopt any new object of love."[31] It lets him turn away from the realm of the living and towards the realm of the dead, but not in order to understand the spiritual implications of the afterlife (like many characters in Walter de la Mare's ghost stories); rather, Enslin does so but to prolong the interaction with what he has lost. On several occasions the film does reveal Enslin's "clinging to the object,"[32] and some examples include when he imagines a crying baby, "sees" Katie on the TV screen, or believes to hold her revived body in his arms. Instead of resolving his trauma and processing his mourning and resulting melancholy, Mike Enslin unconsciously seeks the reception of those stimuli for the purpose of being able to relive the impulses of pleasure and psychological pain. The unconscious externalization of his inner excitations then leads to the confrontation with the spirits of his *own* soul taking the form of the five ghostly manifestations Enslin imagines in the room 1408.

The Return of the Dead and the Remains of Life

In scene 10 (0:43:25–0:48:23), Mike Enslin encounters the first ghostly apparition that, in contrast to the other four manifestations, is the only one trying to harm him. This ghostly aggressor enacts Enslin's pain and disappointment he would still like to take out on everyone who was involved in the unsuccessful attempt of healing his sick daughter Katie. Taking into account that Enslin is ruled by many conflicting emotions and that the essence of being but also of becoming and creating are notions that are associated with the number 1, the existence of the first apparition "gives rise to multiplicity"[33] of meanings and unpleasant surprises while being in the room with the number 1 4 0 8.

It is when the walls close in on him that Enslin notices that the door handle has broken off denying him access to the outside world, that the supernatural manifestations come out of nowhere only to take his life, and that the neighbour across the street is a mere mirror image of his wishful thinking and does not belong to reality. Håfström represents Enslin's realization of enclosure and increase of anxiety through fast alternating shots decreasing in size from eye-level medium-shots to extreme close-up shots. Whereas at first, eye-level medium-shots show Enslin walking around in the room, lying on the bed, or standing in the hotel room window, the director replaces these by extreme close-up shots, revealing, for example, the alarm clock counting down from 60, Enslin recording his fearful apprehension that no one will last longer than an hour, Enslin trying to check out of the room over the phone, and Enslin peeking through the keyhole. All close-ups convey that there is no escape from this room that has turned *bad* and that the viewer already understands the room as an architectural manifestation of Enslin's anxiety-ridden mind.

But why does Mike Enslin suffer from sudden anxiety attacks? Enslin's change of disposition is provoked by the return of the repressed, which causes "the changing of libido into anxiety."[34] In other words, Enslin's still existing love for his deceased daughter and "affective fixation to something that is past"[35] implies an incomplete process or even "a pathological form of mourning."[36] As such, his still existing love for his deceased daughter becomes a source for his developing anxiety finalizing in his extreme fear of death, which manifests itself in the return of and interaction with the dead. The ghostly encounters in Håfström's film, thus, express Enslin's "special interest in the past"[37] that is closely connected to his present life.

In scenes 11 and 12 (0:48:24–0:58:45), Mike Enslin encounters a total of three ghosts: first, an older man jumping out of the window; second, a middle-aged woman crossing the room prior to jumping out of the hotel window; third, Mike Enslin's deceased father sitting in the bathroom complaining about his spiritual existence. In accordance with a traditional ghost narrative, all ghosts personify to some degree "the magical interaction"[38] between Mike Enslin and his universe that somehow belongs to the past; a past that represents a lost perfection of family life consisting of him as the Father, his daughter Katie, and his wife Lily. He notices the first two specters after "seeing" his entire family on TV (scene 11, 0:48:26–0:49:51). This is a moment that juxtaposes this past stability with his present instability provoked by his desire, his pain, and his idealization of and consequential search for his lost life that has become a haunting shadow. This idea of bodily and "natural limits"[39] causing loss and pain opposes Enslin's feelings of "solidity, calmness, and home"[40]: notions that find representation in the room's second number: 4.

The combination of the two first room numbers—number 1 and 4—gives us even more insight into Mike Enslin's disturbed psyche, as the resulting two-digit number 14—the product of 7×2—stands for fusion and, consequently, holds characteristics of both numbers. Even though number 7 has the symbolic meaning of perfection and order, it also contains the notion of the seven capital sins, among which we find wrath (uncontrolled anger and self denial), despair, (sadness and unhappiness) and acedia (melancholy and depression), feelings that rule Mike Enslin's life. Dualism, however, is especially a characteristic of number 2, a number that signifies unity as well as a "movement away from unity."[41] In relation to the scenes 11 and 12, the number 2 symbolizes unity (husband and wife), as well as division (the breaking up of his family) and contrast (his present vs. past life). Consequently, it expresses dualism between opposing poles, which, in Mike Enslin's case, are defined by marriage and divorce, union and separation, life and death, as well as the immortal and mortal. Hence, number 14 reflects Mike Enslin's previous life that he unconsciously cherishes to an utmost perfection and that opposes itself to his present existence and struggle between life and death. In this, the first two room numbers (1 and 4) express change in the sense of becoming oneself without the other. The two-digit number promotes the separation from the "ghosts of the dead, but also [from the] ghosts of the living [...] the living when they were at a quite different period of their lives,"[42] and, in this case, when they were husband and wife.

The realization that this desired family life has elapsed leads to two other dominant feelings of Mike's: emptiness and nothingness—feelings that are symbolically represented in the third room number: 0, a number that is significantly linked to Mike Enslin's grief, loss and depression. Prior to the encounter with the third ghost—his deceased father in the bathroom—he hears a baby crying, a phenomenon that relates to Mike's own past as a young father. When he enters the bathroom, Mike exchanges roles of father and child. He becomes the child himself, ruled by his too vivid imagination that takes over reality and that produces the horrifying events taking place in room 1408. However, whereas the first two ghosts personify death as "the supreme liberation"[43] from all earthly pain and anguish, his father's ghost relates to the folkloric belief of the spirit being earthbound until the cause or matter of death has been clarified. In this last case, death represents the end of life, but not of extreme suffering.

Even though we could easily assume that the novelty of the situation gives Enslin some pleasure in the sense that he has finally found the ghosts he has been looking for, the sudden occurrence of the supernatural entities frightens him as they represent and remind him of his long-ruling desire for as well as fear of death. In accordance with the symbolic reading of the number 3, the three ghosts of scene 12, thus, embody "the beginning, the middle and the end"[44] of something he cannot yet define. And when Mike Enslin envisions the appearance of his daughter Katie walking through the incinerated room towards him (scene 17, 01:23:02– 01:28:32), seeking the everlasting love of her father, he is free of any fear. The imagined existence of his daughter returning from the dead is symbolic for Enslin's still extreme emotional attachment to the loved but lost object. It visualizes that Enslin turns away from reality and clings more than ever "to the object through the medium of a hallucinatory wishful psychosis."[45] It is not surprising that Håfström uses Katie as the fifth ghost, as the number 5 results automatically by adding up the first three numbers of the room ($1 + 4 + 0 = 5$). Moreover, number 5 entails the two most dominant feelings in Mike Enslin's life: love and pain. With the emotional highs and lows associated with the notions of love and pain, number 5 carries yet another connotation that also applies to Mike Enslin's state of mind: it comprises "instability and unpredictability, and radical changes."[46] The ghostly apparition of the deceased daughter is, at first, a source of extreme pleasure. When Katie "dies again" and, when the imaginary dissolves and becomes an empty reality, his source of pleasure transforms, however, into one of extreme un-pleasure. Left behind in complete darkness, Enslin's horror is too strong to endure, leading to his emotional outburst: "No. No no no. You can't take her twice. Not again, please God. You can't. Please. No!"[47]

Disintegration of the Past and Present

We can argue that enclosed in the hotel room, Mike Enslin's almost forgotten past overwhelms him to the extent that it becomes the present reality allowing him to "assess the value of past relationships and [to] comprehend what he [...] lost in losing the other"[48] as well as when losing his own self. It is in this room that his so far successfully repressed emotional pain returns in connection with "instantaneous wish-fulfillments, [the] secret power to do harm, and the return of the dead."[49] The return of the repressed overpowers him to the extent that he is incapable of differentiating between imagination and reality. Lifeless objects and paintings become animated, ghosts appear, and the radio and the TV turn on and off by themselves. As a result, Enslin enters a world that produces a new melody "of disestablishment and disintegration"[50] of the dead and the living, leading to a repetitious visualization of destruction, madness, de-realization, self-alienation, culminating in self-dissolution.

Taking these individual elements of Håfström's film into consideration, it is obvious that his ghost story differs from a traditional ghost story relying on the reader's belief in demonic intervention and the frisson by ghouls disturbing the nightly rest of the living. Even though the film, in accordance with the psychological ghost story, desires the apparitions "to be regarded as symptomatic of mental disturbance,"[51] Håfström's tale diverges from the psychological ghost story in the way that Mike Enslin's mental disturbance is neither caused by misdirected passion, sexual repression, nor by schizophrenia. Mike Enslin's conflicted state of mind has been caused by the unprocessed loss of his daughter.

By combining and developing the folkloristic understanding of ghosts, their depiction in literature throughout the centuries, the psychological understanding of mourning and melancholy, as well as the use of numerology, Håfström goes beyond Wilkie Collins' description of Isaac Scatchard's nightmare in *The Dream Woman* (1855), Sheridan Le Fanu's representation of the alien inner world in "Green Tea" (1869), Guy de Maupassant's illustration of insanity in "Le Horla" (1887) or of delirium and obsession in "Qui sait?" (1890). He also goes beyond Henry James' interpretation of ghosts as evil intruders representing the character's misdirected passion in *The Turn of the Screw* (1898). The spectator of Håfström's film has to realize that the spectral entities haunting the hotel room are not apparitions seeking retribution or an appropriate burial. They are not harmless apparitions trying to disturb playfully Enslin's nightly rest. Håfström's ghosts are mirror images of Enslin's past life and unconscious memory-traces that he has tried to repress. As such, they are reflections of Enslin's emotional trauma that get projected onto the outside. Every single one of the 5 apparitions personifies Enslin's psyche to some extent and proves that, for Mike Enslin, the past has become "more important than the present."[52] Håfström leads the viewer to this conclusion by replacing Enslin's observation of and interaction with the dead with him staring into the bathroom mirror, observing his broken reflection (scene 12, 0:53:34).

Whereas first he seemed convinced of the presence of spectres, he now has to recognize that the only face looking out of the mirror "is also the face looking in."[53] He has to come to terms with the fact that he actually is alone and that there are no ghosts around him. By framing Enslin's face, Håfström recalls Enslin's enclosure and also evokes the idea of him being an integral part of the room in form of a picture. As such, Enslin's self becomes one with the room and with "the power of whatever inhabits [it]."[54] The room with all its ghostly manifestations, then, becomes a symbolic representation of Mike's psychotic mind to which the viewer now is restricted as well. It becomes a representation for Enslin's inner struggle, self-imposed thread and resulting warning: If he does not balance out the "opposing forces"[55] and does not process his so far unresolved trauma, the past will pull him down while being kept in the isolated room of 1 4 0 8.

Conclusion

We can conclude that, unlike King's original text, Håfström's film does not rely on the gruesome and gory alone, but focuses on the illustration of the familiar unknown returning in an unfamiliar disguise. Håfström gives King's "phobic pressure points" a visual image and, by doing so, combines horror with folklore, superstition and psychoanalysis. He lets the ghosts become manifestations of Mike Enslin's self and other. The director leaves no doubt that Mike Enslin's ghosts are part of his memory, at the same time that they are a reflection of his present life, and also of what will happen to him in case he does not fully process his emotional loss. They symbolize the interconnectedness of "all that was, that is, and that will be."[56]

The fact that towards the end of the film Enslin decides to put his experiences into writing illustrates this interconnectedness, as well as that it marks a new beginning in the writer's life. By writing a story—a story that on the outside looks like yet another ghost story, but which on the inside actually is a testimony of Mike Enslin's grief work—Enslin processes his loss. While outlining his fears, hopes, and pain prior to and after Katie's death, the author comes to terms with the death of his only child. The writing of the book then has to be understood as Enslin's attempt to free himself "from the lost object"[57] and to reattach his libido to a new object in order to being able to accept "consolation in the form of a substitute for what has been lost."[58]

His book becomes the key to unlock and close room 1408; a room "whose very numerals add up to thirteen,"[59] which captures everything that the number 13 comprises, and which has to be understood as the architectural manifestation of his mind. In addition to superstitious fears of destruction, suffering, pain and death, this particular place holds Enslin's final step towards transformation. As such, it "symbolizes the death to the matter or to oneself and the birth to the spirit: the passage on a higher level of existence."[60] In this sense, the book is the explanation for all of Mike Enslin's fears, desires, superstitions and hopes.

Even though *1408* can be classified as a ghost story within the field of horror fiction, the viewer has to acknowledge that the director adapts and transforms the long-established folkloristic and literary tradition of ghosts in a way that its result stands for its own and becomes a fictional expression of mourning. By doing so, Håfström accomplishes three things: first, he creates a new type of ghost story, which is composed of the traditional, antiquarian (folkloristic) and psychological ghost story; second, he reshapes King's original text; third, he turns his film into a "fully independent work"[61] of art. In other words, Håfström creates "a work that is second without being secondary."[62] It is, as Linda Hutcheon would say, "its own palimpsestic thing."[63]

Notes

1. This essay originally appeared in *The Popular Culture Review*, Volume 22, Issue 2 (2011): 53–63.

2. Julia Briggs, *Night Visitors: The Rise and Fall of the English Ghost Story* (London: Faber, 1977), 11.

3. Fred Botting, "Horror," in *The Handbook to Gothic Literature*, ed. M. Mulvey-Roberts (New York: New York University Press, 1998), 124.

4. Linda Hutcheon, *A Theory of Adaptation* (New York: Routledge, 2006), 114.

5. Stephen King, "Room 1408," in *Every Thing's Eventual: 14 Dark Tales* (New York: Pocket, 2002), 499.

6. Ibid., 501.

7. Ibid., 500.

8. Ibid.

9. Jack Sullivan, *Elegant Nightmares: The English Ghost Story from Le Fanu to Blackwood* (Athens, OH: Ohio University Press, 1978), 115.

10. Stephen King, *Danse Macabre* (New York: Berkley, 1981), 6.

11. King, "Room 1408," 472.

12. Ibid., 469.

13. M. R. James, Preface to *The Collected Ghost Stories of M. R. James* (London: Edward Arnold, 1949), vii.

14. Hutcheon, *A Theory of Adaptation*, 8.

15. Adam Wadenius, "The Monstruous Masculine: Abjection and Todd Solondz's *Happiness*," *Horror Studies* 1, no. 1 (2010): 131.

16. Emily D. Edwards, "A House that Tries to Be Haunted: Ghostly Narratives in Popular Film and Television," in *Hauntings and Poltergeists. Multidisciplinary Perspectives*, ed. J. Houran and R. Lange (Jefferson, NC: McFarland, 2001), 83.

17. King, "Room 1408," 463.

18. King, *Danse Macabre*, 4.

19. King, "Room 1408," 477.

20. Sullivan, *Elegant Nightmares*, 2.

21. Briggs, *Night Visitors*, 111.

22. King, *Danse Macabre*, 264.

23. Tom Ruffles, *Ghost Images. Cinema of the Afterlife* (Jefferson, NC: McFarland, 2004), 104.

24. King, *Danse Macabre*, 265.

25. Ruffles, *Ghost Images*, 104.

26. King, "Room 1408," 478.

27. Julie Sanders, *Adaptation and Appropriation* (London: Routledge, 2006), 22.

28. Legend has it that twelve Gods were at dinner, when the evil-spirited God

Loki entered the room and provoked a dispute leading to the death of the loving God Baldur. Since then, the number thirteen has been viewed as misfortune, especially "unlucky in terms of dinner parties" (see Donald R. Morse's "Friday, The Thirteenth," in *Journal of Religion & Psychical Research* 24, no. 4 [2001]: 182). Since then this unlucky number has been associated with the fear of destruction, of great suffering, and of the approaching death.

29. According to ancient Egyptian beliefs the number 13 represents "the final step or stage of earthly existence, in which one was merged into permanence or spiritual transformation" (see Claudia De Lys's *A Treasury of American Superstitions* [New York: Philosophical Library, 1948], 481).

30. Tammy Clewell, "Mourning Beyond Melancholia: Freud's Psychoanalysis of Loss," *Journal of the American Psychoanalytic Association* 52 (2004): 44.

31. Sigmund Freud, "Mourning and Melancholia," in *On the History of the Psycho-Analytic Movement. Papers on Metapsychology and Other Works*, eds. and trans. James Strachey and A. Tyson. Vol. 14, (London: Hogarth, 1966), 244.

32. Ibid.

33. Juan E. Cirlot, *A Dictionary of Symbols*, trans. Jack Sage (New York: Philosophical Library, 1962), 221.

34. Sigmund Freud, "Anxiety," in *Introductory Lectures on Psycho-Analysis, Part III*, eds. and trans. James Strachey and A. Tyson, Vol. 16 (London: Hogarth, 1966), 410.

35. Sigmund Freud, "Fixation—The Unconscious," in *Introductory Lectures on Psycho-Analysis, Part III*, eds. and trans. James Strachey and A.Tyson, Vol. 16 (London: Hogarth, 1966), 276.

36. Ibid.

37. Briggs, *Night Visitors*, 11.

38. Ibid., 17.

39. Cirlot, *A Dictionary of Symbols*, 222.

40. Avia Venefica, "Four" and "Five," What's-Your-Sign.Com: The Doorway to Symbolism. The Spiritual Meaning of Numbers, accessed August 31, 2009, http://www.whats-your-sign.com/spiritual-meaning-of-numbers.html. July 24

41. John Michael Greer, *The New Encyclopaedia of the Occult* (St. Paul:: Llewellyn, 2005), 494.

42. Michael Bell Mayerfeld, "The Ghosts of Place," *Theory and Society* 26, no. 6 (2008): 823.

43. Cirlot, *A Dictionary of Symbols*, 74.

44. Claudia De Lys, *A Treasury of American Superstitions* (New York: Philosophical Library, 1948), 472.

45. Freud, "Mourning and Melancholia," 244.

46. Venefica, "Four" and "Five."

47. *1408*, directed by Mikael Håfström (Burbank: Dimension Films, 2007), DVD.

48. Clewell, "Mourning Beyond Melancholia," 44.

49. Sigmund Freud, "Papers on Applied Psychoanalysis. The Uncanny," in *Collected Papers*, trans. James Strachey, Vol. 4, London: Hogarth, 1949), 401.

50. King, *Danse Macabre*, 13.

51. Briggs, *Night Visitors*, 143.

52. King, *Danse Macabre*, 255.

53. Ibid., 259.

54. King, "Room 1408," 479.

55. Cirlot, *A Dictionary of Symbols*, 223.

56. Henry Ole Magga, "Indigenous Peoples' Perspectives on Quality Education," The United Nations, accessed August 31, 2009, http://www.un.org/esa/socdev/unpfii/pfii/members/Magga-Indigenous percent20Education. htm.

57. Freud, "Mourning and Melancholia," 252.

58. Clewell, "Mourning Beyond Melancholia," 44.

59. King, "Room 1408," 478.

60. D. Desrosiers, "Properties of the Number Thirteen," Riding the Beast.com.—Numbers: Symbolism, and Properties, accessed August 31, 2009, http://www.ridingthebeast.com/numbers/nu13.php.

61. Linda Cahir Costanzo, *Literature into Film: Theory and Practical Approaches* (Jefferson, NC: McFarland, 2009), 26.

62. Hutcheon, *A Theory of Adaptation*, 9.

63. Ibid., 9.

"Born in Sin"

Millennial Anxiety in Storm of the Century

PHILIP L. SIMPSON

Stephen King's *Storm of the Century*, an ABC mini-series aired over three nights in February 1999 and directed by Craig R. Baxley, is one of the most unsettling stories in the King canon. Disturbing in its depiction of human nature under immense pressure, the mini-series chronicles the siege of the isolated Maine community of Little Tall Island by a mysterious stranger possessing supernatural powers and the tragic moral decision made by these islanders to buy their safety. The community, closed off from the world, offers up one of its children to the dark god tormenting them to make him, in a mantra constantly repeated in the mini-series, "go away." The story is a damning indictment of what King views as the moral laxity of America as it entered a frightening new millennium. Though written and completed before the terrorist attacks of 9/11 and the resulting erosion of American civil liberties under repressive security measures and a series of international wars, the mini-series is prescient in its dramatization of the lengths to which some Americans freely decide to sacrifice that which is precious to them for some guarantee of safety.

Apocalyptic and Millennial Ideologies

The mini-series articulates what might be called apocalyptic anxiety intersecting with a generalized foreboding about the then-approaching new millennium. Lois Parkinson Zamora may as well be speaking of

Storm when she writes: "And the symbolic nature of a good portion of American fiction [..] owes much to the forms of apocalypse. Indeed, the general dialectical tendency of the American mind to see life as a collision of radically opposed forces and values has its source and its perfect expression in the myth of apocalypse."[1] Certainly, America trembling on the edge of the new millennium in 1999 saw itself as beset from within and without by ideological clashes, political division, economic worries, international tensions, and fear of technology and terrorism. This is the sociopolitical context in which *Storm* exists as a cultural artifact.

In any discussion of apocalyptic themes in literature, it should be noted that apocalypticism is, in David G. Bromley's words, "a borrowed term [...] analytically constrained as a result of having been drawn from theology in the Judeo-Christian tradition."[2] Because the term is essentially theological in origin, referring to revelation of ultimate spiritual truths at the end of history, critics have typically been scrupulous in distinguishing it from more secular applications, such as the routine usage of it as a referent to ultimate disaster. However, as Robbins and Palmer note, "Apocalyptic excitation in contemporary North America [...] transcends the increasingly indeterminate boundary between religious and secular realms of meaning."[3] Put another way, Debra Bergoffen says: "Our visions of ourselves as apocalyptic may indicate that we have not, despite our secular public attitudes, renounced the biblical roots of our American heritage, roots which insist on the essentially moral significance of history and history's end."[4] In keeping with the North American zeitgeist, King's narrative plays with both the secular and theological dimensions of apocalypse. A cosmic, spiritual drama is played out against the backdrop of a once-in-a-lifetime storm threatening the existence of the isolated community.

Martha F. Lee's distinction between apocalyptic and millennial ideologies is instructive in reaching an understanding of King's narrative. In the apocalyptic mode, the emphasis is often on the period of catastrophe itself. The time of destruction and tribulation may also be fairly called the pre-millennial moment. By contrast, millennialism, or postmillennialism, promises that "a perfect postapocalyptic world will emerge" from the wreckage of the first.[5] Within this schema, then, *Storm* in the bulk of its narrative dramatizes apocalyptic or pre-millennial ideology through its visceral images of annihilating snow, destructive wind and water, and a plague of murders spawned by an invasive demon. The presence of Linoge transforms the story from a straightforward, secular "disaster" scenario into a metaphysical drama played out between an evil emissary and a representative of flawed mankind.

This kind of cosmic morality play is also a common feature of apocalyptic texts. The dramaturgical structure requires an escalation of the conflict between the representative(s) of good and the representative(s) of evil until the conflict reaches a peak and is resolved. The resolution involves a judgment in which morally compromised individuals reap the consequences of their actions and the virtuous receive their rewards, or "an end of history when all things will be sorted out and everyone will get what they deserve ('justification')."[6] Within the fallen community of Little Tall Island, the apocalypse brings to town a reckoning enforced by a demon. Since everyone in the town is corrupt to one degree or another, all are judged and found wanting. Even the town's most virtuous and principled man, Mike Anderson, is nevertheless stained with a past sin that brings to him great suffering. In its totality, the narrative is itself a bleak judgment on humanity and its petty, secretive sins.

Yet a modest, melancholy type of post-millennialism is also present in the narrative denouement, when the survivors of the storm move on with their lives in a world forever haunted for them by the memory of the immoral choice they freely made in order to survive. *Storm* does not offer a comforting view of the ability of the community to respond to challenges in any kind of moral way. While it is true that Little Tall Island survives its "Storm of the Century," the cost has been, in the cribbed Biblical framework of the narrative, its communal soul. Through the willing sacrifice of a child to ensure self-preservation, the citizens are spiritually damned, save the one moral man who stood up to collective tyranny even though his own son was lost to him as a result of his principles. The community had a choice in the matter, even if the alternative to the child's sacrifice was for all to die.

Free will is the conceptual hinge upon which this story depends. In that aspect, the narrative runs somewhat counter to a strong tendency in contemporary apocalyptic literature to cast events in a deterministic light. While it may be odd to apply the term "comic" to *Storm*, Stephen D. O'Leary identifies a type of comic apocalyptic drama in which King's narrative could be placed. The comic apocalyptic allows for the possibility of free will and a less destructive, more ambiguous ending than what O'Leary calls the tragic apocalyptic.[7] From another perspective,

Debra Bergoffen makes a distinction between the apocalyptic mood and the prophetic mood: "From the prophetic perspective it is not history per se which is evil, but human choices within history which make it evil."[8] So, while the townsfolk in *Storm* face a terrible moral reckoning, the majority of them remain alive to face the consequences of their choices in a world forever changed by that choice. In its own way, King's story is both hideously bleak and strangely redemptive—apocalyptic, comic, and prophetic all entwined.

As a work of apocalyptic or revelatory literature, *Storm* owes a strong literary debt to Nathaniel Hawthorne, both in its austere New England setting and the moral dilemma that forms the nucleus of the story. In particular, the Hawthorne story "Young Goodman Brown," about another protagonist who refuses to join his fellow villagers in a sinful communion presided over by a dark stranger, is clearly an influence upon King. The apocalyptic communion meeting at the end of the tale, during which the true inner nature of the assembled townspeople is revealed to the shocked Goodman Brown, is recast in King's narrative as the debate between Mike Anderson and everyone else in the town in response to Linoge's demand.

Of Hawthorne's literary deployment of apocalyptic themes, Lakshmi Mani links Hawthorne's work as an expression of concern about the "spiritual myopia" of his time to the "old Puritan theological tradition of Apocalypse which had a hold on most nineteenth century Americans even when they tried to cling to the more optimistic strains of the tradition."[9] From this perspective, Goodman Brown is cognizant of the evil in others but myopic of his own self-righteousness and pride. The "antivision" or "Satanic apocalypse," as Mani calls it,[10] unites the collective soul of the community in sin but destroys Goodman Brown's. Evil rooted in the distortion of the human heart is much on display in Hawthorne's work, as it obviously is in King's. Both writers react against the relative secularism and optimism of their respective eras by choosing to write morality plays disguised as supernatural or apocalyptic horror. King's updated version of the story neatly flips the dynamic, in that the evil antivision destroys the soul of the community but redeems Anderson's. The town itself could have survived a "Storm of the Century" that was only a storm, but it cannot withstand the shattering revelation of its collective nature in the antivision brought to them by the Satanic messenger Linoge.

The Media Apocalypse

The story begins with the community of Little Tall Island in relative normalcy, albeit anxiously preparing for the imminent approach of a major winter storm, dubbed "the Storm of the Century" by the ever-sensationalist media. Yet these stalwart, independent Yankees have the sense of having been here before. Their anxiety is leavened by the communal certainty that they will survive this storm by banding together as they and their parents and grandparents always have. They stock up on supplies from Mike's general store, secure boats to the town dock, and generally batten down the hatches. At first, the threat to the town is believed to be a natural disaster, not a spiritual one. However, King wastes little time in interjecting the theological element into his narrative. He does so by linking Linoge to, of all things, television, the very medium in which *Storm of the Century* itself aired.

This ironic juxtaposition of the sublime metaphysical evil of Linoge to the banality of the media age is established in an early scene wherein the unsuspecting Martha Clarendon interrupts her viewing of the Weather Network and its dire predictions of the oncoming storm to answer her doorbell and then is brutally beaten to death by Linoge wielding a wolf's head cane. The wolf's head comes alive, seemingly alive and snarling, after this baptism in blood. The opening-act murder contextualizes Linoge as an agent of apocalyptic evil, seemingly conjured into being, from Martha's point of view, by the sensationalistic rhetoric of the weather broadcasters. Linoge's slaughter of this elderly woman is the opening act of a judgment or reckoning upon the community of Little Tall Island in which the heavens themselves unleash an elemental cataclysm of wind, snow, and water.

Yet as is typical in a media-saturated culture, the end is announced through the medium of television. The Weather Network reporter speaks in dire tones of a "once-in-a-lifetime supersystem," or winter hurricane that will stall over the coastal regions of Maine to "create the sort of drifting you normally only see on the Arctic tundra."[11] The reporter predicts regional blackouts and is the first character in the narrative to refer to the "Storm of the Century," noting that while the phrase is often overused, this time it is no hyperbole. Disingenuously, the reporter then tells the audience not to panic. The television screen breaks to an ad for a video entitled *Punishments of God*, none too subtly reinforcing the scene's message that what is about to happen to Little Tall Island is not a "mere" natural disaster, but retribution for unspoken and unacknowledged communal sins. On cue, Linoge rings Martha's door bell.

When Martha opens her door to the fateful summons, she sees a stranger hidden in shadow, just as the television forecaster says in the background in reference to the converging storm systems: "These are monster low-pressure areas."[12] Thus the narrative equates Linoge with the oncoming storm and hints at his destructive capacity. His next action speaks to his true nature: he beats Martha to death with his cane. As Martha's corpse lies in ruin on the floor of her house, a blood-spattered Linoge takes her seat in her television-viewing chair and watches an ad for another video, *Punishments of God 2*. By association with the clearly diabolical Linoge, the ads affirm that these disasters truly are punishments inflicted upon sinners by God. The purveyors of disaster for profit are mocked by true evil and figuratively destroyed by Linoge when he smashes Martha's television screen with a basketball. Then he conjures up the weather broadcast from the ruined television with a flick of his supernatural finger and hears the forecaster say: "The forecast calls for destruction tonight, death tomorrow, and Armageddon by the weekend. In fact, this could be the end of life as we know it."[13] The weather forecaster, whether this is part of the actual mainland broadcast or something specially created by Linoge, literally sets out the template for the rest of King's teleplay.

Television makes another key appearance much later in the story, this time in the TV area of the town hall when the assembled villagers fall into a dream-trance brought upon them by Linoge, who chooses to enter the people's subconscious through television, in and of itself a commentary on the powerful effect of pervasive media on the psyche. A television evangelist voices the "moral" of the story for both the audience in the town hall and the audience for *Storm of the Century*: "Brethren, tonight I'd like to speak to you especially of the secret sin….It's easy to say, 'Oh, I can keep that dirty little secret, it's nobody else's business, and it won't hurt me,' and then try to ignore the canker of corruption that begins growing around it."[14] If the town folk are corrupted by secret sin, then it is Linoge who acts upon the message of the television preacher and lances the boil to let the corruption rise into the light of day.

Linoge then inflicts a dream upon the entire town as they sleep uneasily in the town hall. He speaks to their unfettered subconscious minds in the guise of a television reporter covering the mystery of the vanished people of Little Tall Island a few days into the future. By comparing their fate to the mystery of the disappearance of the inhabitants of Roanoke, Virginia, in 1587, Linoge for the first time threatens the entire community if they won't give him "some simple thing ... that would have changed matters for them."[15] He then shows them all a terrifying vision of the townspeople marching en masse into the cold water to their deaths, accompanied by the self-righteous preaching of the televangelist.[16] Linoge chooses to structure this dream vision in the form of television and speak through vapid television reporters and a televangelist, again suggesting that the media commodification of news and religion is the only means by which he can truly penetrate the consciousness of modern humanity, even in this otherwise remote Yankee village. If the end of the world does come, King insists, it will be sold to us in an anxiety-producing brew of cheap sensationalism and religiosity by television.

The Demon of Apocalypse

In many apocalyptic texts, the apocalypse is brought about by a demonic agent. Such agents are personifications of the various social ills that people sense gathering around them at any time of great stress. In *Storm*, that agent is Linoge. As Mike discovers late in the story, Linoge's name is an anagram for "Legion," the collective name in the Gospel of Mark for the demons cast out by Jesus into a herd of swine. Andre Linoge's first on-screen appearance is heralded by a close-up shot of Linoge's silver wolf's-head cane. The wolf's head on the cane implies, none too subtly, that this man is truly a wolf in sheep's clothing. He is garbed in the proletarian fashion of one of King's trademark demons, wearing blue jeans and boots and pea jacket and watch cap. He often sings or whistles a child's tune, "I'm a Little Teapot," which is a foreshadowing of his designs upon the children of Little Tall Island but also cloaks him in a deceptive façade of borrowed innocence. Beneath that surface, however, is a monster with fangs, black or red eyes depending on his mood, long scraggly white hair, and goblin ears. He has great powers of spell-casting, mind control, psychokinesis, longevity, levitation, and no doubt a hundred other dark arts. In the dark glee with which he approaches the chaos he inflicts, he is the genre cousin to the Walkin' Dude or Randall Flagg of King's dark fairy tales *The Stand, The Dark Tower* novels, and *The Eyes of the Dragon.*[17]

When Martha's door opens to him, Linoge's face is shrouded in blackness as he speaks in rhyming couplets to Martha one of the primary themes of King's narrative: "Born in lust, turn to dust. Born in sin, come on in."[18] The euphemistic reference to original sin is reminiscent of the rhetoric of the dark figure in the forest in Nathaniel Hawthorne's tale, "Young Goodman Brown" who tells the assembled townspeople that "Evil is the nature of mankind" and welcomes them to "the communion of your race."[19] References to Hawthorne's fiction abound in *Storm*. The red birthmark or "fairy saddle" on Ralphie Anderson's nose is likely an allusion to Hawthorne's tale "The Birthmark," where the mark is a signifier of some inner corruption of the soul, or at least the potential for it. The people of Little Tall Island resemble Hawthorne's gathering of sinners in "Young Goodman Brown" in that individuals in both communities harbor secret sins that are revealed by outside diabolical figures. Linoge's poetic opening lines to Martha suggest sin is both the uniter ("born in sin, come on in") and the doom ('born in lust, turn to dust") of humanity. As Linoge is the demonic agent that brings these collective sins to light, he holds true to the ancient Greek meaning of apocalypse as "revelation." But in so doing, he wreaks an accounting in the form of physical and moral devastation on the town, thus embodying the more secular connotation of apocalypse as destruction, or "the end of the world."

Linoge's kinship, however distant to humanity, enables him through his powers to see the deepest secrets and fears harbored within any given individual. Rather than use this power for healing or guidance, Linoge wields this information as a cudgel even more brutal in its way than the cane. His revelations are enlightening but they are hateful in intent, intended to harm individual psyches and collective trust. In that Linoge speaks these kinds of secrets aloud, he fulfills the original meaning of "apocalypse" as an act of revealing what is hidden. But to get what he wants from the town, Linoge must first demoralize the residents and disrupt the social glue that connects them. To achieve this goal, he sets out to ruin any respect that any one person in the town holds for another. His signature methodology is to speak out loud any secret that casts a negative moral light on the person holding the secret close. At first, he faces audiences of one, like Robbie Beals, the town manager. To Robbie, Linoge says that Robbie's mother died alone in a nursing home calling Robbie's name while he was with a prostitute in Boston. Other secrets he reveals more publicly, such as telling the townspeople that Peter Godsoe, the owner of the town fish and lobster market, is supplementing his legitimate income with the sale of marijuana, or that Cat Withers, the store cashier, has gone to Derry (one of King's fictional Maine towns) to get an abortion. Of course, as Linoge's push toward public accountability begins, the natural elements intensify their punishment of the islanders.

Prophets or oracles of doomsday are keys to revelation and are often part of the narrative structure of apocalyptic texts, especially those that emphasize the role of free will and human agency in the outcome. *Storm*, too, has its oracles and prophets. The media evangelists as projections of Linoge are oracles who serve as mouthpieces for his supernatural power, as is Angie Carver, abducted out in the blizzard but reappearing to announce the will of Linoge. Through her, the community learns that Linoge wants everyone to gather in the town hall that evening for a special meeting lest they suffer the fate of the villagers of Roanoke. Angie is not only an oracle but prophetess of Linoge, achieving transcendence through his supernatural intervention and then returning to earth to speak of a dire future if the community does not appease its diabolical god.

Linoge has revealed enough of his power by this time that Angie's prophetic voice is accepted uncritically by the fearful islanders. Rather than question the accuracy of what Linoge has put into their minds, they accept his vision of the future as authentic and do not provide alternative actions to compliance (Mike being the sole exception). The only question they ask is that of Job in the face of unbearable suffering, "Why us?" The grim answer from Tavia Godsoe is: "Maybe because [Linoge] knows we can keep a secret."[20] In answer to the same kind of "why is this happening" question, Mike retells the story of Job and concludes it with a sardonic punchline delivered by God to Job when he questioned God's will: "I guess there's just something about you that pisses me off!"[21] Mike repeats a variation of this line in the town meeting when Linoge is asked again why he chose this community: "I guess there's just something about us that pisses him off."[22] Tavia and Mike, in supplying answers to the "why us" question, are thus configured as prophets as Debra Bergoffen deploys the term because what they say cuts right down to the active role that humanity plays in its destiny. So the narrative dialectic is between the community working out its moral choices and Linoge as a representative of the Satanicantivision both exploiting human weakness and punishing it out of divine outrage over that weakness. The prophetic tradition and the notion of secret original sin battle back and forth.

The hypocrisy of self-righteousness is what Linoge spotlights more than anything else. King and Hawthorne are on the same page in arguing that self-righteousness is the deadliest of sins. However, in Hawthorne's moral allegory of "Young Goodman Brown," the majority of the community (save the title character) has reached the point where they freely "own" their nature as sinners. By forcing people to acknowledge their sins in such a brutal way, before they have gone through the appropriate soul-searching that leads to public confession, Linoge creates situations ripe for violent conflict. *Storm* is packed with such incidents, perhaps too many for its own good, but one of the most telling is the fatal confrontation between Billy and Cat, whose argument over each other's respective sins in the supply shed escalates into Cat's murder of Billy.

All of Linoge's hurtful revelations reach their climax in the town hall meeting. In that meeting, Linoge shares various sins committed by some of those present: the theft of thousands of dollars from a place of employment for gambling, the burning down of a planing mill, the beating of a gay man, and of course Robbie's abandonment of his dying mother. But it is a time for ultimate revelations, so Linoge comes to the point of why he has chosen Little Tall: "I'm here because island folks know how to pull together for the common good when they need to [...] and island folks know how to keep a secret. That was true on Roanoke Island in 1587, and it's true on Little Tall in 1989."[23] He then shows his true age as prelude to his request that the town voluntarily hand over one of its children to him so he can raise the child as his heir, or otherwise all the villagers will die. Mike is horrified and rushes to attack Linoge, but others in the assembly hold him back. Even his wife Molly urges him to listen to Linoge. Just as Linoge has revealed his true evil self, the collective is revealing its own true selfish nature. Now that all is out in the open, all deceptions laid bare or stripped away, the storm ends. All that remains is for the town to follow through on what Mike already knows will happen—the selection of which child to hand over to Linoge.

The Compression of the Social Order

One of the key anxieties associated with the apocalyptic narrative is the crumbling of the social institutions by which human beings impose order upon the chaos of existence. *Storm* spends much of its running time subverting the authority of the church, the government, and law enforcement. The church's authority in the town is almost nil, its presence reduced to an ineffectual minister who is at best a minor character quoting useless Scripture and the television evangelists who King consistently mocks. (Significantly, King's cameo in the series is as a televangelist.) Robbie Beals is the representative of secular local government, and as has been discussed earlier, the portrait painted of him is not a pretty one. The most tragic character, or in other words the one who suffers the hardest fall from grace, is Constable Mike Anderson. His suffering is linked to that of Job through frequent narrative references to the Biblical story of the virtuous man who, through no fault of his own, is afflicted with great loss. Through his increasing loss of control over the situation on Little Tall Island, so go the powers of law enforcement during times of great disaster. Without social institutions to protect them, the islanders resort to their natural character.[24]

If Linoge is an avatar of evil, Anderson represents an avatar of decency in this cloistered New England community. Indeed, Linoge may focus on Anderson as his nemesis for this very reason, according to Tony Magistrale.[25] Anderson provides essential goods and services to his community both by running an archetypal small-town general store and serving as chief law-enforcement officer. He achieves a natural and easy balance between these two functions, as geographically literalized by the integration of the constable's office into a small room at the back of the general store. He integrates church and state through his office as church deacon. Just as effectively as Reverend Riggins, he can quote scripture to suit any occasion, as he often demonstrates during the narrative. He is balanced in his personal life as well, with a loving wife and son. Having been educated at the University of Maine, he has also seen something of the world outside of the confines of Little Tall Island.

As the narrative's personification of folksy morality and Yankee self-reliance, Anderson carries an authority both natural and earned. This authority begins with the viewing audience, as Anderson provides the narrative voice-over heard throughout the film and introduces the structuring theme of the story: "Life out on the islands is different. We pull together when we have to."[26] In the opening scenes of the film, it is Anderson who provides the verbal leadership to inspire others to pull together to face the imminent storm. His refreshingly common-sense approach to the challenges of small-town life provides stability for the people in times of crisis, even in the teeth of the "Storm of the Century."

His social skills are given a pseudo-magical overtone in an early scene, when he is summoned by his wife Molly to the town daycare center to help extricate a child, named Pippa, who has somehow managed to wedge her head between two banister posts on a stairway. Molly tells the panicked Pippa that Mike will be on scene shortly to free her even though it is not at all clear how he can accomplish this: "He's just magic that way."[27] Upon arrival, Mike uses his folksy knowledge of psychology to convince Pippa that by pressing her "smaller" button (i.e., her nose) her head will grow smaller. So convinced, she then slides her head easily from between the posts. Her trust in Mike's every word allows her to use her imagination to believe in magic. Mike's pressing of Pippa's nose to make her smaller is, in microcosm, what Linoge does to the town by making it contract or draw together under pressure. The act also references the small birthmark on his son Ralph's nose that marks him as Linoge's heir, an equivalence confirmed in a later scene where Molly laughs about Pippa's "smaller button" and Ralphie then asks about his "lucky fairy saddle" birthmark. But whereas Linoge's influence is palpably demonic and wielded for self-centered reasons to make people morally smaller, Mike uses his natural respect and regard for all children to empower them, to expand their autonomy. By doing so, he is spiritual and secular father to not only his own son but all the children of the community. Linoge's entrance into the town constitutes a dire and ultimately unbeatable threat to Mike's ability to protect the children in his charge. Mike as the town's pater familias cannot withstand the ease with which Linoge turns the town's own insularity inward against its spiritual salvation.

King's screenplay has much to criticize about the herd mentality of these cloistered New Englanders. Mike's opening voice-over introduces this theme when he says: "And [the town] can keep a secret when we have to."[28] His words set the tone for the kind of local pride in insularity that characterizes many of the town's residents. Fireman Lloyd Wishman says in one of the opening scenes: "Trouble don't cross the reach ... ain't that why we live out here?"[29] Of course, this willful retreat from the perceived danger of the mainland is about to put to a severe test by the ultimate Outsider, Andre Linoge. An outsider will always be regarded with suspicion and even paranoia in such a close-knit community, and of course the irony is, this time the people are right. What Linoge does, then, is twofold: he confirms the worst xenophobic fears of his captive audience, shatters their individual belief in their own virtue, and weakens their faith and collective pride. The public spectacle is absolutely necessary to what he does, and so is the breaking down of collective confidence in the ability of their constable to enforce the law and protect them. The crumbling of the lighthouse under the storm surge symbolizes this loss of faith and moral grounding, according to Mary Pharr.[30] Just as the storm physically breaks down waterfront structures, so Linoge destroys the bonds of trust between members of society and those charged with upholding it. If he can fracture the closest interpersonal relationships so that no individual trust and spirit remains, then he can count on the townspeople to resort to the base, instinctive safety of the herd and make decisions to sacrifice the weakest among them for the collective. "Pulling together for the common good" is often invoked as an American virtue, but King asks the uncomfortable question in the introduction to his published screenplay of *Storm*: "Does the idea of 'community' always warm the cockles of the heart, or does it on occasion chill the blood?"[31]

The division of labor by gender is another tradition of the herd that Linoge exploits for his own purposes. The children, as Linoge's true targets, are watched over in the town hall basement by the women of the community. This assignment reflects a traditional social structure, with the men delegated the public sphere of decision-making and the women delegated the domestic sphere of child nurturing, which remains in place in isolated Little Tall Island. If Mike represents all that is patriarchal and paternal about the town's civic organization, then his wife Molly, as daycare provider for Little Tall and de facto leader of the female contingent, embodies the matriarchal. The irony of her position is that even as protector of these children, she too will agree to Linoge's lottery and ultimately sacrifice her own son for self-preservation. Through this development, King engages in a narrative reversal of traditional expectations of motherhood. It is the logical consequence of the power that Molly earlier ceded to Mike because of her inability to handle the mini-crisis with Pippa. Given this story arc, King leaves himself open to the accusations of sexism and even misogyny that have dogged him throughout his career. Mike remains standing as the only defender of the town's children: the patriarch exonerated and redeemed. Little matter that he convinces no one to follow his moral lead; it actually affirms his principles by contrasting them with the self-centered action of the community, including Molly and the other mothers of children at risk. Sexist in tone or not, Molly's failure within the context of the story is one more manifestation of Linoge's apocalyptic power to subject existing social orders to extreme stress.

Linoge does wish to preserve one basic social structure: the will to make decisions based on immediate practicalities, not lofty principle. For instance, the extreme circumstances in which the villagers find themselves lead Robbie to propose a drastic solution to Mike: kill Linoge. Robbie elaborates: "Nobody would have to know. Island business is island business, always has been and always will be. Like whatever Dolores Claiborne did to her husband during the eclipse."[32] Even Molly in a later scene counsels Mike: "Maybe you should get rid of [Linoge]. Make him have an accident."[33] Mike is not shocked by the idea, but neither does he act upon it. Besides the amusing self-referentiality in putting an allusion to King's novel Dolores Claiborne in Robbie's mouth, the exchange reinforces the community conflict between self-interest and higher morality. Robbie, representing the town's civic structure, typically advocates expediency and secrecy over doing the right thing, whereas Mike consistently chooses to follow principle over self-interest.

This dynamic will play itself out in the climactic town hall debate that allows Linoge to claim his prize. When Robbie takes the podium to assert his civic authority, Mike as law enforcer takes the center stage at the front of the room to represent the moral principle of standing firm against thuggery and extortion. He exhorts the town to stand "side by side and shoulder by shoulder"[34] to drive Linoge away. Just when Mike is having some effect on the audience, Robbie reminds them that Linoge will kill all the children if he does not get what he wants. Then others begin to rationalize that Linoge is not going to kill the selected child. "It sounds more like an adoption to me," says Tavia Godsoe from the seats,[35] which in the emerging symbolic landscape of the meeting hall is configured as the "middle way" of moral compromise. The tide quickly turns against Mike, who leaves the stage in defeat. His desperate point that what they are about to do is "damnation" is completely disregarded. When he attempts to take his child away from the meeting hall, he is forcibly prevented from doing so and his wife turns against him. He is alone in opposing the vote that is then taken to give Linoge what he wants. In the self-justifying logic of the collective, Mike has been advocating the murder of the children and becomes more of a villain to his life-long neighbors than the stranger Linoge.

Scorned by all, Mike in turns rejects every one of them, including Molly. Having seen the extent of the community's moral cowardice, Mike is as disillusioned and angry in this moment as Goodman Brown. He can only watch helplessly as the town, in a scene more than a little indebted to Shirley Jackson's famous short story "The Lottery,"[36] draws "weirding" stones from a bag to determine whose child will be given to Linoge. Of course, Ralphie is the child given to Linoge, a development foreshadowed by the "fairy saddle" on his nose marking him as special. As Linoge vanishes with his new protégé Ralphie into the night sky, Mike angrily rejects the society he has lived in: "Don't ever touch me again. Any of you."[37]

Mike leaves Little Tall Island five months after the storm ends as the community continues to hunker down and keep its secrets from the outside world. Hatch tells him he is being self-righteous, an indictment that could also be applied to Goodman Brown. But unlike Hawthorne, King frames his story in such a way that Mike's social exile is the only commendable action in the face of such communal betrayal. Alone on the West Coast as a federal marshal, divorced literally from Molly and figuratively from his former friends and neighbors, Mike lives with the painful awareness that "his fellow citizens are unable to think beyond their own personal safety or to entertain complicated ethical issues, and that when faced with a difficult challenge, his neighbors—like most of us—will opt for the expedient solution," in Tony Magistrale's words.[38]

Mike is granted one more sight of his son Ralphie on a busy city street in San Francisco in the company of Linoge, but Ralphie's hostile reaction to Mike confirms that another of Linoge's predictions has come true: Ralphie now thinks of Linoge as his father. Mike agonizes over whether to write Molly and tell her about this last contact, but finally decides against it. His reflection on that decision can also be read as an affirmation of all his decisions throughout the course of the story: "When every choice hurts, how do you tell which one's the right one? In the end, I kept silent. Sometimes, mostly late at night when I can't sleep, I think that was wrong. But in daylight, I know better."[39] Mike's silence, his refusal to communicate with those he once loved, is the right decision in context, but a lonely one. As Heidi Strengell observes, Mike is innocent but "forced to bear responsibility even for the evil actions of his community."[40] He has suffered the tragic fall of anyone whose stand on principle has led to alienation from the tightly compacted community. Linoge has destroyed what is best about this town's social order, leaving behind only the guilty secret that all save one voted out of selfish expediency to sacrifice a child to a dark god. Yet the final irony: in his exile among out-islanders, Mike still keeps the fatal secret of Little Tall Island.

Conclusion

Storm of the Century as a pre-millennial text, then, says much that is disconcerting about American secrecy, preference of short-term expediency over long-term moral principle, susceptibility to extortion, and inability to tolerate individual dissent when confronted by threats such as natural disasters or terrorism. King gives us a taste of the dread attending the dawn of a new and hostile millennium, and a glimpse into the kind of social havoc that will no doubt attend the end of civilization if or when it does come. But he does argue that in extremis, moral reasoning is still possible, even desirable. Sure, he may have cloaked himself in the clownish vestments of a televangelist to appear in this moral allegory to give his audience an ironic postmodern wink from behind a shattered television screen. But in that he indicts contemporary American trends through his fiction as a warning to his audience in the midst of its entertainment, he is a prophet as sincere as any found in the Old Testament.

Notes

1. Lois Parkinson Zamora, "The Myth of Apocalypse and the American Literary Imagination," in *The Apocalyptic Vision in America: Interdisciplinary Essays on Myth*

and Culture, ed. Lois Parkinson Zamora (Bowling Green, OH: Bowling Green University Popular Press), 98.

2. David G. Bromley, "Constructing Apocalypticism: Social and Cultural Elements of Radical Organization," in *Millennium, Messiahs, and Mayhem: Contemporary Apocalyptic Movements*, ed. Thomas Robbins and Susan J. Palmer (New York: Routledge, 1997), 32.

3. Thomas Robbins and Susan J. Palmer, "Introduction: Patterns of Contemporary Apocalypticism in North America," *in Millennium, Messiahs, and Mayhem: Contemporary Apocalyptic Movements*, ed. Thomas Robbins and Susan J. Palmer (New York: Routledge, 1997), 12.

4. Debra Bergoffen, "The Apocalyptic Meaning of History," *in The Apocalyptic Vision in America: Interdisciplinary Essays on Myth and Culture*, ed. Lois Parkinson Zamora (Bowling Green, OH: Bowling Green University Popular Press), 35.

5. Martha F. Lee, "Environmental Apocalypse: The Millennial Ideology of 'Earth First,'" in *Millennium, Messiahs, and Mayhem: Contemporary Apocalyptic Movements*, ed. Thomas Robbins and Susan J. Palmer (New York: Routledge, 1997), 120.

6. Robbins and Palmer, "Introduction: Patterns of Contemporary Apocalypticism," 7.

7. Stephen D. O'Leary, *Arguing the Apocalypse: A Theory of Millennial Rhetoric* (New York: Oxford, 1994), 63–74.

8. Bergoffen, "The Apocalyptic Meaning of History," 24.

9. Lakshmi Mani, *The Apocalyptic Vision in Nineteenth Century American Fiction: A Study of Cooper, Hawthorne, and Melville* (Washington, D.C.: University Press of America, 1981), 9.

10. Ibid., 10.

11. Stephen King, *Storm of the Century: An Original Screenplay* (New York: Pocket, 1999), 9. Quotations from characters in Storm of the Century are taken from King's published screenplay. There is close alignment between the published screenplay and what was actually aired on ABC.

12. Ibid., 11.

13. Ibid., 44.

14. Ibid., 226–27.

15. Ibid., 231.

16. Stanley Wiater, Christopher Golden, and Hank Wagner make the interesting point that Mike Hanlon, the librarian in King's novel *It*, in his unpublished history of Derry, Maine, compares the disappearance of all of Derry's inhabitants in 1741 to the case of the vanished colonists in Roanoke, Virginia. So, Wiater and his co-authors speculate, has Linoge been to Derry as well? In *The Complete Stephen King Universe: A Guide to the Worlds of Stephen King* (New York: St. Martin's Griffin, 2006), 101.

17. Stanley Wiater, Christopher Golden, and Hank Wagner, as well as Heidi Strengell, all emphasize Linoge's equivalencies to Flagg. Tony Magistrale also observes that Linoge's insights into the secrets of the human heart are similar to those of Leland Gaunt of Needful Things. Wiater, Golden, and Wagner, *The Complete Stephen King Universe*, 233; Heidi Strengell, *Dissecting Stephen King: From the Gothic to Literary Naturalism* (Madison: University of Wisconsin Press, 2005), 145; Tony Magistrale, *Hollywood's Stephen King* (New York: Palgrave Macmillan, 2003), 207.

18. King, *Storm*, 11.

19. Tony Magistrale notes the influence of Hawthorne, particularly his character of Young Goodman Brown, upon the narrative: "*Storm* is one of the most grim,

Hawthorne-like moral fables that Stephen King has written." In *Hollywood's Stephen King*, 208.

20. King, *Storm*, 285.
21. Ibid., 272.
22. Ibid., 321.
23. Ibid., 321.
24. Wiater, Golden, and Wagner say of Little Tall: "It is too tightly woven to be torn asunder so simply. Instead, the neighborhood is drawn together to face the crisis, and to make a terrible decision." Through the outside pressure exerted by Linoge, they have not exploded but rather imploded or compressed into a moral black hole. In *The Complete Stephen King Universe*, 232. Or, as Mary Pharr puts it: "Under pressure, [the islanders] choose expediency rather than morality." In "Only Theoretical: Postmodern Ambiguity in Needful Things and Storm of the Century," in *The Films of Stephen King: From Carrie to Secret Window*, ed. Tony Magistrale (New York: Palgrave Macmillan, 2008), 175.
25. Magistrale, *Hollywood's Stephen King*, 209.
26. King, *Storm*, 4.
27. Ibid., 26.
28. Ibid., 4.
29. Ibid., 6.
30. Pharr, "Only Theoretical," 29.
31. King, *Storm*, ix.
32. Ibid., 191.
33. Ibid., 214.
34. Ibid., 334.
35. Ibid., 335.
36. Strengell, Dissecting Stephen King, 245.
37. King, *Storm*, 357.
38. Magistrale, *Hollywood's Stephen King*, 208.
39. King, *Storm*, 376.
40. Strengell, *Dissecting Stephen King*, 245–46.

The Fallen King(dom)

Surviving Ruin and Decay from The Stand *to* Cell

PATRICK MCALEER

Within Stephen King's fiction, readers are often confronted with images of devastation and destruction which tend to be attached to the Gothic and horror labels by which King is largely known, yet the reduction of King's writing to such limiting categories of literature is problematic if not erroneous. For example, when considering apocalyptic elements present in King's fiction, as "One of King's favorite forms of horror is apocalyptic—he is adept at describing the end of the world and the destruction of life as we know it,"[1] one would do well to conclude that the frightening atrocities contained in his works are more than just horrific (re)constructions of the real world or simplistic and secular reflections of the biblical Apocalypse. Among the purportedly religious undertones found in the apocalyptic inclusions in King's fiction, the weaving of numerous additional genres in his fiction indicates that his brand of horror should not be read or studied as purely apocalyptic, nor as secular, mainstream horror that merely portrays a dark side of the real world. Indeed, the apocalyptic themes that appear throughout King's fiction are certainly difficult to negotiate in that his use of this genre is anything but pure appropriation or even a genuine and devout invoking of the Apocalypse through religion and/or religious beliefs. Of course, it is difficult to deny King's attraction to the many vehicles and faces of horror as well as the numerous manifestations that the Apocalypse takes on in literature. But to claim that King's constant revisiting of the End of Days through different lenses only displays a basic allure to the devastation associated with the end of the world misses the point of his writing. To be sure, King's use of apocalyptic themes in his writing implies that his horrific styling is a complex meshing of various sources and ideas that extend well beyond genre, the Bible, and the commonplace. And among the most highlighted ideas in King's fiction that warrant close attention are not necessarily horror or the Apocalypse or apocalyptic itself, but how one attempts to *endure* and *survive* the atrocities and frights of the apocalyptic, both real and imagined.

Questions and considerations of the apocalyptic in Stephen King's fiction do not constitute necessarily new lenses of reading by scholars and critics. However, the constantly-expanding Stephen King canon is not static, and neither is its treatment of the apocalyptic. When considering the range of King's writing, one must be wary of applying, or forcing, definitive readings to his fiction, especially regarding the presence of the Apocalypse. Although King uses and references apocalyptic ruin on a large scale in several novels like *The Stand* and his later texts such as the *Dark Tower* series, and on the microcosmic level of the small community in *Carrie* and *The Storm of the Century*, the use of apocalyptic allusions in his fiction do not represent a tiresome exercise in appropriation.

While King may, at times, focus on considerations of hope in his apocalyptic writing, adhering to apocalyptic genre in that "Apocalypse [...] counsels genuine hope in a new beginning,"[2] the seemingly consistent sense of hope and optimism found within the Stephen King universe is also witnessed as being absent for numerous characters in King's stories that can be classified within the apocalyptic frame. In short, when King, as an author, denies hope to particular characters in his writing where and when hope is expected from a generic standpoint, it indicates a departure from the apocalyptic formulas set out within this particular genre. This manipulation of the expectations of hope in the face of tragedy results in not only a distinct horror that often denies catharsis, but also a distressing and horrific critique based on the society used as a creative foundation for his fiction.

Indeed, King's apocalyptic writings suggest that hope is often necessarily absent because of the disheartening and hopeless state of humanity that King draws upon for source material in his fiction. When Tony Magistrale says of King and his stories that "at the heart of his universe is a deep-seated awareness of American anxieties about how we live and where we are going, as a nation and as individuals,"[3] he suggests that the cynicism found in King's fiction is only that which he sees among his fellow human beings and within a ruinous, despicable society of their own creation. But this is not to say that King's writing is simply bleak and dreary for the sake of being dark and desolate, or that his fiction has no message or meaning beneath the disturbing and grotesque (or apocalyptic) inclusions.

Rather, as Jonathan Davis says, "the reader of horror fiction is able to explore a distorted picture of the world that might be able to offer some explanations of the unexplainable."[4] And while the cultural criticism in King's fiction does provide more than just critique, King is careful to only provide imaginative speculations in his fiction rather than attempting to promote definitive or absolute answers to various social ills, whether these woes are portrayed as apocalyptic or otherwise. Still, the apocalyptic for King, much like the Gothic, is approached like a genre that may have established norms but receives inconsistent and sometimes even ambiguous treatment in his canon.

Backgrounds of the Genre; or, Generic Backdrops

In the strictest sense of the apocalyptic "genre," Stephen King never fully writes into his fictions of horror and devastation the new world that marks the end of the Apocalypse, which is perhaps an attempt to blanket his fiction with a sense of realism that secularism may afford certain readers. In addition, the departure from seeking or establishing a new world order in his apocalyptic fiction allows King's compositions to almost completely escape designation as "apocalyptic." Still, while there are certainly allusions to new eras in *The Stand* and *The Dark Tower* series, as the Free Zone in the former novel and the gunslinger, Roland Deschain, in the latter text seek some sort of relief and solace for broken worlds that are in dire need of a new direction, King's avoidance of exploring the new worlds that are at the feet of this characterization, and thus an avoidance of pure apocalypticism, is not necessarily problematic.

King has been more than willing to experiment with genre and form, none of which is better witnessed than in his *Dark Tower* series; the manipulation and crafting he exercises regarding pieces and remnants of apocalyptic markers and themes yields a variety of texts that widely diverge in their treatment of the End of Days, that which is largely conceived of from a biblical perspective but is then translated and transformed to resemble a hybrid view and understanding of the Apocalypse. But, as it has been noted that King's fiction is not entirely immersed in the realm of the apocalyptic, especially in a biblical sense, the allusions and selective appropriations of the apocalyptic nonetheless serve King's writing and his audience effectively because "by imagining the end and pondering the reasons for its coming we might help to prevent or at least post-pone it."[5] In other words, despite King's overall reluctance to craft a novel or story that can be wholly categorized as apocalyptic, he invokes the apocalyptic as a means of not only providing a largely familiar scene of ruin to the average reader, but also as a deviation from traditional or common conceptions of the Apocalypse in order to prompt the imagination of his Constant Reader for the purpose of being able to conceive of and adapt to devastation in forms both recognizable and previously inconceivable. To be sure, King purposely resists the definitive lines of genre in his canon, and he does so not out of arrogance or stubbornness but out of a genuine desire to craft fiction that seeks to be more than entertainment.

As King navigates the realms of the known and unknown, and loosely through the vehicle of the apocalyptic, the bulk of his writing within this particular framework, then, asks for a focus on survival, indicating that while destruction and the resulting fears of the apocalyptic are certainly normal if not commonplace regardless of one's faith, there is more to be discovered and considered beyond terror and dread and potential salvation or redemption. Again, King's notably repetitive use of the Apocalypse, or Armageddon, as themes or as images in his writing may insist upon a fascination with death and destruction, but such a simple reduction of a writer's preferred content is a bit diminishing and even inaccurate. As Peter Freese notes, "serious novelists of 'the end' never conjure it up for its own sake, whether they deal with the frightening 'bang' of apocalypse, the ineluctable workings of devolution, or the insidious 'whimper' of entropic inertia. On the contrary, they are interested in how to survive that end."[6] Here Freese iterates the Apocalypse is, more often than not, rarely used for pure shock (or "schlock"), and asks that readers look beyond fear, and even past issues of faith and belief, for a fruitfully instructive, or even didactic, message that is admittedly behind fiction and fiction of the Apocalypse. And nowhere is this better seen in literature than with the treatment of fear produced through technology and scientific innovation.

In beginning to examine the numerous representations and treatments of the apocalyptic and its many masks in King's corpus, it must be reiterated that didacticism is not necessarily at the heart of his tales. King himself has noted on several occasions that he is not aligned with any established or institutionalized religious orthodoxy; he takes the Constant Reader beyond the Bible and inside his own overarching, general understanding and observations on human nature with the apocalyptic as almost a backdrop for the expected horror of a Stephen King novel. One of the clearest examples of such a focused dissection of an individual facing and responding to the crisis of worldly degeneration is found with the gunslinger of *The Dark Tower* series. Roland Deschain, the purported hero of King's seven-volume series that defies generic distinction despite the abundance of apocalyptic references and imagery, "initially lacks an awareness of moral complexity and responsibility,"[7] which is mostly a reflection of selfishness of the gunslinger; he feels his self-righteousness is a justifiable mindset that can actually aid he and others in surviving the collapse of the world. Of course, self-interest is not an uncommon response to large-scale destruction as one must consider typically his or her survival above all else, but it takes all seven books of *The Dark Tower* (roughly 3,000 pages) for the gunslinger to begin to develop any sort of conscience or awareness that his survival, and the survival of the world around him, cannot be accomplished in isolation.

This is not to say that the gunslinger's quest to save the Dark Tower, the lynchpin of all existence in this series of novels, is one which becomes a reflection of adequate or even ethical response to a world in shambles. Rather, "the text of *The Dark Tower* series suggests that Roland's motivation for questing is certainly grounded in his *own* desires and whims,"[8] which makes *The Dark Tower* problematic regarding the theme of survival amidst the apocalyptic in that the focus of the series is limited primarily to a single character seeking relief for only himself and no one else. Although the gunslinger eventually recruits companions to aid him in a quest that appears to have noble intentions—to save the world—his selective cooperation and convenient establishment of a small community does not play out well in *The Dark Tower* series, and even reflects the common theme in King's fiction that cooperation and community are not cure-alls for survival. In the case of *The Dark Tower*, the gunslinger's motives for survival belie his actions involving cooperation and community as his sole reason for survival is not the professed salvation of his world and the people in it but rather the dubious end of simply finding and entering the Dark Tower. Assuredly, within the Stephen King universe, the careful reader must carefully dissect the motives of those who choose to cooperate among their peers for survival, especially if survival is envisioned for ends not shared by all parties involved.

As *The Dark Tower* depicts cooperation as a problematic method of surviving apocalyptic ruin in that not all characters in this series seek the same resolution, some critics tend to view cooperation and harmonious union among his characters in these books and the rest of King's fiction as a catalyst for success. Heidi Strengell says that while "courage and individualism, cooperation and sense of community are qualities necessary for survival in the postapocalyptic world,"[9] one must be careful in assuming that cooperation, in and of itself, is an adequate means of survival in any context. For example, Michael Collings comments on King's tales penned under the pseudonym Richard Bachman: "there are no viable societies in these novels; individuals ultimately survive or die on their own."[10] Collings intimates that cooperation can be quite ineffective, especially if no thought is ever given as to what needs to be accomplished beyond a community simply coming together in the wake of discord. Even though King (and Bachman) seems to create a paradox which suggests neither isolated nor communal action are the keys to survival in his fiction, the more appropriate conclusion to draw is that selfishness or collaborating only to see one's own ends met hardly constitutes the foundations of sensible, intelligent survival, or even compassionate survival that may eventually call for the sacrifice of an individual for the survival of the group. To be sure, survival may be complex, but it is not necessarily difficult, even though "King's flawed social environments are often directly responsible for the night-marish tragedies that proliferate his works,"[11] which effectively positions King's characters as both victims of circumstance and as the root causes underneath the predicaments that they must face. As seen in *Carrie*, where the title character is "metamorphasized into a monster by the society that tried to repress her,"[12] King often creates within his fiction a society that must come face to face with a monster of its own creation, providing a bleak but clearly cautionary tale beneath the veneer of the supernatural, horrific, and apocalyptic. And from this first novel in King's canon to the last, his fiction contains and provides *imagined* preventative measures at best concerning devastating and ruinous scenes akin to the apocalyptic, especially as he cannot, or at least will not, provide his characters or readers a convenient means of escape and endurance. In short, survival, whether within a King novel or in the world outside of the text, must be earned and approached with forethought, especially as survival, unlike certain genres of fiction, is not formulaic.

Divine Navigations of the Apocalyptic: The Stand *and* Desperation

Among the options to consider for surviving apocalyptic situations in King's fiction, religion is one of the more common forms of coping with and confronting The End. As Joseph Reino notes, "Although not all of King's narratives are apocalyptic, almost everything is touched by Scripture (usually negatively) and marked by what can only be called an 'apocalyptic perspective.'"[13] When considering the presence (and persistence) of scripture in King's oeuvre, *The Stand* is perhaps the most well-known example as this text is one of his earliest fictions, has been adapted to television, into graphic novel form, and has received an exceptional amount of critical scholarship. As this text moves from a deadly plague to factions of survivors pitted against one another in a notably biblical battle of good and evil, the lingering image near the end of the novel when the Hand of God detonates an atom bomb in which "the righteous and unrighteous alike were consumed in that holy fire,"[14] seems to point towards a genuinely religious representation of the Apocalypse on King's part as this particular scene positions God as the catalyst for resolution and redemption in the novel. To wit, when Stephen L. Cook states that the blossoming of a "better world, while a fundamental human longing, will never come as a human achievement. It comes only with the advent of God's sovereign rule on earth."[15] Indeed, it could be concluded that *The Stand* is crafted to fit into a purely biblical conception of the Apocalypse with God serving as the ultimate source of resolution and survival.

However, even though God is a constant presence in *The Stand*, whether He is manifested by His hand in the city of Las Vegas where evil lurks or is represented by His voice among the presumably righteous citizens of Boulder through their moral matriarch Mother Abigail, King removes His presence from concluding pages of the text, to which Michael Collings claims: "King does not intend the resolutions of *The Stand* to take on the finality of scripture."[16] Indeed, the final pages of *The Stand* reveal that the devilish antagonist of the novel, Randall Flagg, survives the "holy fire" brought down by God, and that Flagg is left to wreak havoc on the world yet again, and that the people in Boulder are left to their own designs with the presence of evil still living in the shadows. In response to this conclusion, Douglass Winter reflects: "There is almost a compulsion to view *The Stand* as a sustained allegory, but its climax produces instead a sense of brooding mystery."[17]

Indeed, the early pages of *The Stand* prove to be just as mysterious as the last pages concerning the role of God; as S.T. Joshi mockingly yet necessarily asks: "Where was God when the superflu and its effects were ravaging the world?"[18] One response to Joshi's scathing question comes from Ross Douthat who says, "King's God isn't a well-meaning weakling, hold our hands and hoping things turn out OK; rather, he is so far *above* the various adversaries, from Tak to Randall Flagg, that the possibility of their winning passing victories concerns him not at all."[19] Still, consider the conclusion of *The Stand* when Stu Redmond asks Fran Goldsmith, "do you think people ever learn anything?"[20] The clear implication is that people are unable to sustain themselves and live in a world that is subject to human whims and desires, perhaps suggesting that divine guidance, no matter how irregular, may be necessary for survival. Yet, it could also be concluded that King's decision to threaten his seemingly ignorant characters with the menace of Flagg at the conclusion of the novel is one which forces his readers, and maybe even his characters as well, to consider their fate if it must be taken into their own hands without any deity to aid them. And it is this overarching sense of questioning and even doubting divinity that permeates King's 1996 apocalyptic text, *Desperation*.

As ambiguous as King's ultimate message in *The Stand* may be, his later novel *Desperation* also does not provide much more clarity with its own treatment of faith and religion in the battle against the demon entity Tak, a malevolent spirit released unto the world in which faith is in short supply. Although one of the underlying axioms of *Desperation*, at least for the young protagonist David Carver, is to "*don't think, trust*

God,"[21] the ultimate outcome of the novel is founded upon human actions. Belief and adherence to a faith in God is not an infallible means of survival in King's fiction, but it is most certainly a catalyst, and among the ways in which God's Word is received in *Desperation* is that of questioning and even interpreting what is perceived to be divine guidance or intervention as "the questioning of God's goodness and omniscience is common in a number of modern post-apocalyptic novels."[22] And within *Desperation*, the demon Tak utilizes the doubts that are reportedly common among those who are facing death and the possibility that no *deus ex machina* will provide immediate or actual assistance; as Tak tauntingly says to a scared David Carver, "'Do all the praying you want, David, but don't expect it to do you any help. Your God isn't here, any more than he was with Jesus when Jesus hung from the cross with flies in his eyes.'"[23]

In response to Tak's mockery, however, David Carver reflects upon his pathway to belief and recalls his early discussion on faith with his minister, Reverend Martin, who says, "'God's a lousy conversationalist, no question about that, but he left us a user's manual.'"[24] And it is with the reverend's suggestion that action can be taken despite the physical absence of God, and in spite of His mixed or unclear messages, that David ultimately proposes to the survivors of Tak's rampage that "'We do what God tell us [...] That's the plan.'"[25] Of course, this resolution is not easy to adhere to because any instructions left behind are subjected to not only questions of interpretation but also of choice, or "'the free-will covenant,'"[26] which is certainly a frightening monster within the Stephen King universe as choice and autonomy are never easy paths to follow, especially when the author orchestrates a plot that makes such decisions and options even more difficult for the characters contained within the pages. Moreover, as God speaks to and through the survivors of Tak's rampages in *Desperation*, the absence of direct action from Him in addition to the lack of assurances regarding the validity of His suggestions ultimately leaves the characters in this novel to survive own their own, according to their own volitions, and with noted reservations and uncertainties as prompted by numerous examples of God's cruelty, such as the death of David Carver's sister, Pie, by the hands of Tak. In the Stephen King universe, there is almost always blood, and often King's characters must utilize their own intelligence and will to survive in order to endure the devastation and ruin that may not always be cleared away by a divine entity.

The Secrets of Knowledge: The Regulators *and* Cell

Without the guidance of a divine being in *The Regulators*, the characters in this novel are forced to face the fantastical, the mysterious, the deadly, and the apocalyptic with only their own cunning and ingenuity at hand. In this story, one which is populated by many of the same characters from *Desperation* (as King conceived of *The Regulators* as a distorted mirror of the world of the former tale), adaptability and a particular detachment from the inexplicable becomes necessary for surviving the suburban apocalypse that Stephen King/Richard Bachman writes into this story. Indeed, with the strange scene surrounding *The Regulators* and its suburban characters living on Poplar Street in Wentworth, Ohio, a scene which can be best described as a literal melting of reality into the semblance of a child's malformed and disconcerting drawing that attempts to depict the seemingly picturesque neighborhood, complete with agents of death known only as the Regulators, one might conclude that discovery and acquiring some knowledge as to the cause of the distorted reality and onslaught of death in this story is vital to survival. To be sure, in the case of *The Regulators*, the acquisition, and even concealment, of *information*, as well as the willingness to face danger and likely death, becomes vital to the defeat the source of discord and the catalyst to the alterations of reality in *The Regulators*: Tak, the same demon entity from *Desperation*.

All throughout *The Regulators* there are numerous points in the text that focus on the collection of information and the subsequent nod towards the function of the individual's role in working towards a larger goal for the benefit of others, especially with Audrey Wyler, the aunt of the autistic Seth Garin whom Tak possesses and through whom he is able to bend and shape reality. Audrey keeps a journal which the *reader*, and not the other characters in the story, is able to consult; still, Audrey's observations as to the nature of Tak and the seriousness of his possession of Seth do ultimately aid in the defeat of Tak. Additionally, Allen Symes, who works at the China Pit mine from where Tak is originally loosed, is also a source of information, albeit a reluctant one. He composes a letter detailing the strange occurrences at the China Pit that becomes another key piece of information, at least for the reader, as to the context and background surrounding Tak. With the characters lacking immediate or even objective access to information throughout *The Regulators*, their survival becomes dependent on not just the acquisition of information by way of observation, speculation, or deduction, but also through the action of the individual. In this case, survival is dependent upon the unwitting hero, the aforementioned autistic child Seth Garin, whose willing and adept use of knowledge that finds no aid or assistance from God is able to ultimately end the apocalyptic scene that unfolds in the novel.

Regarding the role of knowledge, and the necessity to keep some knowledge hidden rather than shared in *The Regulators*, one must consider the primary catalyst at the heart of Tak's eventual defeat. Seth Garin discovers that Tak loathes the execratory processes of the human body, especially those of a body which Tak possesses. Although Tak despises being in possession of a body while it defecates, Tak is still able to possess a body that is in the process of emptying its bowels. However, throughout the course of *The Regulators*, as Tak has always left Seth Garin's body while the boy has defecated, the creature makes a fatal mistake: Tak surmises that Seth is under the assumption that clearing his bowels is a time when Tak not only will not re-enter but *cannot* re-enter. This assumption leads Tak to believe that Seth will not ever put up a fight against Tak's possessions while the boy is defecating because of the erroneous notion that Tak is indeed unable to enter; hence, Tak believes that Seth feels no need for fortification against Tak when the boy moves his bowels. However, "*Seth has known all along that Tak can re-enter, even during evacuation. Has known and has successfully hidden that knowledge, the way a gambler will hide an extra ace up his sleeve,*"[27] and when Seth positions himself for a final, planned bowel movement to coax Tak out of his body, Seth does indeed prepare for the potential of Tak's re-entry and summons what forces he can to defend against the demon.

As a result, Tak realizes that he had been misinformed about the boy—and by its own poor analysis of available information—and Tak is then forced to seek other, less-stable bodies for possession, which leads to its demise. As "Only Seth was able to contain it [Tak],"[28] when the demon is cleverly forced to possess another body, the possession is limited because possessing a body besides Seth Garin's results in the quick demise of the host. Consequently, Tak is defeated because Seth has cleverly hidden his acquired knowledge as to the nature of Tak, including the information that Tak has attempted to establish a false sense of security in Seth, and he provides the window of opportunity needed to defeat the demon. When Tak becomes subjected to the prospect of limited, temporary possessions rather than finding another stronghold like Seth—as is witnessed in Tak's possession of Cammie Reed whose head explodes only moments after Tak invades her body—the demon loses his foothold in the world, his sway over reality is eliminated, and he is defeated as Tak has little to no power as a non-corporeal entity. Indeed, *The Regulators* suggests that knowledge is of little use if one is not able to utilize information, or keep crucial knowledge hidden away from those who would use such information against those who seek to survive.

Intelligence and ingenuity, then, along with the cunning to know how information is to be used or from whom information is to be kept, and all without the assistance of a divine being, become the center of King's 2006 apocalyptic novel of technology run amok, the text with the short but certainly layered title of *Cell*. Reflecting the sense that apocalyptic occurrences, at least in the loosest sense of the term, can be combated by human communities with the aid of purely human traits, King further explores the boundaries of the people left to their own devices, and their search for and use of knowledge in the wake of the apocalyptic, in *Cell*. In the very first sentences of *Cell*, King immediately informs the reader of not only the primary conflict which threatens the characters, but also that knowledge as to how a resolution might be found will not be easy as the search for answers must be done without the assistance of God or the most specialized and trained human individuals who are assumed to hold keys to information and survival: "The event that came to be known as The Pulse began at 3:03 p.m. eastern standard time, on the afternoon of October 1. The term was a misnomer, of course, but within ten hours of the event, most of the scientists capable of pointing this out were either dead or insane."[29]

Once again, among the chaos of a world gone mad, King creates a story in which the fractures of a community must be mended in order to survive, especially as it would seem to be all too improbable for a single individual (or deity) to solve the enigma behind the apocalyptic Pulse. As *Cell* progresses, the main character, Clayton Riddell, enlists the aid and companionship of a few human survivors, namely Tom McCourt and Alice Maxwell. Their initial quest becomes one of merely surviving the destruction strewn across the land, which includes a majority of the population transforming into zombie-like creatures. Furthermore, they all come to discover that their quest for survival must entail a search for knowledge, knowledge that will help them combat, kill, or even cure the zombies that populate their reality. Their travels eventually take them to Gaiten Academy and its headmaster, Charles Ardai, which provides the text with the convenient metaphor of information provided by an institution of education through its (former) employee. But little information about The Pulse and the victims, known as "phoners," is acquired at this point in the story. Although acute speculations are discussed as to the nature of these phoners, the only information of substance found at Gaiten Academy is the headmaster's theories on the nature of human beings: "'At bottom, you see, we are not *Homo sapiens* at all. Our core is madness. The prime directive is murder. What Darwin was too polite to say, my friends, is that we came to rule the earth not because we were the smartest, or even the meanest, but because we have always been the craziest, most murderous motherfuckers in the jungle.'"[30] While the headmaster's musings on the essential being of humans does not necessarily account for the behaviors of the phoners who, although violent and even cannibalistic, are nonetheless an organized group, the majority of *Cell* depicts investigations that turn up little usable information, which may not necessarily be apocalyptic, but is certainly horrific. Perhaps it is ironic, then, that the antagonist of this novel, the leader of the phoners that is known as the Raggedy Man, dons a hooded sweatshirt proudly pronouncing affiliation with Harvard, reminding readers that not only have the educated fallen victim to The Pulse, but also that sometimes the search for knowledge yields few results.

Making sense of the unknown is an understandable reaction to that which has never been experienced or even conceived. But the quagmire of seeking to understand what will likely never be known, or fully known, generally leads to inertia and the inability to proceed towards a preferable outcome as answers sometimes do not function as solutions. Therefore, it is no surprise to see that the characters in *Cell* redirect their efforts from attempting to understand The Pulse and its catastrophic effects on the general populace and instead focus on surviving by resisting and even destroying those who have been transformed. While the simplicity of this approach—survival by eliminating all threats—appears to be simplistic and even rather primitive in its scope, seeing such a plan through in *Cell* is anything but easy. Just as knowledge, or rather hidden knowledge, becomes the key to survival in *The Regulators*, hidden knowledge also become crucial to the survivors of the apocalyptic scene in *Cell*, even though hidden knowledge in this story is made almost entirely impossible with the telepathic abilities of the phoners.

As *Cell* nears its end and Clay Riddell's group of survivors journeys on to Kashwakamak, a locale that has been advertised as one without any working cellular services, the suicide of one of Clay's companions, Ray Huizenga, seems to only result with Clay taking possession of a cellular phone given to him by Ray before his suicide. Indeed, this scene of death and hopelessness is initially seen as pointless as the narrator suggests, "Ray Huizenga had died for a useless cell phone."[31] But when Clay's group discovers that despite the lack of cellular coverage in the isolated area of Kashwakamak, the fairgrounds in this area, which serve as their prison, actually have cellular technology available as the fair workers brought in their own equipment to allow cellular phone calls to be made. The knowledge, and the importance, of the imported and available cellular technology is never revealed to nor discovered by the Raggedy Man and the rest of the phoners. As Ray Huizenga learns of the technology brought to Kashwakamak, he then rigs a bomb to the underside of the old school bus in which he and his imprisoned companions travel. Further, Ray anticipates that his bomb will be brought into the fairgrounds, undetected, by way of the bus (which proves to be correct), and he cleverly crafts the bomb to be detonated with a cellular phone—like the one which he gives to Clay Riddell. Thus, Ray Huizenga kills himself to keep his knowledge and plan hidden from his friends and his enemies: "'He kept it from you so it wouldn't be in your minds [...] And killed himself so it wouldn't be in his.'"[32] Although Ray's plan needed to be discovered by his companions in that he does not and cannot reveal the ultimate function of a purportedly useless cellular phone prior to his suicide, the key element to his designs is this hidden knowledge, and he ensures the safety of this information with his sacrifice.

Although the Raggedy Man is aware of the cellular phone that Ray gives to Clay, he is unable to completely understand why Clay possesses it as Kashwakamak is, to his knowledge, a zone free of cellular signals. Clay, too, does not initially understand the significance of the phone given to him, especially as he believes Kashwakamak has no cellular coverage, and because his recent experiences with cellular phones suggests to him that cellular phones no longer have a use value besides transforming humans into phoners. But Clay's purely human persistence, intellect, and leadership (along with his inadvertent protection of particular knowledge) allow him and his fellow survivors to ultimately escape from Kashwakamakwith Ray's bomb serving as an exceptional catalyst. But with the rapid movement towards the abrupt ending of *Cell*, which sees little else beyond Clay's group leaving Kashwakamak, it would seem that the extensive focus on the journey for information and knowledge takes precedence over learning of the fates of the characters after they have won their freedom through sacrifice and resourcefulness rather than following some sort of divine or biblical plan to sort out the apocalyptic scene that unfolds throughout the novel.

Conclusion

Admittedly, surviving ruin and decay within the Stephen King canon appears to be a simple matter of possessing much more than a will to live: a willingness to cooperate among one's peers and a willingness to seek knowledge rather than wait for an easy resolution. Such a formula seems to work well, as the Constant Reader can easily see this approach play out rather well in numerous texts beyond those discussed here (such as *The Tommyknockers* and *Under the Dome*). However, part of the horror that King creates within his canon when his characters are faced with overwhelming predicaments is that they do not always readily or immediately band together for the sake of the group or to fight back against the forces that threaten their lives. On one hand, this is merely a matter of plotting—what good would it do for a text to have its characters automatically choose intelligent and decent pathways of survival? On the other hand, hesitancy, doubt, and panic-induced inertia are largely realistic reactions to the unknown and the frightening. As such, despite the simplicity and seemingly repetitive nature of King's horrorscapes, the Master of Horror does his readers a favor by offering tales of hope and redemption, but only after difficult decisions are made, reminding Constant Readers that if they were to ever find themselves in the unbelievable, yet perhaps possible, scenarios that imagined individuals must navigate, survival does not depend upon whom is the fittest.

Survival depends upon the choice to be decent and utilize a sense of rationality that often escapes people trapped within irrational predicaments.

Notes

1. James Egan, "Apocalypticism in the Fiction of Stephen King," *Extrapolation* 25, no. 3 (1984): 214.
2. John R. May, *Toward a New Earth: Apocalypse in the American Novel* (South Bend, IN: University of Notre Dame Press, 1972), 224.
3. Tony Magistrale, introduction to *The Films of Stephen King*, ed. Tony Magistrale (New York: Palgrave Macmillan, 2008), 5.
4. Jonathan P. Davis, *Stephen King's America* (Bowling Green, OH: Bowling Green State University Popular Press, 1994), 14.
5. Peter Freese, "Surviving the End: Apocalypse, Evolution and Entropy in Bernard Malamud, Kurt Vonnegut, and Thomas Pynchon," *Studies in Contemporary Fiction* 36, no. 3 (1995), 175.
6. Ibid., 163
7. Tony Magistrale, *Stephen King: The Second Decade* (New York: Twayne, 1992), 143.
8. Patrick McAleer, *Inside the Dark Tower* (Jefferson, NC: McFarland, 2009), 119, emphasis added.
9. Heidi Strengell, *Dissecting Stephen King* (Madison, WI: Popular, 2005), 133.
10. Michael Collings, *Stephen King as Richard Bachman* (Mercer Island, WA: Starmont House, 1985), 17.
11. Tom Newhouse, "A Blind Date with Disaster: Adolescent Revolt in the Fiction of Stephen King" in *The Gothic World of Stephen Kind*, eds. Ray B. Browne and Gary Hoppenstand (Madison, WI: Popular Press, 1987), 50.
12. Davis, *Stephen King's America*, 61.
13. Joseph Reino, *Stephen King: The First Decade* (New York: Twayne, 1988), 51.
14. Stephen King, *The Stand* – Complete and Uncut Edition (New York: Signet, 1991), 1072.
15. Stephen L. Cook, *The Apocalyptic Literature* (Nashville, TN: Abingdon, 2003), 22.
16. Michael Collings, "*The Stand*: Science Fiction into Fantasy," in *Discovering Stephen King*, ed. Darrel Schweitzer (San Bernardino, CA: Borgo, 1987), 87.
17. Douglass Winter, *Stephen King: The Art of Darkness* (New York: New American Library, 1984), 61.
18. S.T. Joshi, *The Modern Weird Tale* (Jefferson, NC: McFarland, 2001), 81.
19. Ross Douthat, "Stephen King's American Apocalypse," *First Things*, February 2007, 19.
20. King, *The Stand*, 135.
21. Stephen King, *Desperation* (New York: Signet, 1997), 193.
22. Steven Kagle, "Beyond Armageddon: Stephen King's *The Stand* and the Post Catastrophic World in Speculative Fiction," in *A Casebook on* The Stand, ed. Tony Magistrale (San Bernardino, CA: Borgo, 1992), 196.
23. King, *Desperation*, 175.
24. Ibid., 192.

25. Ibid., 512.
26. Ibid., 447.
27. Stephen King, *The Regulators* (New York: Signet, 1997), 465
28. Ibid., 471.
29. Stephen King, *Cell* (New York: Pocket Star, 2006), 3.
30. Ibid., 206.
31. Ibid., 405.
32. Ibid., 409.

"The Word Pool, Where We All Go Down to Drink"

The Irresistible Pull of Language in Lisey's Story

JENNIFER ALBERICO

What is it about Stephen King that keeps a reader reading: the creepiness, the pacing, the folksy stories? I suspect it is his use of language and the casual acceptance of our everyday culture that draws us in. Like a Steven Spielberg movie, we recognize our surroundings, sit back and get comfortable. We feel so at home in the worlds created by King that we need to be there, we want more, even if we get frustrated by the storyline at times. His stories create such intimacy for the reader that we become ensnared; he uses repetition of words and phrases to hypnotize us into belonging. Stephen King's love of language, turns of phrase and the intimate vocabulary shared by people who are close, plays a major role in granting readers access to his novels. In fact, I would argue that the web of comfort he creates between his characters with their unique exchanges of speech and the casual, accepting, almost loving way he writes about American culture common to us all, invites readers to become part of his books. The repetition of phrases and words that readers have never heard before become part of their consciousness and thereby the reader is caught in his net. In *Lisey's Story*, King uses language uniquely developed by his main characters to not only demonstrate the strength of the relationship between husband and wife, sister and sister, father and son, but also to draw the reader down into the language pool so loved by King that his readers cannot resist the pull. Here I will demonstrate ways in which King uses language to envelop his reader into his story: the interior language created by couples and family and the casual references to American culture that imply acceptance (but also represent a dip in the deep, dark end of the pool), as well as an examination of where all of these ideas and words come from in the form of a pool, an allegory for the imagination, which is both a safe and a dangerous place.

King makes repeated mention of the word or myth pool, not only in *Lisey's Story*, but in *Danse Macabre, Bare Bones* and various interviews as well. King inherited the phrase from University of Maine English professor Burton Hatlen, back in 1968, and it stuck with him. King says, "I have trod the path that leads there often in the years since, and I can think of no better place to spend one's days; the water is sweet, and the fish still swim."[1] In fact, the pool is so much a part of *Lisey's Story* (and I'll wager, any other King vehicle) that the "Author's Statement" at the end of the book gives credit to the "literally dozens of novels, poems and songs"[2] that were referenced in order to show readers just how useful and common it is to take a quick dip in the pool. Everyone takes from the word pool, from Yankee old-timers to skilled writers. The ability to retain these catches from the pool remains apparent throughout King's work and demonstrates the great love and respect he has for the art of language.

He finds uses for uncommon words like "widdershins." He mimics the catch phrases of old New Englanders with lines like, "when he went a-choring." Of course, many, if not most, authors use dialect to add a touch of the real to their stories, but these phrases can also make us feel comfortable with the characters King creates. For instance, by using this type of language in reference to Lisey's father, we know what kind of family Lisey is from and the echoes of the world they create still exist in her mind. Phrases like this give us a closer look at Lisey Debusher and her father, Dandy Dave, an old Yankee himself, who used phrases such as "I slang it forth," a beauty of a phrase. Lisey's husband, award-winning author Scott Landon, said the expression "had a weight coming off the tongue that *I threw it away* or even *I flung it away* could never hope to match."[3] Catches such as these charm and entertain in Scott's world and in ours.

Beyond the use of well-worn phrases to create a clearer picture for the reader, catches from the pool also demonstrate the bond that exists between families. Each family has its own culture and with that a unique language. When someone marries into a family, they slowly integrate into that culture. The sisters Debusher (there are four of them, all grown, middle-aged women) had a language and understanding separate from that of their parents, but still their parents' voices continually run in their heads. The matriarch of the Debusher family, referred to as "Good Ma," had phrases that repeated for her daughters long after she was dead. She called scraps of paper "scrids" and often said "third times the charm; third time pays for all." Though she was not as colorful with language as her husband (whose sayings include the gem, he "hung on like a toothache"), she could spin a phrase or two and these phrases popped into Lisey's mind from time to time, keeping her in check. All of our families have their own language. My father called riding a bicycle "giving your ass a ride." This shared experience of words draws us nearer to King's characters. Though the language of the Debusher family does draw a picture for the reader of Lisey's life and heritage, it is the language shared by Lisey and Scott that draws the reader into the story, makes her part of it and stays with her long after the last page has turned.

Scott is a writer and therefore, like King, a harvester of words. When he comes to Lisey, he is fully packed with his unique vocabulary: "bool" for a certain type of gift; "smucking" for its more vulgar rhyming twin; and SOWISA, an acronym for "Strap it on Whenever it Seems Appropriate." As Lisey explains, "*Strapping it on* was a heroic act, an act of will."[4] Scott's playfulness with words influenced Lisey and his vocabulary soon became her's. Early on, "*wait for the wind to change* had become part of their marriage's interior language, like *strap it on* and SOWISA and s*muck*."[5] It meant wait for things to change, hang in there, don't give up yet. The most poignant line of all was the oft used "everything the same." Lisey recalls that, "It had been part of her marriage's inner language. How many times had Scott come breezing in, calling, 'Hey, Lisey, I'm home—everything the same?' Meaning is *everything all right, is everything cool.* But like most phrases of power … it had an inside meaning."[6] As we come to know Scott's brutal past and how he loves Lisey for seeing him "whole," we come to understand this inside meaning. We spend most of the book inside Lisey's mind and so hear these phrases repeated many times, as Scott talking to her or as Lisey repeating these "phrases of power" to herself. She reminds herself to *strap it on (SOWISA, babyluv)*, to *wait for the wind to change*, and that everything is not the same after Scott dies.

We hear not only the words of strength and power from the intimate relationship of Scott and Lisey, but also the nicknames Lisey assigns to people ("Woodsmucky" for Professor Woodbody, and "Toneh," her imitation Southern accent for a man named Tony). As the line of Scott's would-be assassin, just another crazed fan, repeats in Lisey's mind ("Gotta end all this ding-dong for the fresias"), so it repeats for the reader. The quote is so nonsensical and yet oddly lyrical that it takes to repeating. It is a line the mind grabs and wants to ponder, play, and repeat. The repetition of these phrases gives us a close look at Lisey's thinking, and these phrases tend to repeat and repeat in the reader's own mind, becoming part of the reader's store of references.

There were reasons for Lisey and Scott's secret language, reasons Scott's special words did not become part of the Debusher everyday speech. Scott's past was not such a bright one, as Lisey discovers the first time Scott presents her with a "bool, a blood bool, Lisey." A good bool for Scott was a treasure hunt built for him by his older brother, Paul, when they were little. He knew he was at the end of the bool when he found "Bool! The end!" written on a note, usually next to a prize, sometimes an RC Cola. So a bool can be a good thing. It can also be a very bad thing. In this instance, it's both: Scott punishes himself for disappointing Lisey by shoving his hand through a pane of glass, creating a blood bool for Lisey, a gift of apology. Over several months, Scott reveals to Lisey what bools were made of, how they could be good or bad, and how a blood bool could let out the "bad gunky," just as his daddy used to do.

This language can be a bit awkward and sound juvenile, but that's just the point. As Charles DeLint wrote in *The Magazine of Fantasy and Science Fiction*, "Some of King's other writing tricks are present (in *Lisey's Story*): the made-up words used by the characters that seem goofy (like "smucking," or "bool") but acquire poignant resonance the deeper we get into the novel."[7] In a review entitled "A Smuck in the Bools," written for *The Guardian*, Toby Litt wonders whether the language repeatedly used in *Lisey's Story* actually ruins the book and concludes that while it is sometimes annoying, "one of the reasons for (King's) pre-eminence is that (like Dickens) he keeps his readers with him all the time. Throughout *Lisey's Story* there are constant reminders of what has gone before. At points it reads almost like a verbal fugue, with different phrases chiming in from earlier scenes." He continues, "As *Lisey's Story* progresses, a whole lexicon of interior language is introduced and explicated. A passage that reads at the beginning as completely opaque becomes, by the end, highly emotionally charged."[8]

Scott reverts to his childhood as he tells Lisey about his past and so takes her with him. There are words from his father's pool, words he learned from his dear old dad. The "bad gunky" is just the stuff inside that makes him crazy. Scott's father, "Sparky" Landon, has a masterfully unique way with words, especially harsh, demeaning words that he uses against his kids. His is the kind of language that could turn any word into a curse and a sting. "Sparky" called Scott "Scoot, you old Scoot," which shows an affectionate side to this otherwise cruel bastard of a father. Scott's father is a complex, scary and well-drawn character. He's an accurate, if extreme, portrayal of the conflict of good and evil in all of us. When "Sparky" calls Scott's brother an "ugly bug," King writes of Scott: "like *Scooter you old Scoot* and *the bad gunky, ugly bug* is an interior idiom of his family that will haunt his dreams (and his speech) for the rest of his productive but too-short life."[9]

Like Scott, Lisey's sister Amanda experiments with her own blood-letting. When she slips into a catatonic state after one of these episodes, the line between dead Scott and crazy Amanda becomes blurred, and this is represented by language. Amanda never changes into Scott physically, but when Amanda uses words that only Scott would know, Lisey knows the world is not right. In one of the more chilling moments of the book, Lisey is spending the night with Amanda after she purposely cuts herself. When Lisey first arrives on the scene, there is blood all over Amanda's hands. She thinks of her first bool and hears Scott's voice saying, "It's a bool, Lisey! And not any bool, it's a blood bool!"[10] As Lisey is trying to get through to the bloody and far-away Amanda, Amanda looks Lisey full in the face and whispers, "Bool." When they get back from the hospital that night and Lisey gets ready to sleep with Amanda, she is sure some sort of revelation will follow, some sort of explanation for why she used Scott's word.

In the pre-dawn light, Lisey wakes and tries to identify what has awoken her. Then she hears it: "Baby. Babyluv," which is Scott's name for her. Amanda/Scott says, "I left you a bool...You have a blood bool coming...The one you're on is a good bool, Lisey. It goes behind the purple. You've already found the first three stations. A few more and you'll get your prize." And when Lisey asks what the prize is, the voice answers, "Be quiet. We want to watch the hollyhocks"[11] After the voice goes silent, Amanda falls into a catatonic state. Scott had a word for this condition; "in the parlance of the Landon family," when someone checked out in this way: "(s)he had gone gomer."[12]

Where Scott is speaking from, where the hollyhocks are, where Amanda has gone, is the imaginary land he called Boo'Ya Moon. Amanda has her own name for it but she is able to escape to another dimension as well. This is where she goes when she can't handle the pain in our world. In both versions of this place exist the healing and damning waters of the myth pool. And the pool is not just a place of words or a place of myths: initially, yes, the catches of phrase, the inheritance of story and language. But the myth pool goes deeper. The myth pool can heal us or hurt us in the same way. Ronald T. Curran cites King's use of a "myth pool" in both *Danse Macabre* and *Bare Bones* as a place "from which fairy tales come and argue for the existence of an archetypal dimension that they occupy."[13] In Scott's fairy tale world of Boo'Ya Moon, the pool not only has the power to heal but also the power to mesmerize or pull one so far in there is no hope of return.

The fact that Scott and Lisey were so close and had a shared language allowed Lisey access to Scott's imagination. This can only happen in the closest of relationships. Lisey must go to the pool in Boo'Ya Moon to retrieve Scott at one time when Scott loses his grip on reality. The fact that he is a writer not only allows him frequent trips to the pool, but he also knows that it comes at a cost, especially because of the strain his reality was under during his youth. He knew writing stories was a "kind of madness." He had said to Lisey, "You don't understand the gone part. I hope you stay lucky that way, Little Lisey."[14] Of course she doesn't. When she makes it to the pool, "she knows it in her bones, just as she knows Scott has been talking about this place in his lectures and writing about it in his books for years."[15] She looks at the pool and remembers what Scott said:

> It's the pool where we all go down to drink, to swim, to catch a little fish from the edge of the shore; it's also the pool where some hardy souls go out in their flimsy wooden boats after the big ones. It is the pool of life, the cup of the imagination, and she has an idea that different people see different versions of it, but with two things ever in common; it's always about a mile deep in the Fairy Forest, and it's always sad.
>
> Because imagination isn't the only thing this place is about. It's also about

(giving in) waiting. Just sitting … and looking out over those dreamy waters … and waiting. *It's coming*, you think. *It's coming soon, I know it is.* But you don't know exactly what and so the years pass.[16]

What can King mean here? I understand that it would be "a mile deep in the Fairy Forest" because it is an "archetypal dimension," as Curran says. But why is it always sad? He explains, "because imagination isn't the only thing this place is about. It's also about *(giving in)* waiting." If the pool is "the pool of life" as well as the "cup of imagination," then I understand: the sadness comes from the loneliness of creativity, the need for an escape from pain, the endless number of unmet expectations, the duality of love. We wait for things to change, for the wind to change or something to happen before we make our move. We wait (and hope) for things to get better. This doesn't belay action, but it does acknowledge the human tendency to hold out expectations … and wait. Or give in. And to give in, I believe, would mean that you make the decision (or non-decision) to just go with the plan that is already there; just follow the illusion of patriotism, or what have you, down the mile long path into the Fairy Forest. Here, Lisey recalls Scott talking to her about the pool:

> When he talks about the pool he always reaches out, as if he'd put his hands in it if he could, or pull things—language-fishies, maybe—out of it…Sometimes he calls it the myth-pool; sometimes the word-pool. He says that every time you call someone a good egg or a bad apple you're drinking from the pool or catching tadpoles at its edge; that every time you send a child off to war and danger of death because you love the flag and have taught your child to love it, too, you are swimming in that pool … out deep, where the big ones with the hungry teeth also swim.[17]

King is talking about the deeper end of the pool. This is not the pool where we all go to net the amusing phrases, the ones that bear repeating generation after generation. This is the risky end. There is a real dimension here that influences all of us: no, you can't see but you can feel it and taste it. It's the pool of inheritance and culture. It can be full of illusions and false dreams. It's part of what we all buy into when we subscribe to *Good Housekeeping* and take the advice of the columnists. It's the American empire built on our acceptance of this American Fairy Tale: the Hamburger Helper (like that "lurking" on Lisey's back shelf), the lime Kool-Aid, the Pillsbury Dough Boy, a carton of Salem Lights and a six pack of Coke. All of these American products, American ways of living, are sprinkled throughout the novel and, yes, they add to the reality of the picture. We know these are common products in our stores and homes and so would be natural enough to find on Lisey's shelves. But the casual mention of these things brings us closer to Lisey still because we are all drinking from this pool and this can be the deep end, where the fish have teeth.

The book makes it clear that Stephen King is a frequenter of the pool and not just for the obvious reasons: sure, at first there is a writer's affection for language, the craft of writing, the pleasure derived from weighing each word carefully before making a choice. And maybe later comes the knowledge that including readers in the intimate dialogue of his characters would manipulate them in becoming absorbed in his stories, but this novel shows a greater concern. A dip in the pool can be healing, life affirming and necessary. King demonstrates this ability again and again throughout *Lisey's Story*. Spending too much time in the deep end of the pool, however, takes the "really brave fisherfolk—the Austens, the Dostoyevskys, the Faulkners—" those who know when to look away and to not get confused by the composition of the pool.[18] Because the pool is "bigger than it looks, it's deeper than any man can tell, and it changes its aspect, especially after dark."[19] Handling the deep end of the pool, where we all go down to drink, requires discretion and strength and a modicum of craziness. Before you take a dip, I suggest you strap it on tight.

Notes

1. Stephen King, *Lisey's Story* (New York: Scribner, 2006), 656.
2. King, *Lisey's Story*, 654.
3. Ibid., 124.
4. Ibid., 24.
5. Ibid., 83.
6. Ibid.,8.
7. Charles DeLint, review of *Lisey's Story,* by Stephen King. *Magazine of Fantasy and Science Fiction* (Jan. 2007): 38.
8. Toby Litt, "A Smuck in the Bools," review of *Lisey's Story,* by Stephen King. *The Guardian* (October 28 2006):16.
9. King, *Lisey's Story*, 366.
10. Ibid.,111.
11. Ibid.,167–169.
12. Ibid.,352.
13. Ronald T. Curran, "Complex, Archetype, and Primal Fear," in *The Dark Descent: Essays Defining Stephen King's Horrorscapes*, ed. Tony Magistrale, (Westport, CT: Greenwood, 1992), 33.

14. King, *Lisey's Story*, 351.
15. Ibid.,437.
16. Ibid.,437.
17. Ibid.,161.
18. Ibid.,289.
19. Ibid.,289.

Bibliography

Alegre, Sara Martín. "Nightmares of Childhood: The Child and the Monster in Four Novels by Stephen King." *Atlantis* 23, no.1 (2001): 105–114.

"Appalachian Mountains." *Destination 360.* Accessed October 6, 2013. http://www.destination360. com/north-am erica/us/north-carolina/Appalachian-mountains.php.

Ariosto, Ludovico. *Orlando Furioso.* Translated by Guido Waldman. Oxford: Oxford University Press, 1983.

Beatie, Bruce A. "Patterns of Myth in Medieval Narrative." *Symposium* 25, no. 2 (1971): 101–21.

Bergoffen, Debra. "The Apocalyptic Meaning of History." In *The Apocalyptic Vision in America: Interdisciplinary Essays on Myth and Culture*, edited by Lois Parkinson Zamora, 11–36. Bowling Green, OH: Bowling Green University Popular Press.

Bierce, Ambrose. *The Devil's Dictionary*, n.d. http://www.thedevilsdictionary.com.

_____. "The Principles of Literary Art." In *A Sole Survivor*, edited by S.T. Joshi and David E. Shultz, 242–7. Knoxville: University of Tennessee Press, 1998.

Bloom, Harold. "Dumbing Down American Readers." *The Boston Globe.* September 24, 2003. http:// www.boston. com/news/globe/editorial_opinion/oped/articles/2003/09/24/dumbing_down_american_readers/.

_____. "Introduction." In *Stephen King: Modern Critical Views*, edited by Harold Bloom, 1–3. Philadelphia: Chelsea House, 1998.

Botting, Fred. "Horror." In *The Handbook to Gothic Literature*, edited by M. Mulvey-Roberts, 123–131. New York: New York University Press, 1998.

Bourdieu, Pierre. *Distinction: A Social Critique of the Judgment of Taste.* Translated by Richard Nice. Cambridge: Harvard University Press, 1984.

Briggs, Julia. *Night Visitors: The Rise and Fall of the English Ghost Story.* London: Faber, 1977.

Bromley, David G. "Constructing Apocalypticism: Social and Cultural Elements of Radical Organization." In *Millennium, Messiahs, and Mayhem: Contemporary Apocalyptic Movements*, edited by Thomas Robbins and Susan J. Palmer, 31–45. New York: Routledge, 1997.

Browne, Ray. *Against Academia: The History of the Popular Culture Association / American Culture Association and Popular Culture Movement, 1967–1988.* Bowling Green, OH: Bowling Green State University Popular Press, 1989.

Browning, Robert. "Childe Roland to the Dark Tower Came." In *Men and Women and Other Poems*, 57–63, edited by Colin Graham. London: Everyman, 1993.

Bryson, Bill. *A Walk in the Woods.* New York: Broadway, 1998.

Bull Durham. DVD. Directed by Ron Shelton, 1988. Culver City, CA: MGM, 2002.

Burwick, Frederick. "Romantic Supernaturalism: The Case Study as Gothic Tale." *Wordsworth Circle* 34, no.2 (2003): 73–81.

Campbell, Joseph. *The Hero with a Thousand Faces.* 1949. Princeton, NJ: Princeton University Press, 1973.

_____. *The Power of Myth.* New York: Random House, 1988.

Campbell, Joseph, with Bill Moyers. *The Power of Myth*, edited by Betty Sue Flowers. New York: Anchor, 1991.

Chandler, Raymond. "The Simple Art of Murder." In *The Longman Anthology of Detective Fiction*, edited by Deane Mansfield-Kelley and Lois A. Marchino, 208–219. New York: Pearson/Longman, 2005.

"Chanson de Roland, La."*Merriam Webster's Encyclopedia of Literature.* 1995 ed. Springfield, MA: Merriam-Webster, 1995.

Cirlot, Juan. E. *A Dictionary of Symbols.* Translated by Jack Sage. New York: Philosophical Library, 1962.

Clewell, Tammy. "Mourning Beyond Melancholia: Freud's Psychoanalysis of Loss." *Journal of the American Psychoanalytic Association* 52 (2004): 43–67.

Cohen, Jeffrey Jerome. "Medieval Masculinities: Heroism, Sanctity, and Gender." Last updated April 1995. http://www.georgetown.edu/labyrinth/e-center/interscripta/mm.html.

Collings, Michael. "*The Stand*: Science Fiction into Fantasy." In *Discovering Stephen King*, edited by Darrell Schweitzer, 93–90. San Bernardino, CA: Borgo, 1987.

_____. *Stephen King as Richard Bachman.* Mercer Island, WA: Starmont House, 1985.

Cook, Stephen L. *The Apocalyptic Literature.* Nashville, TN: Abingdon, 2003.

Costanzo, Linda Cahir. *Literature into Film: Theory and Practical Approaches.* Jefferson, NC: McFarland, 2009.

Crossley-Holland, Kevin. *The Anglo-Saxon World: An Anthology.* Oxford: Oxford University Press, 1982.

Curran, Ronald T. "Complex, Archetype, and Primal Fear." In *The Dark Descent: Essays Defining Stephen King's Horrorscape*, edited by Tony Magistrale. Westport, CT: Greenwood, 1992.

Dagavarian, Debra A. *Saying It Ain't So: American Values as Revealed in Children's Baseball Stories, 1880–1950.* New York: Peter Lang, 1987.

Dante. *The Divine Comedy Volume I: Inferno.* Translated by Mark Musa. New York: Penguin, 1971.

_____.*The Divine Comedy Volume III: Paradise.* Translated by Mark Musa. New York: Penguin, 1984.

Davis, Jonathan P. *Stephen King's America.* Bowling Green, OH: Bowling Green State University Popular Press, 1994.

DeLint, Charles. Review of *Lisey's Story*, by Stephen King, *The Magazine of Fantasy and Science Fiction*, January 2007: 38.

De Lys, Claudia. *A Treasury of American Superstitions.* New York: Philosophical Library, 1948.

Desrosiers, D. "Properties of the Number Thirteen." Riding the Beast.com.— Numbers: Symbolism, and Properties. Accessed August 31, 2009. http://www.ridingthebeast.com/numbers/nu13.php.

"Diamond," *Minerals Education Coalition.* Accessed October 6, 2013. http://www.mineralseducation coalition.org/minerals/diamond.

Donato, Eugenio. "'Per Selve E Boscherecci Labirint': Desire and Narrative Structure in Ariosto's *Orlando Furioso*." In *Literary Theory/Renaissance Texts*, edited by Patricia Parker and David Quint, 33–62. Baltimore: Johns Hopkins University Press, 1986.

Douthat, Russ. "Stephen King's American Apocalypse." *First Things*, February 2007, 14–19.

Downie, Robin. "Madness in Literature:

Device and Understanding." In *Madness and Creativity in Literature and Culture*, edited by Corinne Saunders and Jane Macnaughton, 49–63. New York: Palgrave Macmillan, 2005.

Edwards, Emily D. "A House that Tries to Be Haunted: Ghostly Narratives in Popular Film and Television." In *Hauntings and Poltergeists: Multidisciplinary Perspectives*, edited by J. Houran and R. Lange, 82–120. Jefferson, NC: McFarland, 2001.

Egan, James. "Apocalypticism in the Fiction of Stephen King." *Extrapolation* 25, no.3 (1984): 214–227.

Eliot, T.S. *T.S. Eliot: Collected Poems 1909–1962.* New York: Harcourt Brace, 1963.

Emerson, Ralph Waldo. *Selections from Ralph Waldo Emerson*, edited by Stephen E. Whicher. Boston: Houghton Mifflin, 1957.

Field of Dreams. DVD. Directed by Phil Alden Robinson. Culver City, CA: Universal Pictures, 1989.

Foucault, Michel. *Madness and Civilization: A History of Insanity in the Age of Reason.* New York: Pantheon, 1965.

1408. DVD. Directed by Mikael Håfström. Burbank: Dimension Films, 2007.

Fowler, Alastair. *Kinds of Literature: An Introduction to the Theory of Genres and Modes.* Cambridge: Harvard University Press, 1982.

Freese, Peter. "Surviving the End: Apocalypse, Evolution, and Entropy in Bernard Malamud, Kurt Vonnegut, and Thomas Pynchon." *Studies in Contemporary Fiction* 36, no.3 (Spring 1995): 163–76.

Freud, Sigmund. "Anxiety." In *Introductory Lectures on Psycho-Analysis, Part III*, edited and translated by James Strachey and A. Tyson. Vol. 16, 392–411. London: Hogarth, 1966.

_____. "Fixation—The Unconscious." In *Introductory Lectures on Psycho-Analysis, Part III*, edited and translated by James Strachey and A. Tyson. Vol. 16, 273–285. London: Hogarth, 1966.

_____. "Mourning and Melancholia." In *On the History of the Psycho-Analytic Movement. Papers on Metapsychology and Other Works*, edited and translated by James Strachey and A. Tyson. Vol. 14, 239–258. London: Hogarth, 1966.

_____. "Papers on Applied Psychoanalysis. The Uncanny." In *Collected Papers.* Translated by James Strachey. Vol. 4, 368–407. London: Hogarth, 1949.

Fronteras, Adam. *The Tarot: The Traditional Tarot Reinterpreted for the Modern World.* New York: Stewart, Tabori, and Chang: 1996.

Furth, Robin. *Stephen King's The Dark Tower: The Complete Concordance.* New York: Scribner, 2006.

Garber, Ralph S. "Baseball in American Fiction." *The English Journal* 56, no. 8 (1967): 1107–1114.

Gatch, Milton McC. *Loyalties and Traditions: Man and His World in Old English Literature.* New York: Pegasus, 1971.

Gerrig, Richard. *Experiencing Narrative Worlds: On the Psychological Activities of Reading.* New Haven, CT: Yale, 1993.

Gish, Nancy K. *The Waste Land: A Poem of Memory and Desire.* Boston: Twayne, 1988.

Glaysher, Frederick. "At the Dark Tower." *Studies in Browning and His Circle* 12 (1984): 34–40.

Greenwood, Susan, and Raje Airey. *The Complete Illustrated Encyclopedia of Witchcraft and Practical Magic.* London: Hermes House, 2006.

Greer, John Michael. *The New Encyclopaedia of the Occult.* St. Paul: Llewellyn, 2005.

Guillén, Claudio. *Literature as System: Essays Toward the Theory of Literary History.* Princeton, NJ: Princeton University Press, 1971.

Hall, J.R. Clark. *A Concise Anglo-Saxon Dictionary.* Toronto: University of Toronto Press, 2004.

Harper, J.W. Introduction to *Men and Women and Other Poems*, edited by Colin Graham, xix-xxvii. London: Everyman, 1993.

Hill, John. M. *The Anglo-Saxon Warrior Ethic: Restructuring Lordship in Early English Literature*. Gainesville: University Press of Florida, 2000.

Hirsch, E. D. *Validity in Interpretation*. New Haven, CT: Yale University Press, 1967.

"How Coal Is Formed." *COAL: Ancient Gift Serving Modern Man*. Accessed October 6, 2013. http:// www.ket.org/ Trips/Coal/AGSMM/agsmmhow.html.

Howells, W. D. "Criticism and Fiction." In *Criticism and Fiction and Other Essays by W. D. Howells*, edited by Clara Marburg Kirk and Rudolf Kirk, 9–87. Westport, CT: Greenwood, 1959.

Hutcheon, Linda. *A Theory of Adaptation*. New York: Routledge, 2006.

Hye, Allen E. *Religion in Modern Baseball Fiction*. Macon, GA: Mercer University Press, 2004.

Indick, Ben P. "Stephen King as an Epic Writer." In *Discovering Modern Horror Fiction*, edited by Darrell Schweitzer, 56–67. Mercer Island, WA: Starmont House, 1985.

James, M. R. Preface to *The Collected Ghost Stories of M. R. James*. London: Edward Arnold, 1949. vii-x.

Jameson, Frederic. "From *Postmodernism, or the Cultural Logic of Late Capitalism*." In *A Critical and Cultural Theory Reader*, edited by Anthony Easthope and Kate McGowan. Toronto: University of Toronto Press, 1994.

_____. *The Political Unconscious: Narrative as a Socially Symbolic Act*. Ithaca, NY: Cornell University Press, 1981.

Jauss, Hans Robert. *Towards an Aesthetic of Reception*. Translated by Timothy Bahti. Minneapolis: University of Minnesota Press, 1999.

Joshi, S.T. *The Modern Weird Tale*. Jefferson, NC: McFarland, 2001.

Kagle, Steven. "Beyond Armageddon: Stephen King's *The Stand* and the Post Catastrophic World in Speculative Fiction." In *A Casebook on The Stand*, edited by Tony Magistrale, 189–202. San Bernardino, CA: Borgo, 1992.

Kepner, Tyler. "The Emotional, Excitable Tom Gordon." *The New York Times*. Last modified April 2, 2005. http:// www.nytimes.com/2005/04/02/sports/ baseball/02gordon.html?_r=0.

King, Stephen. "Acceptance Speech." *National Book Award Acceptance Speech*, 2003. http://www.national book.org/ nbaacceptspeech_sking.html.

_____. "The Best Book You Can't Read." *Entertainment Weekly*. September 19, 2003. http://www.ew.com/ew/article/ 0,,484759,0.html.

_____. *Cell*. New York: Pocket, 2006.

_____. *The Colorado Kid*. New York: Hard Case Crime, 2005.

_____. "Crying Wolfe." *Entertainment Weekly*. January 17, 2005. EW.com. http://www.ew.com/ew/article/0,,1017 532,00.html. November 30, 2006.

_____. *Danse Macabre*. New York: Berkley, 1981.

_____. *The Dark Tower*. Hampton Falls, NH: Donald M. Grant, 2004.

_____. *The Dark Tower*. New York: Scribner, 2004.

_____. *The Dark Tower*. New York: Pocket Books, 2006.

_____. *Desperation*. New York: Signet, 1997.

_____. "Do Movies Matter (Part 2)." *Entertainment Weekly*. November 19, 2003. http://www.ew.com/ew/article/ 0,,546828,00.html.

_____. "Don't Go to Sleep." *Entertainment Weekly*. November 25, 2003. http:// www.ew.com/ew/article/0,,550879,00. html.

_____. *The Drawing of the Three*. New York: Plume, 1989.

_____. *The Drawing of the Three*. New York: Signet, 1990.

_____. *The Drawing of the Three*. New York: Signet, 2003.

_____. *11/22/63*. New York: Scribner, 2011.

_____. *11/22/63*. New York: Gallery Books, 2012.

_____. *The Girl Who Loved Tom Gordon*. New York: Pocket, 1999.

_____. "Graceless and Tasteless." *Entertainment Weekly*. October 6, 2006. 78.

_____. "The Great Escape." *Entertainment Weekly*. October 5, 2007. http://www.ew.com/ew/article/0,,20065612,00.html.

_____. "Goodbye, Harry." *Entertainment Weekly*. July 13, 2007. 76.

_____. *The Gunslinger*. New York: Plume, 1988.

_____. *The Gunslinger*. Rev. ed. New York: Signet, 2003.

_____. "Hail to the Spoken Word." *Entertainment Weekly*, November 3, 2006, 86.

_____. Introduction to *The Gunslinger*, ix-xix. Rev. ed. New York: Signet, 2003.

_____. *IT*. New York: Signet, 1987.

_____. "Kick-Back Books." *Entertainment Weekly*, August 4, 2005. EW.com. http://www.ew.com/ew/article/commentary/0,6115,1089990_5.

_____. "Lights in a Box." *Entertainment Weekly*, November 11, 2005. http://www.ew.com/ew/article/0,,1128488,00.html.

_____. *Lisey's Story*. Scribner: New York, 2006.

_____. "No No No Easy Road." *Entertainment Weekly*, April 27, 2007. 148.

_____. "No Stars, Sorry." *Entertainment Weekly*, March 21, 2005. http://www.ew.com/ew/article/0,,1039066,00.html.

_____. *On Writing: A Memoir of the Craft*. New York: Pocket, 2000.

_____. "Personal Best." *Entertainment Weekly*, December 20, 2004. http://www.ew.com/ew/article/0,,1008401,00.html.

_____. "Potter Gold: Stephen King Takes a Shining to J. K. Rowling's Delightfully Dark *Harry Potter and the Order of the Phoenix*." *Entertainment Weekly*, July 11, 2003. http://www.ew.com/ew/article/0,,462861,00.html.

_____. "The Rating Game." *Entertainment Weekly*, March 5, 2004. http://www.ew.com/ew/article/0,,595367,00.html.

_____. "Ready or Not." *Entertainment Weekly*, June 9, 2006. http://www.ew.com/ew/article/0,,1202235,00.html.

_____. *The Regulators*. New York: Signet, 1997.

_____. "Room 1408." In *Every Thing's Eventual: 14 Dark Tales*, 457–510. New York: Pocket, 2002.

_____. "Scene It." *Entertainment Weekly*, November 9, 2005. http://www.ew.com/ew/article/0,,1138886,00.html.

_____. "The Secret Gardiner." *Entertainment Weekly*. February 15, 2007, 84.

_____. *Song of Susannah*. Hampton Falls, NH: Donald M. Grant, 2004.

_____. *Song of Susannah*. New York: Scribner, 2004.

_____. *Song of Susannah*. New York: Signet, 2006.

_____. *The Stand* (Compete and Uncut Edition). New York: Signet, 1991.

_____. *Storm of the Century: An Original Screenplay*. New York: Pocket, 1999.

_____. "Television Impaired." *Entertainment Weekly*, January 22, 2007. http://www.ew.com/ew/article/0,,20008933,00.html.

_____. "Uncle Stevie's Gotta Have It." *Entertainment Weekly*, June 22, 2007, 144.

_____. *The Waste Lands*. New York: Plume, 1991.

_____. *The Waste Lands*. New York: Signet, 1991.

_____. *The Waste Lands*. New York: Signet, 2006.

_____. *Wizard and Glass*. New York: Signet, 1998.

_____. *Wizard and Glass*. New York: Signet, 2003.

_____. *Wolves of the Calla*. Hampton Falls, NH: Donald M. Grant, 2003.

_____. *Wolves of the Calla*. New York: Scribner, 2003.

"King Winds Real Life into Latest Fiction." CNN.com. Last modified April 5, 1999. http://www.cnn.com/books/news/9904/05/Stephen.King/.

Kinsella, W.P. *Shoeless Joe*. Boston: Houghton Mifflin, 1982.

Kraus, Rebecca. "A Shelter in the Storm: Baseball Responds to September 11." *NINE: A Journal of Baseball History and Culture* 12, no. 1 (2003): 88–101.

Lapidge, Michael, John Blair, Simon Keynes, and Donald. Scragg. *The Blackwell Encyclopedia of Anglo Saxon England*. Oxford: Blackwell, 1999.

Lee, Martha F. "Environmental Apocalypse: The Millennial Ideology of 'Earth First.'" In *Millennium, Messiahs, and Mayhem: Contemporary Apocalyptic Movements*, edited by Thomas Robbins and Susan J. Palmer, 119–37. New York: Routledge, 1997.

Lehmann-Haupt, Christopher. "Books of the Times; A Modern Fairy Tale of the Dark North Woods." *The New York Times*. Last modified April 15, 1999. http://www.nytimes.com/1999/04/15/books/books-of-the-times-a-modern-fairy-tale-of-the-dark-north-woods.html.

Lewis, C.S. *Studies in Medieval and Renaissance Literature*. Cambridge: Cambridge University Press, 1966.

Litt, Toby. "A Smuck in the Bools," rev. of *Lisey's Story* by Stephen King. *The Guardian*, October 28, 2006, 16.

Long, Elizabeth. *Book Clubs: Women and the Uses of Reading in Everyday Life*. Chicago: University of Chicago Press, 2003.

Magga, Henry Ole. "Indigenous Peoples' Perspectives on Quality Education." United Nations. Accessed August 31, 2009. http://www.un.org/esa/socdev/unpfii/pfii/members/Magga-Indigenous%20Education.htm.

Magistrale, Tony. *Hollywood's Stephen King*. New York: Palgrave Macmillan, 2003.

_____. Introduction to *The Films of Stephen King: From* Carrie *to* Secret Window, 1–10. New York: Palgrave Macmillan, 2008.

_____. *Landscape of Fear: Stephen King's American Gothic*. Bowling Green, OH: Bowling Green State University Popular Press, 1988.

_____. Preface to *Stephen King: America's Storyteller*, vii–xi. Santa Barbara: Praeger, 2010.

_____. *Stephen King: America's Storyteller*. Santa Barbara: Praeger, 2010.

_____. *Stephen King: The Second Decade,* Danse Macabre *to* The Dark Half. New York: Twayne, 1992.

Malamud, Bernard. *The Natural*. New York: Farrar, Straus and Giroux, 1952.

Manganiello, Dominic. *T.S. Eliot and Dante*. New York: St. Martin's, 1989.

Mani, Lakshmi. *The Apocalyptic Vision in Nineteenth Century American Fiction: A Study of Cooper, Hawthorne, and Melville*. Washington, D.C.: University Press of America, 1981.

Marlowe, Ann. *How to Stop Time: Heroin from A to Z*. New York: Anchor, 1999.

Maximum Overdrive. DVD. Directed by Stephen King. Wilmington, NC: De Laurentiis, 1986.

May, John R. *Toward a New Earth: Apocalypse in the American Novel*. South Bend, IN: University of Notre Dame Press, 1972.

Mayerfeld, Michael Bell. "The Ghosts of Place." *Theory and Society* 26, no. 6 (2008): 813–836.

McAleer, Patrick. *Inside the Dark Tower Series: Art, Evil and Intertextuality in the Stephen King Novels*. Jefferson, NC: McFarland, 2009.

McComb, John King. "Beyond the Dark Tower: Childe Roland's Painful Memories." *ELH* 42 (1975): 460–470.

Meyers, Joyce C. "'Childe Roland to the Dark Tower Came': A Nightmare

Confrontation with Death." *Victorian Poetry* 8, no. 4 (1970): 335–339.

Morgan, Gwendolyn A. "Dualism and Mirror Imagery in Anglo-Saxon Riddles." *Journal of the Fantastic in the Arts* 5, no. 1 (1992): 74–85.

Morris, Timothy. *Guide to Baseball Fiction*. Accessed October 6, 2013. http://www.uta.edu/english/tim/baseball/.

Morrison, Toni. "The Dancing Mind." *National Book Awards Acceptance Speech*, November 6, 1996. http://www.nationalbook.org/nbaaccept speech_tmorrison.html.

_____. "Memory, Creation, and Writing." *Thought: A Review of Culture and Idea* 54, no. 235 (December 1984): 385–390.

_____. "Rootedness: The Ancestor as Foundation." In *Black Women Writers (1950–1980): A Critical Evaluation*, edited by Mari Evans, 339–45. Garden City, NY: Anchor Press/Doubleday, 1984.

_____. "The Site of Memory." In *Inventing the Truth: The Art and Craft of Memoir*, 2nd ed., edited by William Zinsser, 101–24. Boston: Houghton Mifflin, 1985.

Morse, Donald R. "Friday, The Thirteenth." *Journal of Religion and Psychical Research* 24, no. 4 (2001): 182–183.

Mosley, Walter. "Introduction of Stephen King." *The National Book Foundation*, 2003. http://www. nationalbook.org/nbaacceptspeech_sking_intro.html, March 3, 2007.

Newhouse, Tom. "A Blind Date with Disaster: Adolescent Revolt in the Fiction of Stephen King." In *The Gothic World of Stephen King: Landscapes and Nightmares*, edited by Ray B. Browne and Gary Hoppenstand, 49–55. Bowling Green, OH: Bowling Green State University Popular Press, 1987.

Notkin, Deborah. "Stephen King: Horror and Humanity for Our Time." In *Fear Itself: The Horror Fiction of Stephen King*, edited by Tim Underwood and

Chuck Miller, 149–160. New York: Plume, 1984.

O'Leary, Stephen D. *Arguing the Apocalypse: A Theory of Millennial Rhetoric*. New York: Oxford University Press, 1994.

O'Nan, Stewart and Stephen King. *Faithful*. New York: Scribner, 2004.

Paul, Anne. "Your Brain on Fiction." *New York Times*. March 17, 2012. http://www.nytimes.com/2012/ 03/18/opinion/sun day/the-neuroscience-of-your-brain-on-fiction.html?_r=3&pagewanted=all.

Pharr, Mary. "Only Theoretical: Postmodern Ambiguity in Needful Things and Storm of the Century." In *The Films of Stephen King: From Carrie to Secret Window*, edited by Tony Magistrale, 165–76. New York: Palgrave Macmillan, 2008.

Pinsky, Robert, trans. *The Inferno of Dante*. By Dante. New York: Farrar, Straus, and Giroux, 1994.

Pollan, Michael. *The Botany of Desire*. New York: Random House, 2001.

_____. *Second Nature: A Gardener's Education*. New York: Grove, 1991.

Pollington, Stephen. *The English Warrior from Earliest Times to 1066*. Norfolk, VA: Anglo Saxon, 1996.

_____. *The Mead Hall: Feasting in Anglo-Saxon England*. Norfolk, VA: Anglo Saxon, 2003.

Pondrom, Cyrena N. "*Trilogy* and *Four Quartets*: Contrapuntal Visions of Spiritual Quest." *Agenda* 25, no. 3–4 (1987–88): 155–65.

Proctor, Robert N. "Anti-Agate: The Great Diamond Hoax and the Semi-precious Stone Scam." *Configurations* 9 (2001): 381–412.

Reino, Joseph. *Stephen King: The First Decade,* Carrie *to* Pet Sematary. Boston: Twayne, 1988.

"Riddle 76." Swarthmore College-English Department (Old English Riddles). Last modified 2004. http://www.swarth more.edu/Humanities/english/old english/76.html.

Robbins, Thomas, and Susan J. Palmer. "Introduction: Patterns of Contemporary Apocalypticism in North America." In *Millennium, Messiahs, and Mayhem: Contemporary Apocalyptic Movements*, edited by Thomas Robbins and Susan J. Palmer, 1–27. New York: Routledge, 1997.

Roth, Philip. *The Great American Novel.* New York: Holt, Rinehart and Winston, 1973.

Ruffles, Tom. *Ghost Images: Cinema of the Afterlife.* Jefferson, NC: McFarland, 2004.

Sanders, Julie. *Adaptation and Appropriation.* London: Routledge, 2006.

Schiffhorst, G. "The Rose." Class Handout. LIT 6426: Dante and Eliot. UCF Colbourn Hall, Orlando. 2 April 2002.

Song of Roland, edited by Dorothy Sayers. New York: Penguin, 1957.

"Stephen King Honored at Book Awards." November 20, 2003, http://www.cnn.com/2003/SHOWBIZ/books/11/20/nationalbookawards.ap/index.html. February 2, 2008.

Strengel, Heidi. *Dissecting Stephen King: From the Gothic to Literary Naturalism.* Madison: University of Wisconsin Press, 2005.

Sullivan, Jack. *Elegant Nightmares. The English Ghost Story from Le Fanu to Blackwood.* Athens: Ohio University Press, 1978.

Thoreau, Henry David. *Walden.* New York: Signet, 2004.

Tiffany, Daniel. "Lyric Substance: On Riddles, Materialism, and Poetic Obscurity." *Critical Inquiry* 28, no. 1 (2001): 72–98.

Twain, Mark. "The Art of Authorship." In *The Norton Anthology of American Literature.* 6th ed. Vol. C, edited by Nina Baym, 408–11. New York: W. W. Norton, 2003.

_____. "Fenimore Cooper's Literary Offences." In *The Norton Anthology of American Literature.* 6th ed. Vol. C, edited by Nina Baym, 412–20. New York: W. W. Norton, 2003.

_____. "How to Tell a Story." In *The Norton Anthology of American Literature.* 6th ed. Vol. C, edited by Nina Baym, 407–8. New York: W. W. Norton, 2003.

Venefica, Avia. "Four" and "Five." What's-Your-Sign.Com: The Doorway to Symbolism. The Spiritual Meaning of Numbers. Accessed August 31, 2009. http://www.whats-your-sign.com/spiritual-meaning-of-numbers.html.

Vincent, Bev. *The Road to the Dark Tower: Exploring Stephen King's Magnum Opus.* New York: New American Library, 2004.

Wadenius, Adam. "The Monstruous Masculine: Abjection and Todd Solondz's *Happiness.*" *Horror Studies* 1, no. 1 (2010): 129–141.

Walton, Marsha, and Michael Coren. "Scientist: Man in Americas Earlier than Thought." CNN.com. Last modified November 18, 2004. http://www.cnn.com/2005/TECH/science/11/17/Carolina. dig/index.html.

Watt, Ian. "From the Rise of the Novel: Studies in Defoe, Richardson, and Fielding." In *Theory of the Novel: A Historical Approach*, edited by M. McKeon, 363–381. Baltimore: Johns Hopkins University Press, 2000.

White, Paul. "Sounds of Silence Bring Peace to Game." 19 September 2001. USAToday.com. Last modified September 19, 2001. http://www.usatoday.com/sport/bbw/2001–09-19/2001–09-19-leadingoff. htm.

Wiater, Stanley, Christopher Golden, and Hank Wagner. *The Complete Stephen King Universe: A Guide to the Worlds of Stephen King.* New York: St. Martin's Griffin, 2006.

Williams, Anne. "Browning's 'Childe Roland,' Apprentice for Night." *Victorian Poetry* 21:1 (1983), 27–42.

Williams, Edith Whitehurst. "The Anglo-Saxon Theme of Exile in Renaissance Lyrics: A Perspective on Two

Sonnets of Sir Walter Raleigh." *Journal of English Literary History* 42, no. 2 (1975): 171–188.

_____. "Auden, Yeats, and the Word 'Silly': A Study in Semantic Change. *South Atlantic Review* 46, no. 4 (1981): 17–33.

Williamson, Craig. *Feast of Creatures: Anglo Saxon Riddle-Songs*. Philadelphia: University of Pennsylvania Press, 1982.

Winter, Douglass. *Stephen King: The Art of Darkness*. New York: New American Library, 1984.

Woolf, Virginia. "Mr. Bennet and Mrs. Brown." In *Theory of the Novel: A Historical Approach*, edited by M. McKeon. Baltimore: Johns Hopkins University Press, 2000. 745–758.

Yacowar, Maurice. "Negotiating the Loner." *Queen's Quarterly* 105, 4 (1998): 543–555.

Zajdel, Melody M. "'I See Her Differently': H.D.'s *Trilogy* as Feminist Response to Masculine Modernism." *Sagetrieb: A Journal Devoted to Poets in the Pound-H.D.-Williams Tradition* 5, no. 1 (1986): 7–16.

Zamora, Lois Parkinson. "The Myth of Apocalypse and the American Literary Imagination." In *The Apocalyptic Vision in America: Interdisciplinary Essays on Myth and Culture*, edited by Lois Parkinson Zamora, 97–138. Bowling Green, OH: Bowling Green University Popular Press.

Zatti, Sergio. *The Quest for Epic: From Ariosto to Tasso*. Translated by Sally Hill and Dennis Looney. Toronto: University of Toronto Press, 2006.

About the Contributors

Jennifer **Alberico** teaches writing and humanities courses at the Community College of Vermont and lives in Brattleboro.

Scott **Ash** is a professor of English at Nassau Community College (Garden City, New York). He teaches American literature surveys as well as courses in film and literature, mystery and detective fiction, and the American short story.

Abigail L. **Bowers** is an assistant professor of English at Kent State University-Ashtabula. Her areas of specialization include contemporary American literature, addiction narratives, and popular culture.

Michele **Braun**, an independent scholar and professional communicator who specializes in ghostwriting, is president of the Popular Culture Association of Canada. Her research interests in popular film and literature include zombies and King Arthur.

Mary **Findley** is a tenured faculty member at Vermont Technical College where she teaches "The Films and Novels of Stephen King," "Gothic Themes and Social Issues in Film," "Popular Culture: Zombies and Consumerism" and others. She has published various essays on Stephen King's fiction.

Jennifer **Jenkins**' interests include science fiction and nineteenth century Gothic literature. She lives in Carrollton, Georgia, and works in the Office of Research and Sponsored Projects at the University of West Georgia.

Jennifer D. **Loman** is a Ph.D. candidate in English at the University of Iowa where she studies religion and science in American literature. Her concentration is in nineteenth and early twentieth-century works; her research interests in science fiction include more contemporary works.

Patrick **McAleer** is co-chair of the Stephen King Area of the Popular Culture Association's Annual National Conference. He is the author of *Inside the Dark Tower Series* (2009) and *The Writing Family of Stephen King* (2011), both from McFarland. He teaches King's work in his English courses at Inver Hills Community College in Minnesota.

Georgianna O. **Miller**'s essay was inspired by a graduate course on Dante and T.S. Eliot. She works at Arizona State University.

Michael A. **Perry** is an associate professor of English at Rockford University in Illinois. He has presented papers connecting Stephen King to Toni Morrison, Mark Twain, and Ambrose Bierce. He has also presented a paper on *Duma Key* and its connection to literary modernism and blues.

Alexandra **Reuber** is a professor of French and director of the French language program at Tulane University, New Orleans. She focuses her research on the development of gothic and fantastic writing from the nineteenth century onward, as well as on the adaptation of classical works in popular culture and their use in the classroom.

Philip L. **Simpson** is provost of the Titusville Campus of Eastern Florida State College. He has served as president of the Popular Culture Association and area chair of Horror for the Association. He is co-chair of the Stephen King Area and sits on the editorial board of the *Journal of Popular Culture*.

Lowell Mick **White** is an assistant professor of English at Pittsburg State University, where he teaches creative writing and literature. He is the author of a story collection, *Long Time Ago Good*, and two novels, *The Demon Life* and *Professed*.

T. Gilchrist **White** teaches at College of the Mainland in Texas City, Texas. She has used King's fiction to teach composition to college freshmen.

Index